teach yourself...
PageMaker 6
for Windows 95

David Browne

A Subsidiary of
Henry Holt and Co., Inc.

First Edition—1996

Printed in the United States of America.

Library of Congress Cataloging-in-Publication Data

Browne, David.
　　Teach yourself—PageMaker 6 for Windows / by David Browne.
　　　　p.　　cm.
　　ISBN 1-55828-419-2
　　1. Aldus PageMaker. 2. Desktop publishing. I. Title.
Z253.532.P333B77　　1996
686.2'2544536—dc20　　　　　　　　　　　　　　　　　　　95-53876
　　　　　　　　　　　　　　　　　　　　　　　　　　　　　　　CIP

10 9 8 7 6 5 4 3 2 1

MIS:Press books are available at special discounts for bulk purchases for sales promotions, premiums, fund-raising, or educational use. Special editions or book excerpts can also be created to specification.

For details contact:　　Special Sales Director
　　　　　　　　　　　　MIS:Press
　　　　　　　　　　　　a subsidiary of Henry Holt and Company, Inc.
　　　　　　　　　　　　115 West 18th Street
　　　　　　　　　　　　New York, New York 10011

Associate Publisher: *Paul Farrell*
Managing Editor: *Cary Sullivan*
Development/Technical Editor: *Jono Hardjowirogo*
Copy Edit Manager: *Shari Chappell*
Production Editor: *Anne Incao*

Dedication

To Sally, Michael, and Kathleen.

CONTENTS

Introduction   1

CHAPTER 3: Editing Your Work 91

CHAPTER 4: Adding Design Elements   125

CHAPTER 5: Setting Up Templates   155

CHAPTER 6: Setting Up Custom Styles   185

CHAPTER 7: Printing   195

CHAPTER 8: Adding Color 215

CHAPTER 9: Developing Long Documents 241

INTRODUCTION

- ❖ The highlights of version 6.0
- ❖ The advantages of Windows 95
- ❖ Desktop publishing: how it all started
- ❖ First the Mac, then Windows
- ❖ What this book is about
- ❖ Who should read this book
- ❖ To sum up

This book is about PageMaker, a page-composition software program that automates all the steps in developing a printed document. *Composition* is the process of laying out text and graphics—typography, lines, boxes, pictures, drawings, and colors—on a page. PageMaker is considered by many industry experts, and by many users, to be one of the most functional expert systems available for the design and composition of documents. I think it is also the easiest, most intuitive page-composition software to learn. PageMaker is taught in high schools and colleges, art schools, trade schools, and vocational centers (it's probably even offered in some advanced elementary schools). It is used by graphic designers and artists, technical writers and illustrators, corporate communications departments, marketing groups, newspapers, magazines, and book publishers. The beauty of PageMaker is that it can be simple to use to those who want to just scratch the surface of its resources, and at the same time, it is just as sophisticated for complex, four-color designs. Its long-document capabilities are better than the best word processors, and it presents a simple, friendly workplace for the novice.

The Highlights of Version 6.0

Version 6 is the first effort by Adobe Systems—following the merger of Aldus with Adobe—to improve PageMaker. They've not only succeeded, but the program is now a more mature package that includes much versatility. When combined with Windows 95, it's difficult not to fall in love with PageMaker, even if you are a QuarkXPress fan.

Color Management

PageMaker uses Kodak's Color Management System (CMS) to provide standardized colors across all areas of design and production. This means that the color you see on your color monitor will match the color proofs from your dye sublimation printers, which will come very close to matching press proofs from your commercial printer's presses. CMS lets you add drivers for just the devices (monitors, proof printers, and printing presses) that you specifically need, so you can tailor PageMaker to your exact needs.

Minute Trapping Control

Finally, PageMaker comes with the trapping controls that let you get upfront and personal with your trapping specifications. PageMaker can now handle trapping as precisely as QuarkXPress.

Multiple Master Pages

Again, after pleading for years, we finally get as many master pages as we want. And PageMaker comes with a handy Master Pages palette to create and configure all those master pages.

Adobe Plug-Ins

Aldus additions have become Adobe plug-ins—often doing exactly the same thing, but less shaky and less likely to fail. Moreover, PageMaker now accepts other Adobe plug-ins and third-party plug-ins. You can expect a lot of new development in the plug-in area in the near future.

New Time-Saving Commands

Forget the awful Group-it PS addition from version 5; PageMaker now has **Group** and **Ungroup** commands (on the new Arrange menu), just like Quark. Once grouped, you can lock the group's position on the page.

When you wish not to print a graphic (or any object), simply use the **Non-Printing** command on the Element menu to prevent printing.

The **Align Objects** command, also on the Arrange menu handles the same job as the addition of the same name from version 5; it's just quicker and easier to use now. Same for the **Sort Pages** command (on the Layout menu).

Printer Styles (on the File menu) is also like the old addition, it lets you assign similar documents to a printing style and then let PageMaker handle the job of printing automatically.

Finally, version 6 offers the **Move Forward** and **Move Backward** commands (on the Arrange menu); these provide more finite control than the **Move to Front** and **Move to Back** commands.

The Advantages of Windows 95

While PageMaker 6 for Windows will run perfectly well in Windows 3.11 or Windows for WorkGroups, the real key to PageMaker's power is found when you add it to a Windows 95 computer. Then PageMaker's 32-bit speed and Windows 95's multitasking capabilities give desktop publishers and designers more time, energy, and help than they've had in the past.

Flexible File Management

PageMaker's Windows 95 document management dialog boxes (for opening files, saving files, placing files and exporting files) gives you capabilities never before seen on either PCs or the Macintosh.

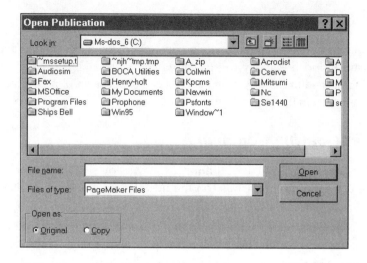

❖ First of all, you can change icon shape to whatever you want, from small folder icons (shown here) to large icons

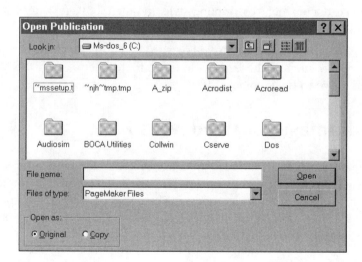

❖ To a list of folders showing date stamp information, like this:

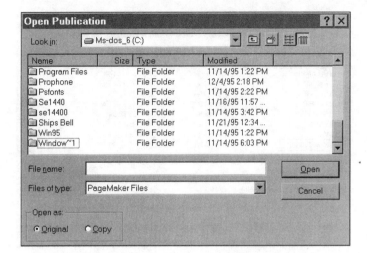

❖ Simply click the right mouse button inside the dialog box and choose from the standard menu:

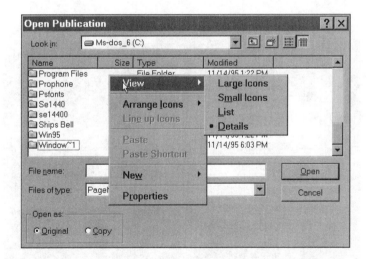

❖ Likewise, if you want to create a new folder, simply right-click the mouse, choose **New** and **Folder** from the menu. Windows will instantly add a new folder in the dialog box:

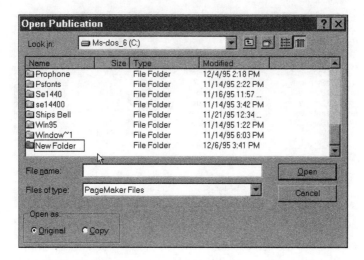

❖ Now, type name, as long as you want it.

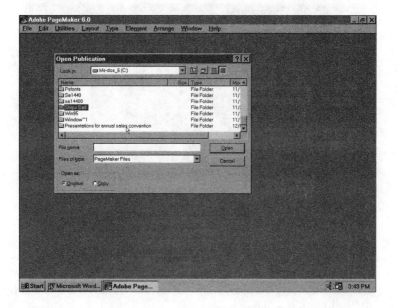

Flexible Printing

You can print from any file management dialog box as easily as you can create new folders and documents. Simply right-click the document that you want to print and choose **Print** from the menu:

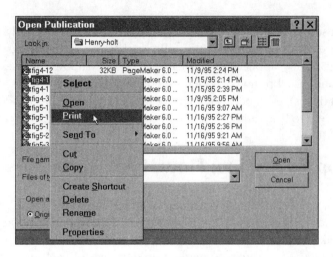

PageMaker will open the document you clicked and begin printing.

True Multitasking

Unlike Windows 3.1 which prioritizes multiple jobs but never actually lets you do two things at once, Windows 95 is multithreaded, meaning it can dance and chew gum at the same time. This means that you, the designer/publisher, can print any number of documents in the background and never be disturbed. While you are printing, you can dial up the Internet, upload or download files, and format a floppy disk in your **A:** drive. Try that in Windows 3.1!

Long Document Names

As I mentioned a moment ago, Windows 95 lets you assign long names to documents. Gone are the days of DOS name conventions, including the eight-character limit on file names. And the long names are completely compatible with Windows 3.1 and MS-DOS, where the name is simply truncated to the first eight characters.

Wizards

If you've used previous Microsoft Office applications, you already know what *Wizards* are. They are clever little fellows that configure things for you. In Windows 95, every application can have Wizards. Windows 95 uses Wizards to configure and install printers, modems, peripheral hardware (like SCSI controllers or SyQuest drives), even network interface cards. Wizards make Windows 95 computers a breeze to learn and use, and they make you work fast in PageMaker 6.0.

Desktop Publishing: How It All Started

My first job, while still in college, was rewriting news copy on the city desk of a daily morning newspaper. This was more than 20 years ago, before the advent of personal computers—or even digital typesetters. Back then, pages were designed by layout editors who marked up dummies of each page, told us how many lines of copy each story had to be, and fit the advertisements around the stories. The dummy was the layout specification for the newspaper page. We writers had little idea of how the stories would look or their location until the page was ready to be printed. If a story broke and needed to be added at the last minute, it would often mean an entire remake of the page, which meant completely redesigning the page resetting the type.

The dummies and typed stories were sent to composing, where hot lead typesetting machines set the type in melted lead, one justified line at a time (the line came out in a *slug*, or strip of lead). If one word was misspelled, the entire line had to be reset. The machines were gigantic, hot, noisy, and smelly. There were 16 of them in the composing room; several were always being repaired.

In 1970, these machines were still considered pretty much state-of-the-art for a large newspaper. Working with hot lead was a lot faster than working with cold type. *Cold type* meant that the lead characters were already cast, and you had to manually arrange the type in a galley tray, set as the mirror image of the printed page (that is, backward and reading right to left). The classified ad pages were set in cold type. Around the year 1460, Johannes Gutenberg came up with the idea of printing from movable type. There was very little difference between setting classified ads at most daily newspapers in 1970 and the way Gutenberg set the type for his Bible in 1465; in both instances the type was cast individually in lead and placed by hand in a galley.

First the Mac, Then Windows

Regardless of the method for setting type, page composition remained a completely manual process for the most part, until the mid-1980s, when small, personal laser printers were invented, the PostScript page description language for laser printers was refined, and a graphics-based personal computer called the Apple Macintosh was introduced. The Mac could run a most unorthodox program called *PageMaker*, which displayed a page laid out exactly as it would be printed—a radically new concept called *What-You-See-Is-What-You-Get*, or *WYSIWYG* (pronounced "wizzy wig"). Until the Macintosh, most personal computers were IBM PCs, character-based systems that could not display the shapes of typeset characters or graphic symbols—they weren't WYSIWYG. The Mac, PageMaker, and the Apple LaserWriter were the impetus for a new computer-designed, computer-generated graphic composition industry that came to be known as *desktop publishing*.

While Apple computers were the first to run graphic-based software, it wasn't long before a graphical user interface (GUI) was developed for IBM-compatible PCs. The interface, developed by Microsoft Corporation, was called *Window*s. It brought the graphics power of the Macintosh and much of its look and feel to the world of personal computers. Today, Adobe Systems offers both Mac and Windows versions of PageMaker; they are virtually identical in operation, and they work with other programs in similar ways.

What This Book is About

This book does exactly what its title says: it helps you teach yourself PageMaker 6.0 for Windows. If you're like me, you're probably standing in a bookstore, reading this introduction, trying to decide whether this is the book to buy. I'll tell you a secret: if you start Chapter 2, "A Weekend Tour of PageMaker," on Saturday morning, by Monday you'll understand PageMaker. This book covers all the basic functions of PageMaker in depth, and in most cases, it gives you an overview of PageMaker's high-powered functions. It is arranged to introduce you to the capabilities in the order in which you will probably need them. That is, it explains how to install the software before telling you how to use it, it covers how to create a basic document before telling you how to print it, and so forth.

Who Should Read This Book

You won't need to know very much about computers, software, or Windows to understand this book. It is a basic text on PageMaker that starts at the beginning and assumes you know very little. Since the chapters are arranged functionally, if you already know what I'm talking about in a section, feel free to jump ahead. You will also find a comprehensive reference section (Appendix B) explaining each command on each pull-down menu, arranged in the left-to-right order of the menus across the top of the PageMaker window.

If You Work in the Graphic Arts

While you don't need to know anything about art, design, typography, or composition, if you are a graphic artist, you will continually be surprised at how simple it is to do many repetitious, handworked chores in PageMaker. I use examples of documents in this book to fit the beginner's as well as the expert's needs. If you are a graphic designer, or if you have some creative juices, you will find that PageMaker can accomplish in seconds things that take hours manually. All the graphic artists to whom I have introduced PageMaker (and there have been quite a few over the years) have taken to it like ducks to water. PageMaker becomes a natural extention of their fingertips.

If You are a Writer or Editor

If you write for a living, you will be pleasantly surprised at how easy it is to develop copy for manuals, brochures, and fact sheets in PageMaker. You'll find it just as easy to import stories from your favorite word processor and graphics from Windows and Macintosh graphics programs. You will find yourself looking forward to laying out and composing the page as you did to writing the page. And you'll learn that it is indeed painless to try our new ideas and experiment with graphic designs.

To Sum Up

I first saw PageMaker demonstrated in 1985. It was running on a Macintosh hooked up to a Linotronic typesetter. The typesetter was actually printing out typesetting that had been composed on the Mac in PageMaker—unbelievable! I was exuberant; I had waited for such a marvelous invention for many years, and I was hungry for it. Those of us who worked in graphic arts and publishing before the advent of desktop publishing know how time-consuming, restrictive, and difficult manual page composition could be. Just as computers and computer users have matured over the past few years, so has PageMaker. It is now an extremely powerful publishing and graphics tool, made even more significant by Windows and the family of Windows applications.

David Browne
1361 Queen Elaine Drive
Casselberry, FL 32707
Internet:71045.1103@compuserve.com

CHAPTER 1

Getting Started

❖ The PageMaker advantage

❖ The Windows advantage

❖ Installing PageMaker

❖ A quick Windows primer

❖ To sum up

If there is one central advantage to PageMaker for Windows, it is creative freedom. PageMaker and Windows are naturally intuitive, inviting places to work. Start up your Windows computer, open up PageMaker, and before you realize it, you're using commands and tools without referring to this book or Adobe's documentation—your computer running PageMaker makes logical sense and just seems to feel right.

Documents that communicate are developed from creative skill that comes, in part, from having the freedom to explore a palette of ideas—and to discard those ideas that don't work. PageMaker frees you to experiment; it buys you more time to try more ideas. And with PageMaker, documents can continue to evolve as they are designed, written, laid out, revised, and printed.

The PageMaker Advantage

PageMaker makes your work more efficiently and your time more productive. Over the course of the 10 years that I've used PageMaker, I've found that an hour working in PageMaker can equal as many as 12 hours of handwork. For the graphic designer, layout artist, or draftsperson, repetitive tasks—including inking lines, pasting down type, painstakingly searching for typographical errors, aligning art to the page frame, even drawing crop marks and registration bullets—are gone. You can put away your razor blades and artist's tape. PageMaker gives you better things to do with your time. And the writer or editor, accustomed to turning in typed stories to a graphic arts group, can now design documents and carry that design through to a finished, camera-ready mechanical that is ready to print.

PageMaker is a great vehicle for playing "What if?" You can use some of your newfound time playing around with ideas. As shown in Figure 1.1, creating rough layouts for an ad can be easy and creative.

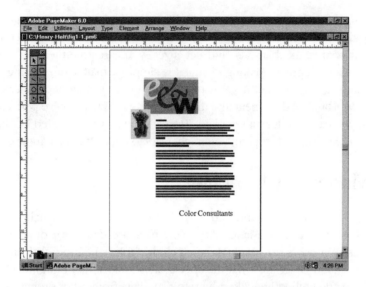

Figure 1.1 *Rough layouts for an ad.*

One important benefit to designing and producing documents in PageMaker is the ease with which you can revise your documents. Instead of storing documents in stacks of art boards, mechanicals, and negatives, you can store them on your hard disk or on a few floppies. Making changes is simply a matter of opening the file, editing it, and saving the file. If you save the file under a different name, you will have both your original document and the changed one. When you've perfected your document, you can save it as a template. *Templates,* which are covered in Chapter 5, are master copies of any document you might want to duplicate in the future.

The Windows Advantage

Windows not only provides the rich graphical environment in which PageMaker operates, it also gives PageMaker the ability to share data with other Windows applications. Windows and PageMaker include Object Linking and Embedding capabilities. Called *OLE* (like what the spectators shout to the bullfighter) for short, object linking and embedding allows you to plant data from other programs directly in your PageMaker documents. OLE is explained in Chapter 4, "Adding Design Elements." When used with PageMaker's powerful import filters, along with cutting and pasting with the Windows Clipboard, OLE gives you the most flexibility possible in working with different software on your PC. When OLE is combined with the inherent power of PageMaker, your computer becomes an automated publishing system that can support your creative efforts and your imagination.

Installing PageMaker

The PageMaker installation program is a Windows program, which means you must have Windows 95 installed and running before you can install PageMaker. Insert Disk One of the installation diskettes in the **A:** drive of your computer, and follow these steps:

1. Click the Windows **Start** button to open the Start menu.

2. Choose the **Run** command to open the Run dialog box and enter **A:\Setup**.

3. Use the Setup Main window to select which PageMaker components you want to install along with the PageMaker program:

   ❖ **Install** everything.Everything means about 30 MB of stuff.

   ❖ **Filters**. PageMaker comes with a wide variety of import filters. You can add all the filters to your system, but they will take up a lot of room. Instead, click the **Filters** option and choose **Setup** to see the list of available filters and choose only the ones you need. You'll see quite a few, including filters for dBASE, DCA, AutoCAD, DEC, Encapsulated PostScript, Excel, Lotus, Write, Word, WordPerfect, and Kodak Photo CD.

   ❖ **Plug-ins**. *Plug-ins* are programs that Adobe and third-party developers have created to do certain chores in PageMaker. You can install close to two dozen plug-ins.

   ❖ **PostScript Printer Description files**. Choose this option to install PostScript printer description (PPD) files for the printers you have and those for which you will be creating print-to-disk files (such as the high-resolution imagesetter your service bureau uses).

   ❖ **Dictionaries**. If you have ordered foreign language dictionaries, you can install them now.

4. Highlight the features you want by positioning the mouse pointer over the feature and clicking the left mouse button. When you are finished, click the **Setup** button.

N O T E

The setup program will ask you to enter the serial number of your software package. You will find the number on the installation diskettes. Enter the number exactly as you see it, including dashes between sets of numbers, but without any alphabetic characters. If you purchased PageMaker 6.0 as an upgrade from version 5.0, look on your 5.0 installation diskettes for the serial number.

It is not necessary to make up your mind right now about what accessories to install. A copy of the setup program will be installed in the Adobe folder. You can start the setup program at any time and install any of the features you want to work with. This is particularly important when hard disk space is limited: install PageMaker right away and load more features as you need them.

As the installation program copies programs and files onto your hard disk, it will ask you to insert various disks in the **A:** drive. When the installation is completed, you will see the Adobe program folder in the Program menu, like Figure 1.2, with icons representing the PageMaker program, the installation program, and so forth. To start PageMaker, simply double-click the **PageMaker** program icon.

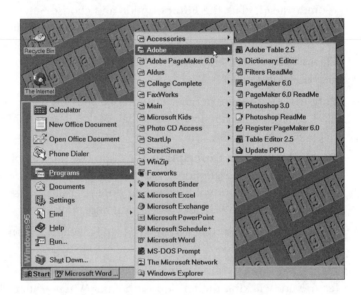

Figure 1.2 *Adobe program folder in the Program menu after installation.*

A Quick Windows Primer

Windows is a creative, graphical environment that allows you to use your software in much the same way that you work at your desk or drawing board. Windows applications display text and graphics very close to the way they will look when printed; typefaces are shown in their actual sizes and styles, and graphics and scanned images look realistic. Windows gives a natural, intuitive feel to programs and allows you the personal flexibility to:

❖ Use the mouse to pick up and move graphic elements or to stretch, shrink, and otherwise resize graphics. You select commands and menus directly with the mouse instead of having to remember complicated Function- or **Ctrl**-key commands.

❖ Arrange programs on your computer screen in much the same way that you arrange work on your desk. In Windows, the blank screen is known as the *desktop*. You can open many different programs simultaneously, arranging them on the desktop any way you like to help optimize your work. An example of this is shown in Figure 1.3.

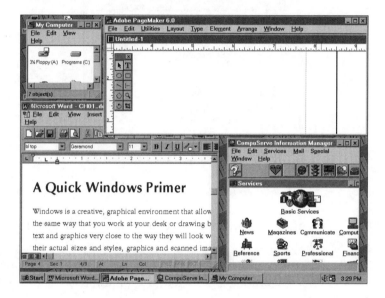

Figure 1.3 *Multiple open windows on the desktop.*

❖ Exchange information between programs. Analyze financial data in your spreadsheet and import the results into a financial report written with your word processor. Create a graphic in a paint program and import it directly into PageMaker to use as part of a page layout. Copy information from one program and paste it into another, without worrying about inconsistent formatting or data incompatibility.

Windows provides a standardized operating environment for different software programs. All Windows applications work with your monitor and printer in exactly the same way:

❖ Forget about having to load different printer drivers for different programs or to define your display monitor differently for different software. In Windows, every program shares the Windows printer drivers and display drivers; there's never a question of incompatibility. The Printers window, shown in Figure 1.4, lets you select the printer you want to use.

Figure 1.4 *The Printers window.*

❖ Install screen and printer fonts once, and they're available for all your Windows programs.

❖ Installing a new printer is simple in Windows. Make the addition using the Add Printer Wizard, and all Windows applications will recognize the new printer.

Windows provides standardized commands for applications:

❖ You no longer have to remember the program name to type in order to start a program. With Windows, you simply double-click the program's icon.

❖ Windows applications share the same commands to activate similar functions. For example, you can always press **Ctrl+Insert** to copy and **Shift+Insert** to paste. Pressing **F1** always gets you to the Help window, shown in Figure 1.5 Pressing **Alt+Tab** lets you cycle among all open applications.

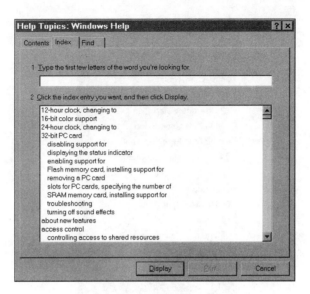

Figure 1.5 *The Help window.*

In addition, Windows provides standardized functionality for all Windows applications:

❖ All Windows applications have a similar look and feel. For example, all applications have command menus at the tops of their screens. All use dialog boxes, pull-down menus, and drop-down lists to present command choices and user selections. All open, close, and save files in similar ways.

❖ Windows applications are easy to learn. Once you've learned how to operate one application, learning other applications is easier.

❖ Windows gives you a common set of accessories and tools to use with your applications, including a card file for addresses, an appointment calendar, a communications program, a calculator, a note pad, a clock, a print spooler, and a file manager, called *Explorer*, that performs many common management tasks. Some of these accessories are shown in Figure 1.6.

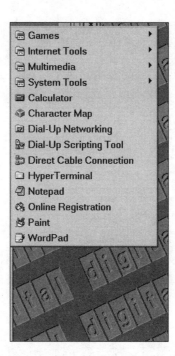

Figure 1.6 *Some of the accessories in the Accessories menu.*

Using the Mouse

The mouse is one of the most important features of Windows. While Windows and its applications can be operated from the keyboard, running Windows without the mouse is like mashing potatoes without a potato masher; you can do it, but it takes a lot longer. Many PageMaker functions can be activated with the keyboard, but the mouse is your most important tool. Once you get used to it, you'll wonder how you ever managed to work without it. If you return to working in DOS programs, you'll find yourself constantly reaching for the mouse, only to remember that you must stick to the keyboard.

CLICKING

When you see the word *click*, it means press quickly on the left mouse button. You can think of clicking as the keyboard equivalent of pressing the **Enter** key, in that it activates commands, but it does much more. Clicking the left mouse button twice quickly is called *double-clicking*. To highlight a word in PageMaker, double-click anywhere in the word. The word and the space following it will be highlighted. *Triple-clicking* highlights all the words and spaces up to the next hard return (created by pressing the **Enter** key at the end of a paragraph). Triple-clicking could highlight a line, a group of lines, or a paragraph.

SELECTING

In PageMaker, you select graphic elements by clicking the element with the mouse. Place the mouse pointer within the area of the graphic element and click once. PageMaker will display sizing handles around the object, as shown in Figure 1.7. To cancel the selection, click anywhere outside the graphic element.

Figure 1.7 *Active sizing handles around a selected object.*

When you have stacked graphics on top of one another, clicking the mouse will usually select only the topmost graphic. To see and select graphics underneath, hold down the **Ctrl** key and click on the top graphic. With each click, the next layer of graphics will rotate to the top for you to select. You'll learn how to work with graphics in Chapter 4.

HIGHLIGHTING

In PageMaker, there are two ways to choose a block of text: select it with the Pointer tool, or highlight it with the Text tool. Selecting text with the Pointer tool selects the entire text block, as shown in Figure 1.8. The text block can then be copied, cut, or deleted; or it can be stretched by dragging a sizing handle. Working with text blocks is covered in Chapters 2 and 3.

Figure 1.8 *A selected text block.*

Highlighting text with the Text tool marks only the words you highlight, as shown in Figure 1.9. Highlight text when you want to change the specifications of type, indents and tabs, color, or style. You can also cut, copy, or delete highlighted text. To highlight text, position the Text tool insertion point before the first letter of the first word you want to highlight. Hold down the left mouse button and pull the mouse to the right. As the insertion point moves over the words, they will be marked with a black highlight bar (the characters will be reversed in white). Pulling the mouse down will highlight a line from your insertion point forward.

Figure 1.9 *Highlighting text with the Text tool.*

Understanding Dialog Boxes

The *dialog box* is the common way Windows displays command choices and options for you to choose. A typical dialog box is shown in Figure 1.10.

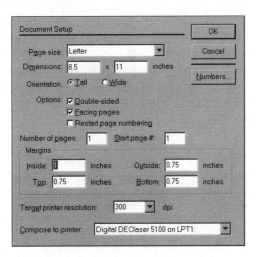

Figure 1.10 *Command choices in a typical dialog box.*

Dialog boxes can be simple or complex; they can offer a list of choices to choose from, options to select, text boxes to type into, or buttons that lead to more dialog boxes. Let's look at some of the characteristics of dialog boxes:

❖ *List boxes* inside dialog boxes display a list of items from which to choose. If there are more items than will fit within its borders, the box will have a scroll bar to let you scroll down the list of items. Or you can type the first few letters of the item and Windows will automatically scroll to find the first occurrence of the letters you typed. The Compose to Printer list box, shown in Figure 1.11, is a list box of available printers.

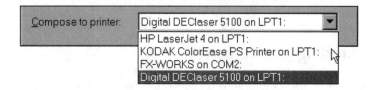

Figure 1.11 *The Compose to Printer list box.*

❖ *Buttons* activate whatever command or function is printed on them. The most common buttons in dialog boxes are the **OK** and **Cancel** buttons. Choose the **OK** button to activate whatever choices you've selected in the dialog box and return to your document. Choose the **Cancel** button to ignore the choices you've made and return to your document. Choosing the **Setup** button displays the Printer Setup dialog box.

❖ *List buttons* note the currently selected (or default) choice. List buttons have arrows indicating if there are more choices available on a drop-down list. Figure 1.12 shows the Page Type list button in the Document Setup dialog box.

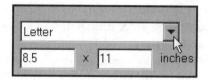

Figure 1.12 *The arrow on a list button indicates more choices.*

❖ *Drop-down lists* are displayed by pressing a list button (see Figure 1.13). Drop-down lists may actually pop up above the list button, and therefore they are sometimes called *pop-up lists*. If there are more choices than there is room to display them, use the scroll bar on the side of the list to move through the choices, or type the first few letters of the choice and Windows will automatically scroll to find the first occurrence of the letters you typed.

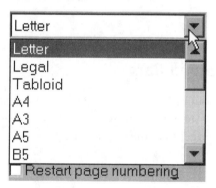

Figure 1.13 *Clicking on the arrow opens the drop-down list.*

❖ *Text boxes* usually show a current value. To change the value, position the insertion point in the box and type the new value. The Inside Margin text box, for example, appears in the Document Setup dialog box.

❖ *Check boxes* present options or choices that can be toggled on and off. A check box containing an **X** means the option is on. Select it again to remove the **X** and toggle the option off. Check boxes may be *dimmed* (and unavailable) at times, based on other selected options in a dialog box. Check boxes in the Document Setup dialog box, for example, indicate which options are currently on and off.

❖ *Option buttons* present choices that are mutually exclusive. Only one in a list of option buttons can be selected at a time. When an option is selected it has a black dot in the center. Often, option buttons will be tied to text boxes; choosing a certain option button enters corresponding values in nearby text boxes. For example, in the Document Setup dialog box, you can select one of two page orientations with the Orientation Option buttons. Choosing the other orientation reverses the page dimensions in the Page Dimensions text boxes above the buttons. Option buttons are sometimes referred to as *radio buttons* because, when selected, they look like the knobs on old-time radios.

Understanding Scroll Bars

Scroll bars along the bottom and right edges of windows, shown in Figure 1.14, are used to move the contents of the window up and down and left and right when the page size is larger than the window size.

Figure 1.14 Scroll bar along the bottom edge of PageMaker's window.

MOVING IN SMALL STEPS

To move about the page in relatively small steps, position the mouse pointer over the appropriate arrow at the end of one of the scroll bars, and click the left mouse button. Each time you click the arrow the document page will scroll in the opposite direction. For example, if you click the right arrow once, the scroll box will jump slightly to the right, which scrolls the page slightly to the left.

MOVING IN LARGER STEPS

To move in larger steps, position the mouse pointer over the scroll box and depress the left mouse button. You will see a dotted outline of the scroll box. Hold down the mouse button and drag the scroll box outline in the direction you want to move the page. Release the mouse button. The scroll box will jump to the new position indicated by the outline, and the page will be repositioned in the direction you want. You can also reposition the page in larger steps by clicking on the gray part of the scroll bar (Figure 1.15) in the direction you want to move. The further along the scroll bar (away from the scroll box) you click, the more the page will move.

Figure 1.15 *To reposition the text in larger steps, click on the gray part of the scroll bar.*

MOVING IN GIANT STEPS

To move the page in very large steps, position the mouse pointer on the scroll bar very near the arrow that points in the desired direction. Hold down the left mouse button and the scroll box will rapidly move toward the mouse pointer.

Arranging Windows

Virtually every Windows application, including PageMaker, has a **Window** command. Use it to arrange multiple windows on your desktop. The command allows you to arrange windows in cascaded or tiled order. *Cascaded windows* are stacked one on top of another, with the title bars of each window visible, as shown in Figure 1.16.

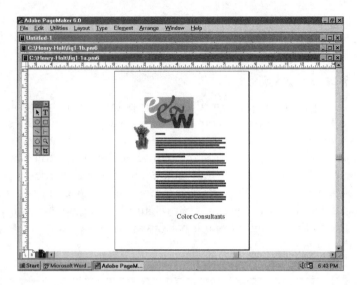

Figure 1.16 *Windows (in this use PageMaker documents) in a cascade arrangement.*

Tiled windows are positioned side by side, like tiles on a floor, as shown in Figure 1.17. The more windows you add to the tiled arrangement, the smaller each tile is made in order to fit. In other words, with three groups or programs opened, the individual tiled windows will be larger than with six groups or programs opened.

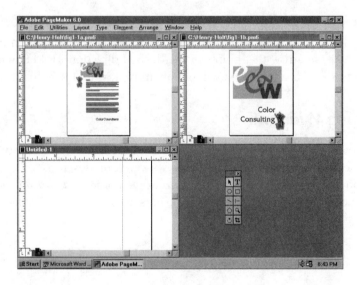

Figure 1.17 *Windows (in this example PageMaker documents) in a tiled arrangement.*

You can cascade or tile various Windows applications, Windows and DOS applications (running in Windows), or different documents in the same application.

To Sum Up

If you have limited experience with Windows and Windows applications, you will find PageMaker very easy to learn. If you are an old-timer with Windows, you'll have absolutely no trouble getting up to speed with PageMaker. Once you have gained some experience, PageMaker's natural feel and intuitive commands will have you thinking of new ways to use the software and produce finished work in a very short time.

In the next chapter you'll walk through a tour of PageMaker that will have you using the program before you know it.

CHAPTER 2

A Weekend Tour of PageMaker

- ❖ Components of the PageMaker windows
- ❖ Creating a new document
- ❖ New document windows
- ❖ Entering text
- ❖ Formatting type
- ❖ Changing type specifications
- ❖ Saving your document
- ❖ Developing paragraphs
- ❖ Formatting paragraphs
- ❖ To sum up

Get ready to take a big bite out of PageMaker and start chewing. This chapter gives you a solid overview of using PageMaker and provides a number of useful examples. I call this chapter "A Weekend Tour of PageMaker" because in the better part of two days, you will be working comfortably and confidently with PageMaker. If you left work Friday night not knowing PageMaker and vowing to do something about it, here's your chance. This chapter walks you through the basics of designing, laying out, and preparing to print a document—everything you need to know to become productive in PageMaker. So grab a cup of coffee and get comfortable; we're going to cover a lot of ground.

To start PageMaker:

1. Move your mouse over the **Start** button at the bottom of your Windows screen, and click to open the Start menu.

2. Slide the mouse arrow up the menu to **Programs**. Don't click; the menu will open by itself.

3. Now slide the arrow up the Programs menu to the **Adobe** folder. After a second, the Adobe menu will pop open. Now choose the **PageMaker** program icon and double-click to start PageMaker. The main window is shown in Figure 2.1.

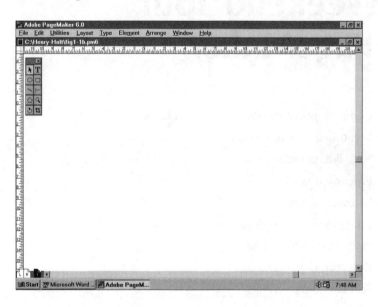

Figure 2.1 *The main window of PageMaker 6.0.*

Components of the PageMaker Window

The *PageMaker window* is the working space for creating and producing documents. Since you haven't yet created a new document or opened an existing document, there is nothing in the main window. Let's take a brief look at all the components in the window. I'll cover them in greater detail later in this chapter and in the chapters that follow:

❖ **Title bar**. Across the top of the screen is the PageMaker *title bar.* When the size of the window is less than the maximum size, you can move the entire window by clicking on the title bar and dragging the mouse to a new position.

Control-menu icon. The symbol at the upper left of the title bar is called the Control-menu icon. Click it to open the Control menu. Use the Control menu to resize the current window or close the application.

Minimize button. Click the **Minimize** button, on the upper-right side of the title bar, to shrink PageMaker to an icon on the Windows desktop. Double-click the icon to maximize PageMaker.

Maximize button. If PageMaker is the full size of the screen, clicking the **Maximize** button (to the right of the Minimize button) reduces the size of PageMaker so that you can see the Windows desktop. To increase the size of the PageMaker window, click the **Maximize** button again.

Close button. To close PageMaker in one click, use the **Close** button.

❖ **Pull-down menus**. The main pull-down menus control all PageMaker functions. Click on a menu title in the menu bar to pull down the menu. Pull-down menus contain five types of commands:

Hyphenation...   **Commands with ellipsis (...).** Choosing a command with an ellipsis displays a dialog box. Command dialog boxes require you to enter more information or present more choices.

Size ▶   **Commands with arrows.** A right-pointing arrow means there is a second menu level (called a submenu) to follow. For example, choosing **Size** displays a size submenu showing all the currently installed font-sizes in your system.

✔ No Track   Sh^Q   **Commands with check marks.** A check mark beside a command means the command is toggled on (turned on). Choosing a command with a check mark removes the mark and toggles the command off. The check mark beside the No Track command means that tracking is not possible.

Expert Kerning...   **Commands that are dimmed.** A dimmed command is not currently available. Often, you must select or highlight some text or a graphic before dimmed commands will darken and become available.

Type Specs...   ^T   **Commands with keyboard shortcuts.** Sometimes a keyboard equivalent is displayed to the right of the command. Pressing the keys gives you the same result as selecting the command indicated from the menu. (In this example, the caret before the T means to hold down the **Ctrl** key while pressing the **T** key.)

There are two ways to pull down menus:

❖ **Using the mouse.** Position the mouse pointer over the pull-down menu name you want to activate and click once. The menu drops down. To see a submenu or invoke a menu command, reposition the mouse pointer over the menu command title (a right-facing arrow points to another level of menus) and click the left mouse button. If you hold down the left mouse button as the pointer passes over a menu name, that menu drops down. To pull the menu back up, click in the title bar above the menus or anywhere in the document window.

❖ **Using the Alt key**. If you press the **Alt** key and the underlined letter in the pull-down menu name, the menu drops down. For example, to see the Edit menu, hold down the **Alt** key and press **E**. To see any other menu, use the **Left** and **Right Arrow** keys. To pull the menu back up, press **Esc** twice.

Using PageMaker Shortcuts

In addition to the **Alt**-key shortcuts, PageMaker uses a number of unique shortcuts. The key combinations are a carryover from the Macintosh version of PageMaker's **Command**-key shortcuts; in the Windows version, the **Ctrl** key replaces the Macintosh **Command** key.

Activating a Menu Command

Menu commands can be activated by the mouse or the keyboard. With the mouse, click the appropriate pull-down menu and choose the command by clicking it. If you are using the keyboard, press the **Alt** key and the underlined pull-down menu letter, then press the letter underlined in the command you want. For example, to paste (**Edit > Paste**), press **Alt+E P**. Some commands can be activated with keyboard shortcuts (the **Paste** command is also activated by holding down the **Shift** key and pressing the **Insert** key). In this book, combination keystrokes are indicated by a plus sign (+), which means you should hold down the first key while you press the second key. For example, **Shift+Insert** means to hold down the **Shift** key and press the **Insert** key.

Creating a New Document

Creating a new document is similar to taping a clean sheet of paper to your drawing board. Before you can begin to work, you must tell PageMaker some things about the paper, such as the margin specifications, paper size, and how many pages long your document will be. Follow these steps to create a new document:

1. Move the mouse to the **File** pull-down menu and click the left mouse button (or press **Alt+F**).

2. Move the mouse to select **New** (or press **N**). PageMaker displays the Document Setup dialog box, shown in Figure 2.2.

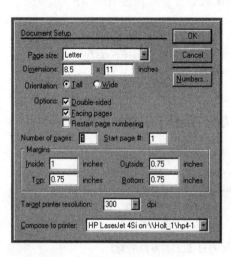

Figure 2.2 *PageMaker's Document Setup dialog box.*

Use the Document Setup dialog box to set the initial specifications for your paper, including:

❖ **Page**. Indicates the size of paper for this document, based on the printer you have selected.

❖ **Page dimensions**. Indicates the overall width and height of the paper specified in the Page list box. Enter your own dimensions here to define a custom page size. The default measurement system in PageMaker is inches. Chapter 3 tells you how to change the measurements to another standard, such as picas or millimeters.

❖ **Orientation**. The default orientation is tall (also called *portrait*). Wide orientation turns the page 90 degrees (also called *landscape*). Depending on the page dimensions you entered, PageMaker selects the tall or wide orientation automatically. If you click on the opposite orientation, the values you entered in the dimension text boxes are switched.

❖ **Start page #**. Indicates which number to start numbering the pages with (for example, if you want your first page number to be 7 and your second page to be 8, and so on, enter **7** in the text box).

❖ **Options**. If you will be printing on both sides of the page, click the **Double-sided** check box. If your document will be bound on the left side and you want PageMaker to compensate for the binding or hole punch, click the **Facing pages** check box.

❖ **Margins**. The default margins for a new document are displayed. You can change the margins if you wish.

Changing the margins after formatting one or more pages of text may produce some unexpected results. Save the document before changing the margins. Then, if you change your mind, simply close the current document without saving it and reopen the version of the document you saved before changing the margins.

Setting the Margins

For many types of documents, including reports, proposals, stationery, business forms, fact sheets, and flyers, the default margin settings may be satisfactory. But you can change the margin size and the page size to suit practically any need. Remember, the page size is the overall size of the printed page. Margins are the inner boundaries of that page, which normally designate where the printer prints text and graphics. To change the margin settings:

1. Position the mouse pointer in the Margin Measurement text box you want to change, and double-click the left mouse button.

2. Type the new margin value. If the default margins are in inches and you want to enter a pica value, simply type **P** after the value. When you click **OK** or press **Enter** to leave the dialog box, PageMaker converts the pica measurement to the equivalent number of inches (for example, *6 picas* is converted to *1 inch*). PageMaker also recognizes millimeters (mm) and ciceros (c). See "Changing Design Preferences," in Chapter 3.

3. Press **Tab** to move to the next margin text box you want to change.

4. When you are finished, click **OK** or press **Enter** to display the new document window.

Setting the Page Size

PageMaker comes configured with standard paper sizes, based on the capability of your laser printer. You can't print a larger page size than your printer can physically handle, but you can specify a smaller size. Why would you want to? Because PageMaker prints crop marks, based on the page-size dimensions, that indicate the trim size of the finished page. To change the page-size dimensions:

1. Position the mouse pointer over the first dimension text box and double-click the left mouse button.

2. Type the new dimension. If the default dimensions are in inches and you want to enter a pica value, simply type **P** after the value. When you click **OK** or press **Enter** to leave the dialog box, PageMaker converts the pica measurement to inches (for example, 51 by 84 picas is converted to 8.5 by 14 inches).

3. Press **Tab** to move to the second dimension text box. Enter a value.

4. When you're finished, click **OK** or press **Enter** to move to the new document window.

Using the **Tile** option in the Print Document dialog box, you can print pages larger than the physical size of the paper by printing tiles that fit together to form the larger size. You'll learn more about tiling in Chapter 7, "Printing."

Using printed crop marks helps your commercial printer align, print, and trim your PageMaker documents. This saves time, and thus money.

Changing the Page Orientation

If after setting a page size you find that the page width is actually the height (because you entered the page dimension values in the wrong order), you can change the orientation without re-entering the page dimensions. Here's how:

1. From the document window, click on the **File** pull-down menu and select **Document Setup** (or press **Alt+F M**) to display the Document Setup dialog box.

2. To change a tall document to a wide document, click the **Wide** option button. To change wide to tall orientation, click the **Tall** option button. Notice that the page dimensions switch text boxes when you change orientation.

3. Click **OK** or press **Enter** to return to the document window. You can change page orientation at any point while composing a page, but doing so may disturb the placement of text and graphics. It is a good idea to settle the orientation issue before you begin work.

Setting Page Numbers

When you create a new document, PageMaker sets the number of pages to 1 and highlights the text box. You can enter any number of pages up to 9999. To change the number of pages (assuming all else is correct in the dialog box), simply type the number of pages and click **OK** or press **Enter**. Follow these steps:

1. If you want the page numbers to start with a number other than 1, place the insertion point in the Start Page # text box and double-click the left mouse button.

2. Type the new beginning page number. Press **Tab** to move to the # of Pages text box.

3. If you only want to increase the number of pages, type the number in the highlighted text box. It's safer to break up extremely large documents into individual chapters. PageMaker runs faster when working with smaller files. See Chapter 9, "Developing Long Documents," for more information about the Book and Link features.

4. Click **OK** or press **Enter** to move to the new document window. For multipage documents, you needn't be concerned with setting the correct number of pages—you can add more pages or delete excess pages any time. See "Inserting and Removing Pages" in Chapter 3.

Targeting the Correct Printer

It is a good idea to decide which printer will print the document when you are setting the page configuration in the Document Setup dialog box. If you click the **Compose to Printer** list box arrow you will see a list of all installed Windows printers. Choose the one you want for this particular document, if possible. If not, you can always change the printer setting later. While PageMaker warns you that making changes later can affect the layout of the page, as long as you are selecting another PostScript printer, the changes should make little, if any, difference. See

"Targeting the Right Printer" in Chapter 7 for more details about choosing the printer to print your documents.

Changing the Page Size View

PageMaker offers a number of perspectives, or *views*, of your document pages. You can shrink the image down to see the whole page or see varying enlargements of the page up to 400% of actual size. When a new document is created, it is initially displayed in the Fit in Window view, shown in Figure 2.3. You see the whole page and the edges of the PageMaker pasteboard at each side of the page. This perspective is ideal for seeing the overall design of your page. Body copy that is 16 points or smaller is represented by gray bars, type 17 points and bigger is readable in this view.

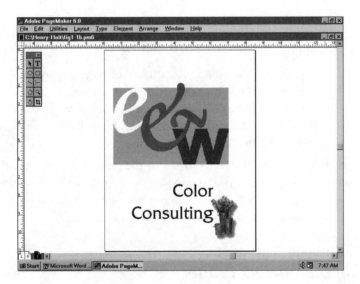

Figure 2.3 *Fit in window view.*

You can change views of the page at any time. To increase the size of your page: choose the **Layout** pull-down menu (or press **Alt+L**) and select the **View** command to display the View submenu. Then choose one of the page view options:

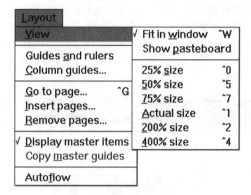

- ❖ **Fit in window (Ctrl+0)**—Shows the full size of the page, no matter how large, as in Figure 2.3.

- ❖ **Show pasteboard**—This view shrinks the page to a postage-stamp size and shows the entire size (and contents) of the pasteboard. If you're sure you moved something to the pasteboard but you can't find it, choose this view and you'll see it right away.

- ❖ **25% size**—Displays a very small rendering of the page, as shown in Figure 2.4. Only large headlines are readable in this thumbnail sketch of the page.

Figure 2.4 *The 25% view displays a very small rendering of the page.*

❖ **50% size** (**Ctrl+5** or **Alt+5**)—Displays a half-size view of the page, as shown in Figure 2.5. Normal body copy is *greeked* (displayed in gray lines) below 13 points, but there is good definition to larger headings and graphics.

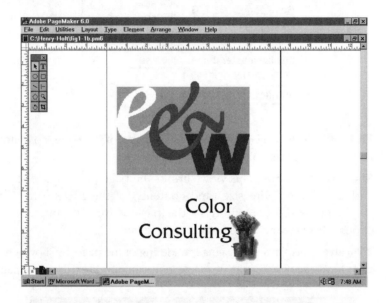

Figure 2.5 *The 50% view displays a half-size view of the page.*

❖ **75% size**—Displays body copy clearly, as shown in Figure 2.6. This is probably the most useful view if you have a 12- or 13-inch monitor because more of the page is visible than with the full-size view. In this view, the full width of an 8-inch page is visible. It takes very little movement of the scroll box to move to the top or bottom of the page. Of course, if you have a big full- or dual-page monitor, you can see everything in the Actual Size view.

Figure 2.6 *The 75% view displays body copy clearly.*

❖ **Actual size** (**Ctrl+1** or **Alt+A**)—Shows an exact one-to-one representation of the page, as shown in Figure 2.7. Use this perspective when adjusting lines, text, or graphics or when typing text on the page.

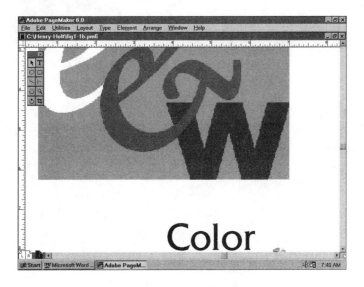

Figure 2.7 *Actual size shows an exact representation of the page.*

❖ **200% size** (**Ctrl+2** or **Alt+2**)—Doubles the actual view size, as shown in Figure 2.8, giving you very fine control over the placement of text and graphics. You may find it awkward to use the scroll boxes to move around the page in this view. If so, hold down the **Alt** key and press the left mouse button. The mouse pointer changes to a hand icon. While holding down the **Alt** key and mouse button, push the page in the direction you want it to move, just as you would push a piece of paper on your desk.

Figure 2.8 *The 200% view doubles the actual size.*

❖ **400% size**—Again doubles the size of the page, as shown in Figure 2.9. At this perspective, you're seeing less than a 2-by-2 inch area of the page—great for extra-fine work, but it may take your computer a moment to refresh the screen when you move the page with either the hand icon or the scroll boxes.

Figure 2.9 *The 400% view is useful for extra-fine work.*

The New Document Window

When you leave the Document Setup dialog box, PageMaker displays a new document window, shown in Figure 2.10. Page 1 is displayed in the Fit in Window view, with rulers along the top and left edges. In the upper-left corner is the toolbox palette. The toolbox contains all the tools you need to compose your page. When you click the mouse pointer on a tool, the mouse changes to that tool when you move the pointer outside the boundaries of the toolbox. The tools include:

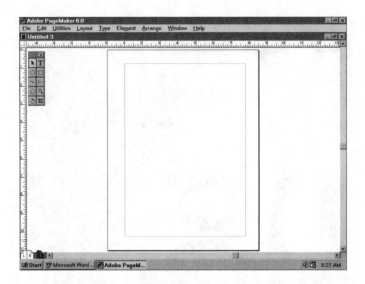

Figure 2.10 *A new page 1 in the Fit in Window view.*

Pointer tool (**F9**)—Use the pointer to select any kind of object on the page, including blocks of text, lines, boxes, circles, and imported graphics. When selected, the objects display sizing handles, as shown in Figure 2.11. Moving text is covered later in this chapter. See Chapter 3 for more information about selecting and moving text and Chapter 4 concerning resizing and moving graphic objects and images.

Figure 2.11 *Objects display sizing handles when selected with the Pointer tool.*

Text tool (**Shift+F2**)—Clicking the **Text** tool changes the pointer to an insertion point for typing and highlighting text.

Ellipse tool (**Shift+F3**)—Use this tool to draw circles and ellipses. You draw ellipses much like boxes: start in the upper-left side and drag down and to the right. Holding down the **Shift** key while drawing creates a perfect circle.

Rectangle tool (**Shift+F4**)—This tool draws square-cornered boxes. Click the mouse button to position the upper-left corner of the box and drag the mouse to the right and down to create the box. Holding down the **Shift** key while drawing creates a perfect square.

Line tool (**Shift+F5**)—Use this tool to draw diagonal lines. You can select a diagonal line with the Pointer tool and click on either handle to resize the line or change its angle.

Constrained-line tool (**Shift+F6**)—This tool draws vertical and horizontal lines. You can shorten or lengthen the lines with the Pointer tool by clicking on either handle.

Polygon tool (**Shift+F7**)—Use this tool to create multisided objects. While its default setting is to create pentagons, you can modify the shape using the Polygon Settings dialog box, found on the Elements menu.

Zoom tool (**Shift+F8**)—Control the current view of your page with the Zoom tool. Click to increase or decrease the magnification of the page.

Rotating tool (**Shift+F9**)—Allows you to rotate a selected item to any of 360 degrees of rotation in .01-degree increments. To use the tool, first click the item you want to rotate with the Pointer tool. Then click the **Rotating** tool. Move the crosshairs to the center of rotation for the item, press and hold down the left mouse button, and draw a line with the crosshairs in the direction you want to rotate. Pretend that the line is the rotating lever, and while still holding down the left mouse button, position the crosshairs at the outboard end of the lever and drag the lever clockwise or counterclockwise. When you have established the degree of rotation you want, release the mouse button. You can force the rotation to 45-degree increments by holding down the **Shift** key while you drag the rotating lever.

Cropping tool (F11)—Use this tool to *crop* (reduce the image area of) graphics and scanned photos. In the lower-left corner of the window are the master page icons (discussed in Chapters 4 and 5) and the page icon, displaying the page numbers. You'll learn how to use the page icons to move around the document later in this chapter.

Displaying the Rulers

If rulers are not displayed in the document window, you can activate them by choosing the **Guides and Rulers** submenu from the Layout menu. Then choose the **Show Rulers** command to display the horizontal and vertical rulers. A check mark next to the option indicates that the rulers are displayed. Selecting the option again removes the check mark and hides the rulers. The default measurement system for the rulers is inches, but you can change to any of several systems. To save time, you might want to use the PageMaker keyboard shortcut **Ctrl+R** to toggle the display of rulers on and off.

Changing the Ruler Measurement System

By default, the rulers are calibrated in inches. However, you can change PageMaker's measuring system at any time by following these steps:

1. Choose the **File** pull-down menu and select **Preferences** (or press **Alt+F F**) to display the Preferences dialog box, shown in Figure 2.12.

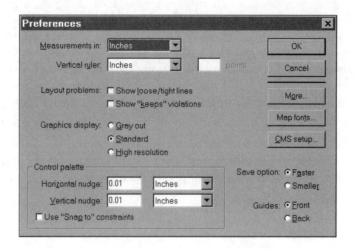

Figure 2.12 *The Preferences dialog box.*

2. In the Layout area, click the **Measurement System** list box arrow to see the drop-down list. You can choose among:

   ❖ **Inches**. The default measurement system.

   ❖ **Decimal inches**. The rulers display ten tick marks (when the page view allows) to the inch. Values are entered in decimals.

   ❖ **Millimeters**. 25.4 millimeters equal 1 inch.

   ❖ **Picas**. There are 12 points to the pica and 6 picas to the inch. The length of a text line (known as the *line measure*) is traditionally specified in picas.

   ❖ **Ciceros**. A *cicero* is slightly smaller than a pica; there are 5.58 ciceros to an inch.

3. Select the measurement system you want. The system you select is displayed in the top ruler and in all dialog text boxes requiring a measurement value. For example, if you select picas as the measurement system, the top ruler displays picas, and the margin values you originally set up in inches are converted to picas.

4. Next, click the **Vertical Ruler** list box arrow to see its drop-down list. Notice that the same measurement choices are displayed, with the addition of **Custom**.

5. Choose a measurement system for the vertical ruler. It can be the same as your selection for the Measurement System text box (which controls the top horizontal ruler), or you can choose a different system. Choose **Custom** if you want to establish point-measurement tick marks on the vertical ruler that equal the amount of leading for your type. Then, if you turn on **Snap to Rulers** in the Guides and Rulers submenu (from the Layout menu), the baselines of the text align to the tick marks on the vertical ruler.

6. If you selected **Custom** in step 5, enter the number of points of leading in the Points list box. Click **OK** or press **Enter** to return to your document.

Using the Rulers

The rulers give you the most accuracy in laying out a page. As you move the mouse pointer or tool icon across the page, reference marks also move on the horizontal and vertical rulers, indicating the current position of the mouse, as shown in Figure 2.13.

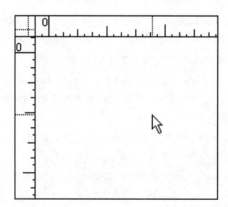

Figure 2.13 *Horizontal and vertical reference marks indicate the current position of the mouse.*

You may find it helpful at times to reset the zero point of either ruler to measure a specific area of the page, for example, if you add a line to a page and want to place it exactly one inch from the bottom margin. You can gauge the measurement on the vertical ruler (although you may have to change the measurement system to inches first), or you can pull down the zero point of the vertical ruler to be even with the bottom margin. To reset the vertical ruler's zero point:

1. Position the page in the area you want to work. Consider enlarging the page view to get a more accurate picture.

2. Place the pointer in the junction of the two rulers (upper-left corner of the document screen) and do one of the following:

    ❖ To pull the horizontal ruler's zero point down the page, click in the ruler junction box, hold down the left mouse button, and drag the pointer down the vertical ruler to the position you want. When you release the mouse, the new zero point is established. To accurately position the box in the preceding example, drag the zero point down until it is even with the bottom margin. Then position the box at the one-inch tick mark on the ruler.

    ❖ To pull the vertical ruler's zero point across the page, click in the ruler junction box, hold down the left mouse button, and drag the pointer along the horizontal ruler to the position you want.

    ❖ To reposition both zero points, click in the ruler junction box, hold down the left mouse button, and drag both zero points off the rulers onto the page to the position you want. As you drag the zero marks out of the rulers, you see a pair of intersecting lines extend down and across the page, like crosshairs, to help you align the ruler zero points accurately on your page.

    ❖ While you can change the zero points of the rulers at any time, you may want to lock a particular adjustment so that they can't be accidentally moved. To do so, choose the **Layout** pull-down menu and select the **Guides and Rulers** submenu. Choose **Zero lock** to toggle the option on (you will see a check mark by the option if you choose the submenu again). To unlock the zero points, simply choose the option again, toggling it off.

Using Guidelines

A fundamental aid to page layout is the *grid*. Grids help you to visualize the basic symmetry of a page and provide an accurate reference for positioning text and graphics. On a drawing board, you drew grids with a T-square and a blue pencil.

In PageMaker it's much simpler: position the mouse pointer on either ruler and click and drag a horizontal or vertical guideline onto the page. Guidelines are the equivalent of nonreproducible blue pencil lines (on a color monitor, the guidelines are displayed in blue) and, just like the nonrepro pencil lines, they do not print. Guidelines are used for alignment only.

POSITIONING GUIDELINES

Guidelines are a basic building block of PageMaker's design and layout capabilities. You can use as many of them as you need, and each page can contain a unique arrangement of guidelines. You can also set up master guidelines that are the same for all pages.

To position a unique set of guidelines on an individual page:

1. Select the page view needed to accurately position the guideline. You might want to start out in the Fit in Window size (**Ctrl+0**) to see the overall page, position the guideline in the general area, then select **Actual size (Ctrl+1)** or **200% (Ctrl+2)** to finalize the guideline's position.

2. Regardless of which toolbox tool you are using, move it onto the horizontal ruler if you need a horizontal guideline or onto the vertical ruler if you need a vertical guideline. The tool icon changes to a pointer once inside the ruler.

    You can click anywhere on the ruler to grab a guideline, except in the junction box of the two rulers. Clicking there repositions the zero points.

3. Hold down the left mouse button. The pointer changes to a two-headed arrow, indicating you have grabbed a guideline. Now drag the arrow onto the page. As soon as the arrow moves out of the boundary of the ruler, you'll see a guideline the width or height of the displayed page size. Continue dragging the guideline to the position you want. As you drag the guideline, the guideline reference mark moves an equal amount on the ruler, indicating the guideline's position.

4. Release the left mouse button to fix the guideline's position. You can adjust the guideline at any time by clicking it with the Pointer tool. The pointer changes back to the two-headed arrow. Drag the arrow to reposition the guideline.

NOTE

You may have noticed that guidelines do not appear on the PageMaker pasteboard. If you need a guideline on the pasteboard, position the guideline on the page in relation to where you want it on the pasteboard. Then select the **Constrained Line** tool and draw a line over the guideline, but continue it off the page. Unless you specifically want the line leading off the page to print, delete it or shorten it so that it is completely on the pasteboard before printing.

ADDING GUIDELINES TO MASTER PAGES

Each PageMaker document includes a set of master pages that are used to contain document-wide text, graphics, and formatting. The Master Pages feature is explained in detail in Chapters 4 and 5, but let's look at it briefly now to see how guidelines work with it. To set up master guidelines that are the same for all the pages in your document:

1. The **Master Pages** icon is located beside the Pages icon in the lower-left corner of the document window. Click the **Master Pages** icon to display the master pages window. If you selected **Double-Sided pages** in the Document Setup dialog box, you see a blank two-page spread consisting of the left and right master pages. Anything added to the left page is added to all left pages (usually the even-numbered pages). Anything added to the right page is added to all right pages (usually the odd-numbered pages).

    For example, let's say you wanted to add a logo in the top margin of both pages of a two-page document, to be printed on the front and back. By positioning the logo on the right master page, it is automatically displayed on the front page of the document, locked in position. By adding an additional logo to the left master page, the logo is also displayed on the back of the page (page 2). You don't have to manually position the logo on each page in exactly the same spot. Likewise, if you add more pages to your document, the logos are displayed automatically on every page. Finally, if you decide you really want the logo in the bottom margins, all you have to do is click on the **Master Pages** icon and move the two logos to the bottom of the pages. The logos are then automatically repositioned throughout your document.

2. Move the mouse pointer to the ruler, grab a guideline, and drag it onto the master page. Position the guideline exactly where you want it. Add as many guidelines as you like. You can add or remove them at any point in your work.

3. When you're finished, click on the appropriate page number, beside the Master Pages icon, to move back to that page of your document.

You will see the guidelines you just added to the master pages. Notice that you can't move these guidelines. You must go back to the Master Page feature to adjust them.

N O T E

While PageMaker comes ready to configure only one left and right master page, you can create as many master pages as your document needs. See Chapter 5, "Setting Up Templates," for complete details.

ALIGNING TO GUIDELINES

Guidelines make it easy to align text and graphics. It's even easier if you turn on the Snap To Guides feature. *Snap* means that if you get the object you're aligning close to the guideline and release the mouse button, the object automatically jumps to the guideline, giving you perfect alignment (within 1/2880-inch). To turn on the Snap To feature:

1. Choose the **Layout** pull-down menu (or press **Alt+L**). Next, choose the **Guides and Rulers** submenu.

2. Select **Snap To Guides**. Choose the submenu again to see a check mark next to Snap To Guides, indicating the feature is toggled on. Select it again to toggle the feature off. The shortcut for this command is **Ctrl+Shift+5**.

3. You can differentiate between guides and rulers with the Snap To feature. Notice that the Guides and Rulers submenu allows you to set the Snap To feature differently for guides and rulers.

N O T E

When the Snap To option is on, it is in effect for all pages in your document.

DISPLAYING GUIDELINES

Sometimes you may want to see guidelines; other times you might want to hide them. The display of guidelines is controlled by the Layout menu. Follow these steps:

1. Choose the **Layout** pull-down menu (or press **Alt+L**) and click the **Guides and Rulers** command to display the submenu.

2. Select **Guides** to toggle the display of guidelines on and off. A check next to the option means the option is on. Select the option again to toggle it off. The shortcut for this command is **Ctrl+J**.

You may also want to change whether guidelines are displayed over the top of items on the page or behind items. Each mode has its advantages. I like to display the guide on top of other items so that I'm sure the items align to the guides, but sometimes the guides are annoying when they are visible in front of text and graphics. To control their placement, let's go back to Guides and Rulers submenu. Follow these steps:

1. Choose the **Layout** pull-down menu (or press **Alt+L**) and click the **Guides and Rulers** command to display the submenu.

2. Now, choose the guides' placement: **Guides in Front** or **Guides in Back**. The placement can be changed at any time without affecting what is aligned to the guidelines.

LOCKING GUIDELINES

Once the guidelines are positioned correctly, it's a good idea to lock them in place. To lock guidelines:

1. Choose the **Layout** pull-down menu (or press **Alt+L**) and click the **Guides and Rulers** command to display the submenu.

2. Select **Lock Guides** (or press **L**) to lock the guidelines on the pages of your document. A check mark means the guides are locked. Select the option again to remove the check mark and unlock the guides.

Entering Text

There are two things to remember about entering text in PageMaker: first, select the **Text** tool. Second, position the text insertion point where you want to begin typing and click the mouse. Let's try entering some text on your new document page:

1. Move the pointer to the toolbox and click on the **Text** tool. The Text tool icon darkens, indicating the Text tool is active.

2. Move the pointer onto the document page. As soon as the pointer leaves the toolbox it changes to an insertion point. Position the insertion point where you wish to begin typing, and click the mouse.

   You may notice that if you click in the middle of the document, the insertion point and your typing skips to the left margin. Clicking the insertion point on the document invokes whatever page formatting is currently in effect—in this case, PageMaker defaults to left justification. Overriding current type alignment is discussed later in this chapter.

Before starting to type text, let's get a closer view of your work. To change the view of this page from Fit in Window to the full-size view:

1. Move the mouse up to the Layout pull-down menu. Notice that the insertion point changes back to the pointer when it leaves the boundaries of the document.

2. Choose the **Layout** pull-down menu and choose the **View** submenu to display your view choices. Now choose **Actual**. The document resizes to a 1:1 perspective, and the rulers automatically recalibrate to actual size. Hold a real ruler up to the PageMaker ruler and compare them if you like; they're the same.

3. Use the scroll bars to reposition the portion of the page you want to work in.

4. Move the pointer back onto the page—the pointer changes back to the Text tool insertion point—and click where you want to begin typing.

Whatever you type is displayed in the PageMaker default type style and font. We'll cover changing the type specifications in a minute, but first let's learn how to place the text where you want it—instead of where PageMaker wants it.

Opening a Text Block

In PageMaker, text is actually typed in text blocks, not on the paper of the document window. A text block is basically defined by the amount of text and the margins of the page. Think of typing in a text block as typing onto one or more windowshades: they are normally as wide as the column or margins, and they unroll as you add more text. When selected with the Pointer tool, you see handles at the top and bottom of each windowshade, as shown in Figure 2.14. Use the handles to roll the windowshade up and down, covering up or revealing text. Windowshade handles are also used to thread text blocks together, as explained in Chapter 3.

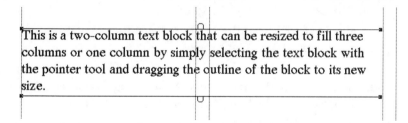

This is a two-column text block that can be resized to fill three columns or one column by simply selecting the text block with the pointer tool and dragging the outline of the block to its new size.

Figure 2.14 *Handles at the top and bottom roll the windowshade up and down to cover or reveal text.*

N O T E

Because text blocks have their own identity in PageMaker, you can move them just like any other graphic object or image. When typing in a text block, you can continue adding text right off the bottom of the page. You can just as easily click on a text block and drag it off the page, just like you might move a piece of type off to the side of the drawing board. Text blocks, like all other objects in PageMaker, have sizing handles that allow you to resize their width. You can easily stretch a one-column text block across two columns simply by clicking and dragging a text block handle. When you do this, the text inside the box is rearranged to fit the new width—the size of the type is not affected. Figure 2.15 shows some examples of resized text blocks.

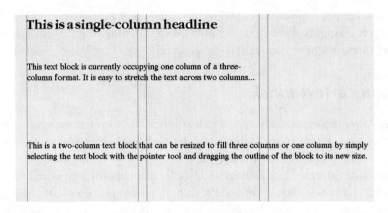

Figure 2.15 *Some examples of resized text blocks.*

To open a new text block positioned where you want:

1. Select the **Text** tool from the toolbox. Place the insertion point where you want to type.

2. Press the left mouse button and drag the insertion point to the right, the width that you want the line of text. As you drag, you'll see a box open up. This box defines the boundaries of your text block.

3. When you have opened the box to the correct size, release the mouse button. The insertion point snaps to the beginning of the new, now-invisible, text block.

4. Begin typing. The text moves to the right until it reaches the right edge of the text block you defined and then wraps back to the next line, as shown in Figure 2.16.

This is an example of text wrapping: when the insertion point gets to the end of a line, it automatically jumps back to the first character position in the next line

Figure 2.16 *Text wraps automatically in text blocks.*

You can see the boundaries of the text block by selecting it with the Pointer tool.

Moving a Text Block

To move a text block:

1. Select the **Pointer** tool and click anywhere inside the text block. The windowshade and sizing handles will appear.
2. Position the pointer anywhere inside the block, other than on one of the four corner sizing handles.
3. Hold down the left mouse button—the pointer changes to the positioning icon—and drag the text block to a new position.
4. When you are sure of the new position, release the left mouse button.

Resizing a Text Block

To resize the width of a text block:

1. Select the **Pointer** tool and click anywhere inside the text block. The windowshade and sizing handles will appear.
2. Position the Pointer tool over one of the four corner sizing handles.
3. Hold down the left mouse button and drag the handle to a new location, stretching or shrinking the text block.
4. When you release the handle, the text fills the newly sized text block.

Formatting Type

When you create a new document in PageMaker, it contains a set of default formatting specifications that may or may not be complementary to what you want to do. The default format is easily changed; once it is, it remains in effect for that document.

PageMaker offers extremely accurate typographic control of letters, words, lines, and paragraphs. One of the advantages of PageMaker is that you don't have to spend a lot of time specifying type for simple jobs. The default specifications do nicely for many designs. Other documents might require only a few changes to customize the type or layout to exactly what you want.

With PageMaker, you are free to experiment with different formats. You can make as many changes in the format of a document as you wish. Each page of a brochure could contain text in a different number of columns, for example, set in different typefaces (although I can't say how attractive such a design would be). Only two things cannot change within a document: the size of the page and the width of the margins.

Changing Font Families

A *font family* consists of the basic typeface, and usually bold, italic, and bold italic styles of the typeface. Some typefaces also have extra light, extra bold, condensed, and extended versions. An example of a font family is Helvetica, one of the standard fonts that comes installed on all PostScript printers. You could define a letter, word, sentence, paragraph, or an entire document with any combination of Helvetica, Helvetica Bold, Helvetica Italic, and Helvetica Bold Italic and remain within the Helvetica family. (Additionally, there are a number of Helvetica downloadable fonts that you can buy, including Helvetica Black, Condensed, Compressed, Extended, Light, Rounded, and Narrow.)

To change font families in a document, follow these steps:

1. If you are not in the Actual Size page view, select it by pressing **Ctrl+1**.

2. Let's create some personalized stationery. Position the Text tool in the upper-left corner of the page and type your name on the document page.

3. Highlight the name by placing the Text tool anywhere on it and quickly clicking the left mouse button three times.

N O T E — Double-clicking a word in a text block highlights the word. Triple-clicking 'a word highlights that word and all the words around it until a paragraph code (made when you press the **Enter** key) is encountered. Normally, this means that all the text in a paragraph is highlighted.

4. Move the mouse to the Type menu and select **Font** (or press **Alt+T F**). The system displays a drop-down submenu of available font families. You will see a check mark beside the family for the currently selected font.

NOTE If you have installed many font families on your computer, all may not be displayed in the Font submenu. Choose **More** to see additional font menus or use the Type Specification dialog box, described later in this chapter.

5. Move the mouse pointer down the submenu or scroll down the submenu with the down arrow to select a new family. Click the left mouse button on the new family name or press **Enter**. Notice that the selected text is now formatted in the font you selected.

6. Position the Text tool to the right of the last letter in your last name and press **Enter** to move down to a new line in the text block. Type your street address, press **Enter** to move down another line, and then type your city, state, and zip code. Move down one more line with the **Enter** key and add your phone number.

Changing Font Sizes

PostScript and TrueType fonts are *scalable*, meaning you can display and print type in any size from 4 to 650 points. PageMaker comes set with a default type size of 10 points, but you can change the size as often as you like. To change the size of your type, do the following:

1. Position the insertion point anywhere in your name on the first line of the letterhead. Select the entire line by quickly clicking the left mouse button three times.

2. Choose the **Type** pull-down menu and choose **Size** (or press **Alt+T Z**) to display the Size submenu. You can choose any size from this list or select **Other** (or press **O**) to enter a different size. Selecting **Other** displays a dialog box for you to enter the type size you want. Click **OK** or press **Enter** to return to your document.

When you return to your document, the new size is in effect for the selected type.

Changing Typeface Styles

Styles are changed as easily as sizes. There are six different styles for any typeface. They are:

❖ **Normal** (**Ctrl+Shift+Spacebar**). The look of the font without any styles added. If you want to undo styles that you've added to text, just redefine the text as **Normal**.

❖ **Bold** (**Ctrl+Shift+B**). Adds blackness and thickness to the type.

❖ **Italic** (**Ctrl+Shift+I**). Slants the type to the right and often gives the font a script-like appearance.

❖ **Underline** (**Ctrl+Shift+U**). Underlines text and spaces between words if the spaces are included in the text selected to be changed.

❖ **Reverse** (**Ctrl+Shift+V**). Reverses the color of the type from black to white (to see reversed type you must color the background).

❖ **Strikethru** (**Ctrl+Shift+S**). Draws a horizontal line through the middle of each letter selected. This style is often used in legal correspondence and contracts to indicate text changes.

You can change any highlighted text to All Caps by pressing **Ctrl+Shift+K**.

You can undo any style by pressing the keyboard shortcut a second time. For example, if you highlight several words and press **Ctrl+Shift+B** to make them bold, pressing the same key combination again toggles the style off. Or you can press **Ctrl+Shift+Spacebar** to undo the style.

You can combine any or all of the styles in one font to create a custom look. For example, if you select both **Reverse** and **Bold**, you will have a white, bold type that must be placed on a black or colored background. This has a striking effect, as shown in Figure 2.17.

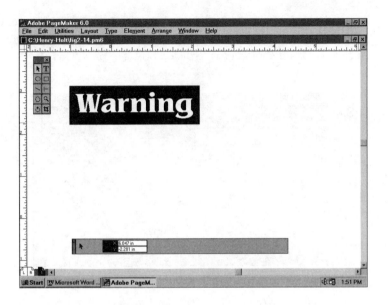

Figure 2.17 *Creating a custom look of text for a striking effect.*

To change the font style of text:

1. Position the insertion point of the Text tool in the name portion of the letterhead you just created.

2. Highlight the entire line by quickly clicking the mouse button three times.

3. Choose the **Type** pull-down menu and choose **Type Style** (or press **Alt+T Y**) and select the style you want. In this case, select **Bold**.

4. When you return to your document, the new bold style is in effect for the selected text.

Changing Type Specifications

Occasionally you will want to change several aspects of a line of type all at once. A quick way to do so is with the Type Specifications dialog box. Let's take a look:

1. Select some text to change. For this example, select the two-line address of your letterhead.

2. Choose the **Type** pull-down menu and choose **Type Specs** (or press **Alt+T T**) to display the Type Specifications dialog box, shown in Figure 2.18. A nice PageMaker shortcut to the dialog box is to press **Ctrl+T**.

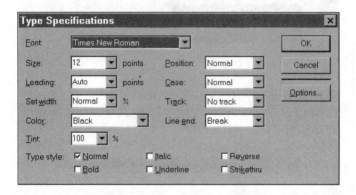

Figure 2.18 *The Type Specifications dialog box.*

As you can see, the dialog box allows you to make all the changes to type we've just covered, plus many others. Let's look at the remaining capabilities briefly and then use the dialog box to change the type you have selected:

❖ **Leading** (pronounced "ledding")—*Leading* constitutes the height of the font plus the space above the font, based on its size. As the font size is changed, so must the leading measurement. The correct leading for a given size is normally about 120% of the type size (so that if the type size is 10 points, the leading is usually 12 points). PageMaker uses two different measurement systems for leading. Luckily, you don't normally have to worry about leading because PageMaker has a nifty Auto feature that automatically determines and sets the correct amount of leading. When you change the type size, PageMaker adjusts the leading size accordingly. See "Changing Type Leading" later in this chapter.

❖ **Set Width**—Changes the width of individual characters proportionally from 70 to 130% of Normal. See "Changing Character Widths" later in this chapter.

❖ **Color**—Assigns the selected type a color based on the colors you have defined for this document. See Chapter 8, "Adding Color."

❖ **Position**—Used mostly in typesetting equations, this feature allows you to set type as subscript characters (dropped below the baseline) or superscript characters (raised above the baseline).

❖ **Case**—Allows you to set type in all capital letters, all small capital letters, or to leave it as typed.

❖ **Track**—Tracking is similar to kerning, except *tracking* applies to a group of selected letters or words and the spaces between those words. *Kerning* applies to only certain pairs of letter combinations. The looser the tracking, the longer the line. Tighter tracking results in a shorter line. See "Changing Tracking" later in this chapter.

❖ **Type style**—Gives you access to the same style features we have already discussed. It doesn't matter whether you change a type style with the Type Specifications dialog box or by selecting the **Type Styles** submenu from the Type pull-down menu.

Let's change that address you selected:

1. Position the mouse pointer over the Case text box and click the arrow to open it. Notice that **Normal** is currently checked. Double-click on **Small Caps** to select it and close the list box.

2. Click **OK** or press **Enter**. When you return to the document window, the address is in small caps.

Changing Type Leading

The easiest way to think of leading is the space between two lines of type. If there is too little leading, the descenders of the upper line (the tails of the lowercase *g*s and *p*s, for example) overlap the ascenders of the lower line, as shown in Figure 2.19. If there is too much space between the two lines, it is difficult for the eye to track down the page. Too little space, and the autonomy of the line is lost—again making a paragraph of such lines difficult to read. The leading measurement for a given line depends on the size of the type. The larger the type, the more leading is needed. With dedicated typesetting equipment (back in the good old days before PageMaker and personal computers), leading had to be specified for each type size change, just as the type size had to be specified. Fortunately, PageMaker makes it easier. Just use the **Auto** option, and PageMaker adjusts the leading automatically each time you change the size of the type.

Leading for these lines is set correctly with the Auto option in the Type Specifications dialog box. The correct amount of leading lets the type breathe and helps your eyes read a line at a time.

Leading for these lines is set to tightly: there is not enough space between the lines of type, so they seem to run together, making them dificult to read. You probably find the words in this column jumbled together and more dificult to follow.

Figure 2.19 *Examples of correct and incorrect type leading.*

PageMaker defaults to the **Auto Leading** option, in which leading is automatically adjusted based on the size of the type. However, there may be instances where you deliberately want to manually adjust the leading, such as in Figure 2.20.

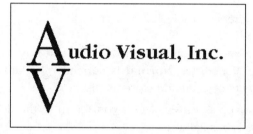

Figure 2.20 *Manually adjusted leading creates an interestig effect for a logo.*

To manually adjust leading:

1. Choose the **Type** pull-down menu and choose **Type Specs** (or press **Ctrl+T**). PageMaker displays the Type Specifications dialog box.

2. Click the **Leading** text box arrow. Notice that **Auto** is selected.

3. Select a specific leading value. Remember, the rule for the correct amount of leading is generally to use 120% more leading than the type size. For example, 12-point type needs about 14.5 points of leading. Or, like the example in Figure 2.20, you can select a specific value to gain a special effect.

4. Click **OK** or press **Enter** to return to the document window.

Changing Character Widths

Character width, like leading, is something you generally don't think about with PageMaker. However, for special effects, very bold headlines, or designing a unique logo, changing the character width can help you achieve a special look. The default width of all characters is normal, or 100% of the width. You can change the percentage width value from 5 to 250% of normal in as small as .1% increments.

To change the character width:

1. Use the Text tool to highlight your name on the first line of the stationery.

2. Choose the **Type** pull-down menu and select **Type Specs** (or press **Ctrl+T**) to display the Type Specifications dialog box.

3. Click the **Set Widths** text box arrow and select **130%**.

4. Click **OK** or press **Enter** to return to your document. Notice that your stationery name is now considerably wider than before.

Changing Tracking

Tracking stretches or squeezes text. Tracking is similar to kerning in that it adjusts the space between letters, but kerning only adjusts the space between certain pairs of letters and does not affect the spacing between words. On the other hand, tracking adjusts the spaces between letters and words in equal proportion, so that if you select a headline to squeeze, everything in the headline shifts toward the margin the text is aligned to. Figure 2.21 shows an example of tracking.

> Old-fashioned barbeque tonight
> Old-fashioned barbeque tonight
> Old-fashioned barbeque tonight

Figure 2.21 *An example of diffrent tracking settings.*

To adjust the tracking of selected text:

1. Highlight the address and phone number portion of your letterhead with the Text tool.

2. Choose the **Type** pull-down menu and choose **Type Specs** (or press **Ctrl+T**) to display the Type Specifications dialog box.

3. Click the **Track** list box arrow and select **Loose.**

4. Click **OK** or press **Enter** to return to your document.

Notice that the address lines appear longer and that there is slightly more space between the letters and words.

Changing Type Options

The Type Options dialog box contains little-used options for altering the look of small caps, superscript characters, and subscript characters. The default values are fine for most documents, but if you wish to change the proportional size of these type styles, do this:

1. Choose the **Type** pull-down menu and select **Type Specs** (or press **Ctrl+T**) to display the Type Specifications dialog box.

2. Click the **Options** button to display the Type Options dialog box, shown in Figure 2.22.

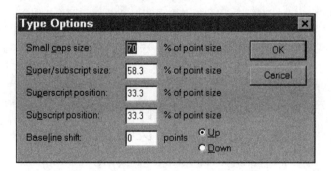

Figure 2.22 *The Type Options dialog box.*

Use the Type Options dialog box to adjust the size of these special type styles:

❖ **Small caps size**—To change the size of small caps, enter a different percentage in the text box. The percentage you enter is proportional to the type size. For example, if you enter **60%** and the typeface is set to 24 points, then the small cap size would be about 14.5 points.

❖ **Super/subscript size**—Superscript characters are positioned above the normal baseline of the type (like a footnote in-text reference). Subscript characters drop below the baseline. To change the size of these characters, enter a different percentage in the text box. The percentage you enter is proportional to the type size.

❖ **Superscript (or subscript) position**—Adjusts the position above or below the baseline, relative to the surrounding type. In other words, the default value of **33.3%** means that a superscript character is **33.3%** of the character's em size above the baseline of the surrounding type. (The *em size* is the width of the letter *m* in the size and typeface you have selected.)

❖ **Baseline shift**—The *baseline* is an invisible line on which all type rests. If you were to specify points for the vertical ruler to align the tick marks on the ruler to the leading value of your text, the invisible baselines would actually be aligned to the ruler. To *shift the baseline* is to move the baseline for selected type up or down. Enter the amount of shift you want in the Points text box, in as small as .1-point values. Then choose either the **Up** or **Down** option button to tell PageMaker in which direction you want to shift the baseline.

When you are finished, click **OK** or press **Enter** to move back to the Type Specifications dialog box, and click **OK** again to return to your document.

Saving Your Document

Up to this point haven't saved your sample letterhead document. You also haven't assigned a name to the document, which is done the first time you save it. If you lose power to the computer right now, there would be no hint that the document ever existed when you restart the computer system. Clearly, saving your work is important and should be done often.

How often really depends on the complexity and importance of the document you are creating. Saving your work once an hour means you risk losing an hour's work. I generally save every ten minutes, more often if I'm working on a very complex document. Luckily, PageMaker realizes the possibility of a power failure and automatically saves a miniature version of the file whenever any one of a number of certain tasks are performed, including adding or removing pages from the document, switching to the story editor, switching back to the document window, printing, copying, and changing the Document Setup options.

If you lose power and lose some of the work you entered prior to saving, you may be able to recover the work by opening the mini-version using the **Revert** command. If you lost power before assigning a file name to the new document, the mini-version of the document is saved as a temporary file in the **Windows\temp** folder, where other temporary files are stored. Look for a file with a tile (**~**), the initials **PM**, and a **.tmp** extension (such as **~pm21112.tmp**).

Saving a New Document

The first time you save your document, use the Save dialog box to assign a file name and directory path. To save your new document, do this:

1. From the File pull-down menu choose **Save** to display the Save Publication dialog box, shown in Figure 2.23. The shortcut for this command is **Ctrl+S**.

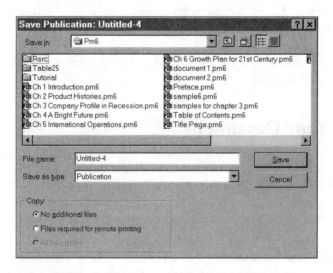

Figure 2.23 *The Save Publication dialog box.*

2. The insertion point is positioned in the Name text box. Type a file name for this document (up to eight characters). PageMaker adds the extension **.pm6** to the file name, so you don't have to add an extension.

3. The default folder for the dialog box is the **PM6** folder, where PageMaker's programs are located. To change the folder, click the **Save in** text box and move to the folder you want, as shown in Figure 2.24.

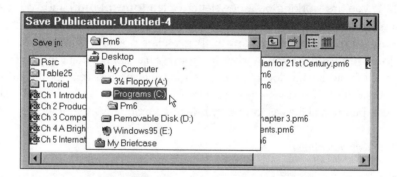

Figure 2.24 *Changing from the default folder.*

4. Click **OK** or press **Enter** to return to your document.

You only assign a file name once to a new document. Each subsequent time you open the document, you in fact open a copy of the document. Any changes made to the opened document are made to the copy until it is saved, then the original is updated with the changes. Remember, if you open an existing document and make some changes you don't like, the simplest thing to do is to close the document without saving it and then reopen it and start again.

Saving an Existing Document

It's always a good idea to save your work often; it takes only a moment. To save your document:

1. Choose the **File** pull-down menu and choose **Save** (or press **Ctrl+S**).

2. The mouse pointer momentarily changes to an hourglass icon as the file is being saved.

Saving a Document as Another Document

An easy way to try out different ideas as you develop a document is to save it as an experimental file. Then you can try your idea and see if it flies. If it doesn't, you haven't altered the original document; just close the test document and reopen the original. If your idea worked, simply rename the experimental document with the name of the original document to replace it. For example, as illustrated in Table 2.1, you are working on a newsletter called **jonesnl.pm6** and you want to try a tabloid size instead of the 8.5-by-11-inch size. Use the **Save As** command to save **jonesnl.pm6** as **jonesnlx.pm6**. PageMaker opens a duplicate of the file name **jonesnlx.pm6** for you to work in. Nothing has happened to the original file, and if the tabloid layout doesn't work, nothing will be lost (except the duplicate experimental file). If it does work, you can use the **Save As** command again to save the experimental files as **jonesnl.pm6** and continue with your work.

Table 2.1 *Experimenting with different file layouts.*

Start with this	New Save As name	To get this
Original file	**jonesnlx.pm6**	Duplicate test **jonesnl.pm6** file
Duplicate test file	**jonesnl.pm6**	Duplicate test **joneslx.pm6** file renamed as original

To use the **Save As** command:

1. Choose the **File** menu and click **Save as** (or press **Alt+F A**) to display the Save Publication dialog box.

2. The name of the current document is highlighted in the Name text box. Type a new name for the document.

3. Click **OK** or press **Enter** to save the new document and return to the document window.

PageMaker saves the old document and closes it, makes a copy of the document with the new assigned name, and opens the new document in the document window. Notice that the title bar of the document window now reflects the new document's name.

Another way of protecting the original version of a document is to save it as a template. Then you can open as many versions of it as you like. See Chapter 5 for more information on templates.

Reverting to a Previously Saved Version

Sometimes the easiest way to fix a problem is to revert to an earlier version of your document. That's what the **Revert** command does. It takes the document back to the way it was the last time it was saved, and deletes everything you have done since the last save (another reason to save often!). Using **Revert** is easy—simply choose it on the File pull-down menu—the rest is automatic.

Developing Paragraphs

There are three ways to type copy in PageMaker: type copy on your laid-out page on the pasteboard, type copy using the story editor (the story editor is covered in Chapter 9), or type copy using a word processing program and import the file into PageMaker (importing files, called *placing*, is covered in Chapter 4).

Typing Text

You can type in your document much the same way you type in your word processor:

1. Select the **Text** tool from the toolbox. Position the insertion point where you want to begin typing and click the left mouse button.
2. Type the text as you normally would. If the Page View size is too small, enlarge the view of the page by choosing the **Page** pull-down menu and selecting a different view.

3. Press the **Spacebar** once after periods. Press the **Tab** key if you wish to move the insertion point more than one space to the right. At the end of a line, the insertion point automatically wraps to the next line (don't press the **Enter** key at the end of a line like you would press the carriage return key on a typewriter).

It's a good idea not to use the **Spacebar** in formatting columnar or indented text in PageMaker. While you can't see spaces, each time you press the **Spacebar** you insert a hidden code in your document. Although the text may look aligned properly on your screen, it may not print correctly. Instead, press the **Tab** key if you wish to move the insertion point more than one space forward. Similarly, if you are typing your text in a word processor to place in PageMaker, use the **Tab** key, not the **Spacebar**.

Adding Special Characters to Text

PageMaker has a number of special characters available to insert in your text, including copyright and trademark symbols, em and en dashes, and open and close quotation marks. Table 2.2 details the list of special characters and the keyboard shortcuts that insert them.

Table 2.2 Special characters and their keyboard shortcuts.

To insert this	Press this	You'll see this
Nonbreaking hyphen	**Ctrl+Shift+-**	-
Nonbreaking slash	**Ctrl+Shift+/**	/
Em dash	**Ctrl+Shift+=**	—
En dash	**Ctrl+=**	–
Open double quote	**Ctrl+Shift+[**	"
Close double quote	**Ctrl+Shift+]**	"
Open single quote	**Ctrl+[**	'
Close single quote	**Ctrl+]**	'
Auto page numbers	**Ctrl+Shift+3**	# LM RM

Bullet	**Ctrl+Shift+8**	•
Registered trademark	**Ctrl+Shift+G**	®
Copyright	**Ctrl+Shift+O**	©
Paragraph marker	**Ctrl+Shift+7**	¶
Section marker	**Ctrl+Shift+6**	§
Discretionary hyphen	**Ctrl+-**	-
Em space	**Ctrl+Shift+M**	
En space	**Ctrl+Shift+N**	
Thin space	**Ctrl+Shift+T**	
Fixed space	**Ctrl+Spacebar**	

Aligning Text

Aligning text determines how the text will be oriented in columns, pages, and headlines (see Figure 2.25). There are five different alignment orientations for text: centered, aligned left, aligned right, justified, and force justified.

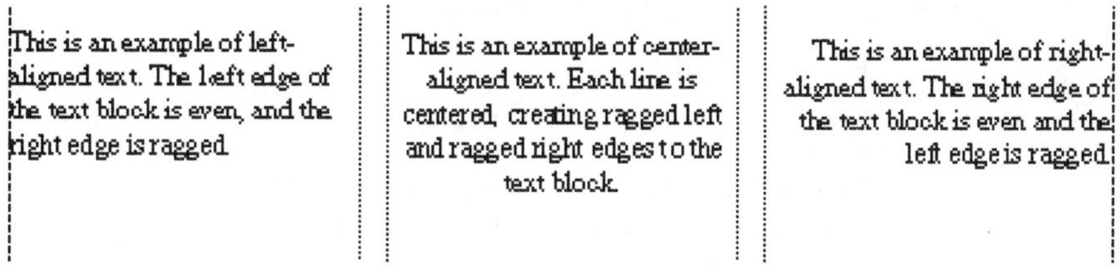

This is an example of left-aligned text. The left edge of the text block is even, and the right edge is ragged.

This is an example of center-aligned text. Each line is centered, creating ragged left and ragged right edges to the text block.

This is an example of right-aligned text. The right edge of the text block is even and the left edge is ragged.

Figure 2.25 *Alignment text orientations: left, centered, and right justified.*

❖ **Align left** (**Ctrl+Shift+L**)—Lines up the left edge of the text evenly. The right edge is not aligned (called a *ragged-right* edge). Left-aligned text is commonly used in personalized letters, informal newsletters, and the body text in many books.

❖ **Center** (**Ctrl+Shift+C**)—Centers text between the left and right margins or within columns. Centered text is often used for headlines in ads and headings in newsletters and brochures. Several centered lines of text can be difficult to read because neither edge is even, making it difficult for the eye to track down the page.

❖ **Align right** (**Ctrl+Shift+R**)—Lines up the right edge of text evenly, producing a ragged-left edge. Right-aligned text (if used sparingly) can produce a refreshing change to body copy. Right-aligned heads in a brochure can contribute to a fresh, unusual look.

❖ **Justified** (**Ctrl+Shift+J**)—Lines of text are even on both edges, made so by adjusting the internal spacing of letters and words in the line, as shown in Figure 2.26. To reduce increased spaces in the line, justified text is normally *hyphenated*, meaning words are broken at the ends of lines that would normally be too short or long for the line, thus evening out the spacing.

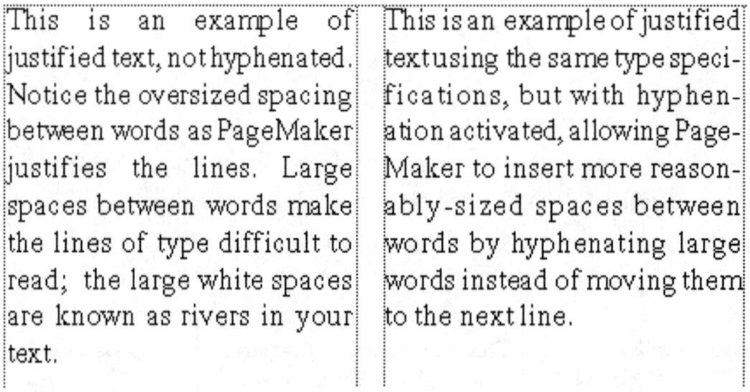

> This is an example of justified text, not hyphenated. Notice the oversized spacing between words as PageMaker justifies the lines. Large spaces between words make the lines of type difficult to read; the large white spaces are known as rivers in your text.
>
> This is an example of justified text using the same type specifications, but with hyphenation activated, allowing PageMaker to insert more reasonably-sized spaces between words by hyphenating large words instead of moving them to the next line.

Figure 2.26 *Hypebnated text in right column*
fills up excessive word space (in left column).

❖ **Force justified** (**Ctrl+Shift+F**)—Stretches a word or words across a line (forcing it to be justified). Force justify is normally used to add spaces to the letters of a word, as shown in Figure 2.27.

Figure 2.27 *An example of force justified text.*

The default alignment for text in PageMaker is align left. To change the alignment:

1. Use the Text tool to highlight the text you want to change. If you are about to type new text, select the **Text** tool and click on the page where you want to begin typing.

2. Choose the **Type** pull-down menu (or press **Alt+T**) and select **Alignment** (or press **A**) to display the Alignment submenu.

3. Click the alignment orientation you want or press **L** for align left, **C** for align center, **R** for align right, **J** for justify, or **F** for force justify. A check mark next to the alignment choice indicates that it is in effect.

The keyboard shortcuts in the table below allow you to select an alignment orientation without using the pull-down menus.

Table 2.3 *Alignment orientation keyboard shortcuts* .

Orientation	Shortcut
Align left	Shift+Ctrl+L
Align center	Shift+Ctrl+C
Align right	Shift+Ctrl+R
Justify	Shift+Ctrl+J
Force justify	Shift+Ctrl+F

Formatting Paragraphs

Paragraph formatting includes setting indent values in paragraphs, specifying the space above and below a paragraph, setting the text alignment orientation, and controlling how paragraphs split among columns and between pages. To make formatting changes to a paragraph, follow these steps:

1. Determine what paragraph text you want to format:
   ❖ To change the format of a series of paragraphs, but not the whole document, highlight the paragraphs with the Text tool and choose the **Type** pull-down menu (or press **Alt+T**).
   ❖ To change just one paragraph, click the **Text** tool anywhere in the paragraph and choose the **Type** pull-down menu (or press **Alt+T**).
   ❖ To change the paragraph default settings for this document, do not click in the document, just choose the **Type** pull-down menu (or press **Alt+T**).
2. Select the **Paragraph** command (or press **P**) to display the Paragraph Specifications dialog box, shown in Figure 2.28.

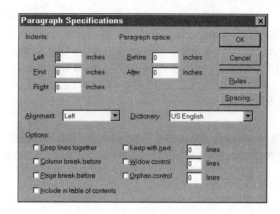

Figure 2.28 *The Paragraph Specifications dialog box.*

Changing Indents

To change the indent specifications for a paragraph:

1. Change the left indent amount by clicking in the **Left** text box and entering a value. The left margin of the paragraph is indented by the amount of the value entered, as shown in Figure 2.29.

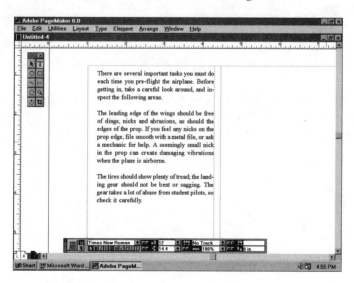

Figure 2.29 *Changing the left indent amount.*

2. Change the first line indent amount by clicking in the **First** text box and entering a value. If a value has been entered in the Left text box, entering a negative value here outdents the first line by the amount of the negative value entered, while the remaining lines of the paragraph are indented the amount entered in the Left text box, as shown in Figure 2.30.

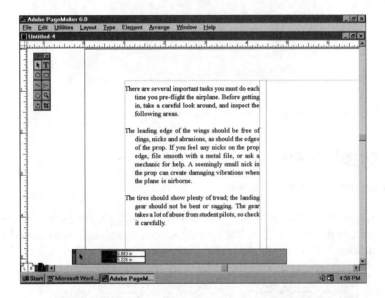

Figure 2.30 *Changing the first line indent amount.*

3. Change the right indent amount by clicking in the **Right** text box and entering a value. The right edge of the paragraph is indented by the amount of the value entered, as shown in Figure 2.31.

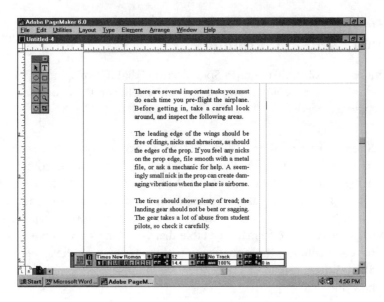

Figure 2.31 *Changing the right indent amount.*

Changing the Space Around Paragraphs

The Paragraph Specifications dialog box gives you the option of adjusting the amount of space above and below paragraphs. The default amount of space is zero, meaning no extra space. Instead of double-spacing after each paragraph, you can use the **Paragraph Space** option to enter a space value above, below, or above and below the paragraph.

Enter the amount of space you want in the Before and After text box(s). Once values are entered in either of these text boxes, you should only press the **Enter** key once between paragraphs. Pressing the key twice will result in twice the amount of space you specified between paragraphs.

Changing Paragraph Alignment

You can change the alignment of text in a paragraph in the Paragraph Specifications dialog box instead of using the **Alignment** command on the Type pull-down menu. Click the list box button to make your choice of left, right, center, justify, or force justify.

Controlling How Paragraphs Break Between Pages and Columns

The Options area of the Paragraph Specifications dialog box controls how paragraphs are affected by column and page breaks. Choose those options that suit your document's needs:

❖ **Keep lines together**—Click this check box to keep all the lines in a paragraph together on the same page or in the same column. If the paragraph falls at the bottom of the page or column—and PageMaker would normally break the paragraph—with this option checked, the whole paragraph is moved to the next page or column. This option is useful if you have formatted a table that you don't want to break between pages or columns. In formatting a table to be kept on the same page, use **Shift+Enter** instead of **Enter** to move the insertion point down for each new line.

NOTE

If the paragraph is longer than the column it's in, PageMaker breaks the paragraph at the bottom of the column even if **Keep lines together** is checked.

❖ **Column break before**—Click this check box to force a paragraph to start at the top of a new column. Check this option if you have a heading that you always want to start in a new column.

❖ **Page break before**—Click this check box to force a paragraph to start on a new page. Check this option if you have a heading (a new chapter title, for example) that you always want to start on a new page.

❖ **Keep with next _ lines**—Click this check box to designate that highlighted text be kept up with the next one to three lines of text on the same page. This option is used mostly to keep headings connected to the first few lines (you can specify 1, 2, or 3 lines) of the paragraph that follows, so that a page break won't fall between the head and its body copy. In Chapter 6, you'll learn how to create a style that automatically designates this option for heads and body copy.

❖ **Widow control _ lines**—A *widow line* is the last line of a paragraph isolated at the top of the next page or the next column. Enter **1**, **2**, or **3** in this text box to indicate the number of lines of the paragraph to keep together at the bottom of a page to prevent widowing.

❖ **Orphan control _ lines**—An *orphan line* is the opposite of a widow; it is the first line of a paragraph left at the bottom of a page or column, with the rest of the paragraph continuing on the next page or at the top of the next column. Enter **1**, **2**, or **3** in this text box to indicate the number of lines of the paragraph to move to the beginning of the next page to prevent the orphan.

Adding Lines Above or Below Your Paragraphs

One way of emphasizing a paragraph is to add lines (called *rules*) above and below the paragraph. For example, to relieve the visual monotony of a long column of text, a pull quote is often added. A *pull quote* is a sentence or part of a sentence, taken from the column of text, that is treated as a graphic to add visual interest and act as a teaser to get the reader's attention. Figure 2.32 contains an example of a pull quote.

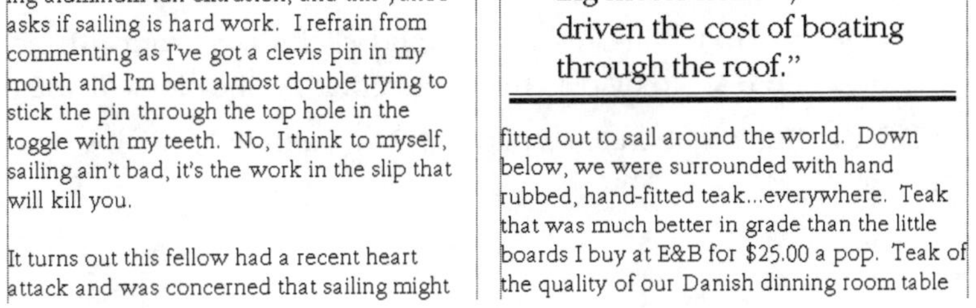

in the process of installing a Hood roller furling system on my old Bristol and busier than a one-armed paper hanger. It's not the sort of job to take on without some able-bodied help, and in the middle of all this a pleasant looking older gentleman strolls my way and asks if sailing is a lot of trouble.

Here I am juggling 70 or 80 pounds of gyrating aluminum luff extrusion, and this yahoo asks if sailing is hard work. I refrain from commenting as I've got a clevis pin in my mouth and I'm bent almost double trying to stick the pin through the top hole in the toggle with my teeth. No, I think to myself, sailing ain't bad, it's the work in the slip that will kill you.

It turns out this fellow had a recent heart attack and was concerned that sailing might

cal little 27 footer we were sitting in was $89,000! Now, to be fair, the little 27 footer was built like a brick you-know-what, and

---
"It's this nesting instinct, this need to turn perfectly sound sailboats into floating motor homes, that has driven the cost of boating through the roof."
---

fitted out to sail around the world. Down below, we were surrounded with hand rubbed, hand-fitted teak...everywhere. Teak that was much better in grade than the little boards I buy at E&B for $25.00 a pop. Teak of the quality of our Danish dinning room table

Figure 2.32 *Adding lines above and below pull quote.*

Another use of lines above or below a paragraph is to create a certain style. For example, you could add rules to a note or caution, as shown in Figure 2.33.

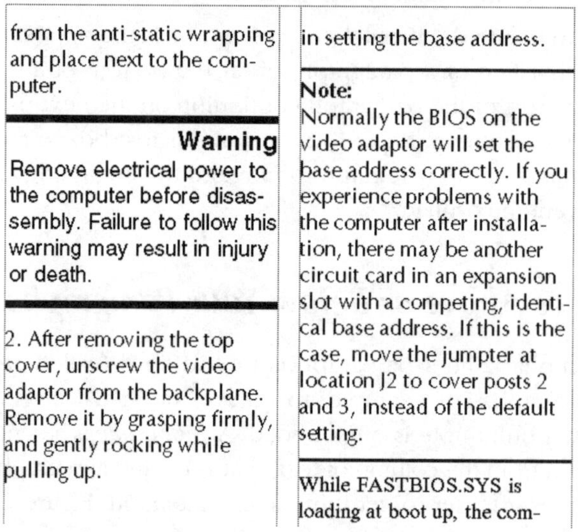

from the anti-static wrapping and place next to the computer.

Warning
Remove electrical power to the computer before disassembly. Failure to follow this warning may result in injury or death.

2. After removing the top cover, unscrew the video adaptor from the backplane. Remove it by grasping firmly, and gently rocking while pulling up.

in setting the base address.

Note:
Normally the BIOS on the video adaptor will set the base address correctly. If you experience problems with the computer after installation, there may be another circuit card in an expansion slot with a competing, identical base address. If this is the case, move the jumpter at location J2 to cover posts 2 and 3, instead of the default setting.

While FASTBIOS.SYS is loading at boot up, the com-

Figure 2.33 *Add rules around a note or caution to set it apart from the rest of the text.*

To add rules to paragraphs, follow these steps:

1. Highlight the paragraph you want to change by triple-clicking the **Text** tool anywhere inside the paragraph.

2. Choose the **Text** pull-down menu and click the **Paragraph** command (or press **Ctrl+M**) to display the Paragraph Specifications dialog box.

3. Click the **Rules** button to display the Paragraph Rules dialog box, shown in Figure 2.34.

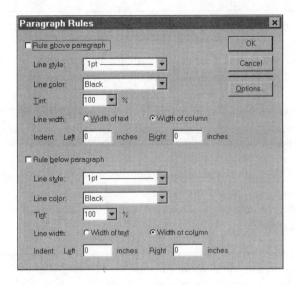

Figure 2.34 *The Paragraph Rules dialog box.*

Use the Paragraph Rules dialog box to set up a line style, line color, or line width for rules above and below the paragraph you have highlighted:

❖ **Changing the line style of paragraph rules**—The default line style for paragraph rules is a one-point line. To change the weight of the line, click the **Line style** list box button and choose from the styles.

❖ **Changing the line color of paragraph rules**—The default line color is black. To change the color, click on the **Line color** list box arrow and choose a different color. The color choices will include any colors you have added with the Define Colors dialog box (all the colors shown on the Color palette are available in the Line color list box).

❖ **Changing line width**—The default line width is the width of the column. To make the line width the same as the text width, click the **Width of text** option button.

Since a *paragraph* is defined as anything typed after pressing the **Enter** key, paragraph headings are considered paragraphs (to type a heading, you must press the **Enter** key, type the heading for a new paragraph, and press the **Enter** key again to begin typing the copy for the paragraph). It's easy to dress up headings by adding a line just above or below. After highlighting the heading, simply select the **Width of text** option button in the Paragraph Rules dialog box.

❖ **Indent**—To indent the rule in from the left column or page margin, enter the amount of the indent in the Left text box. To indent the rule in from the right column or page margin, enter the amount of the indent in the Right text box.

Entering the same value in both the Left and Right text boxes centers the line over or under the paragraph. To change the amount of space between the paragraph text and the rules, click the **Option** button to display the Paragraph Rule Options dialog box, shown in Figure 2.35.

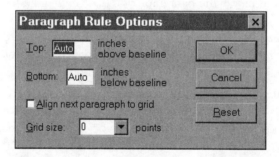

Figure 2.35 *The Paragraph Rule Options dialog box.*

Use the Paragraph Rule Options dialog box to choose among the following:

❖ **Top**—The auto default value aligns a rule to the top edge of the leading slug. To raise the rule higher, enter the height in this text box.

❖ **Bottom**—Again, the auto default value places the rule at the bottom edge of the leading slug. To lower the rule, enter the value in the third text box.

❖ **Align next paragraph to grid**—If you have two or more columns on the page and are having difficulty aligning the baseline of one column to the other(s), clicking this check box aligns the selected text to PageMaker's invisible grid.

❖ **Grid size**—Enter the amount of leading for the type you want to align to the grid or click the list box arrow and scroll down the list to select the leading.

❖ **Reset**—Resets the top and bottom values to **Auto** and unchecks the **Align next paragraph to grid** check box.

When you are finished, press **OK** to return to your document.

To Sum Up

Whew! A lot to cover in a weekend but now you're ready to push the drawing board and light table out of the way and fire up your PC. In this chapter, you have touched on most of the basic commands of PageMaker. You've learned to create and open documents, type text in documents, add headlines to text blocks, and change type specifications and alignment. You have also learned how to set tab stops for tabs and indents and fine-tune the look of paragraphs. You're now ready for the next step: editing your work.

In the next chapter you'll learn how PageMaker text is threaded together and how you can change that invisible thread that connects your story from page to page.

CHAPTER 3

Editing Your Work

❖ Threading and unthreading text
❖ Selecting text
❖ Editing text
❖ Inserting and removing pages
❖ Adjusting spacing between characters, words, and lines
❖ Adjusting indents and tabs
❖ To sum up

Before I became enamored of desktop publishing and began using PageMaker, I had a desk drawer devoted to what I called my quick-fix kit. The kit contained razor blades, white tape, press-type letters and numbers, adhesive spray, little scraps of leftover type in my favorite typefaces, and a folder stuffed full of page numbers printed on adhesive-backed paper. I saved the little bits of type in case I had to make a last-minute change to camera-ready copy. The sheets of numbers were cut apart into tiny numbered squares and carefully stuck down with the tip of an X-acto knife. (You haven't lived until you've had to renumber a long, technical document with little stick-down numbers!) When it came time to edit the work, I'd roll up my sleeves and dig out my quick-fix kit.

Editing a hand-worked mechanical is a messy affair—and not fun. Waxed or pasted type refuses to pull up and be moved—if you can get the type pulled up, it probably will never stick firmly again. Art boards soon take on a dirty, tattered appearance. With all the mess and rework, it's easy to lose sight of the design theme and overall purpose of the piece. Luckily, all that has changed with PageMaker—my quick-fix kit drawer was cleaned out years ago.

Editing a document with PageMaker is as simple and straightforward as creating a document. Open the file, make the needed changes, print the revised version, and close the file. Proof your changes on a 300-dpi laser printer, and print your final mechanical on either a laser printer or a laser imagesetter at 1200 to 2500 dpi. You can edit text right on the document screen or in the story editor (explained in Chapter 9). You can grab text blocks and resize them or drag them to new positions. In fact, you have complete control over all text and graphic elements on the page: you can change their position, size, or color; change margin or column settings; and change page orientation or overall page size. With a laser printer, you can instantly see the printed results of your editing.

Threading and Unthreading Text

When text blocks are selected, they are displayed as windowshades of text, with handles like windowshade pulls at the top and bottom, and sizing handles at the four corners. A text block can be so small that it contains only one character (or no characters) or as long as the page is tall. (Effectively, the maximum size of a single text block is a little more than 20 inches by 20 inches on a single page.) When a story in a text block extends to the next or subsequent pages, it is broken up into individual page text blocks, each connected to the next, or *threaded* together, as it's called in PageMaker. When text is added or deleted on one page of a threaded text block, the threaded text blocks on subsequent pages are automatically reformatted.

You can have more than one threaded text block on a page. For example, in a two-column newsletter, Story A may fill the first column and be continued on (and threaded to) the first column of page 2, and Story B may reside in the second column of page 1 and be continued on (and threaded to) the second column of page 2. The newsletter contains two independent stories: each story is made up of threaded text blocks on pages 1 and 2, but the blocks are independent of each other.

The concept of threaded text blocks is central to PageMaker's ability to manage long stories that flow across many pages. Threading enables you to edit a story on page 1 and know that the words you add will push the text forward on all the following pages of the story. Likewise, if you delete a sentence on page 3, the pagination for all the following pages of the story will be reformatted for you.

The windowshade handles, displayed when a text block is selected, denote one of several possible conditions:

An *empty handle* indicates the beginning of a text block if it is at the top or the end of a text block if it is at the bottom. The empty handles essentially mean there's no more text stored for this text block. All of it is displayed, and there are no text blocks threaded to this text block, either before or after it.

A *plus sign* in the top handle of a text block means that it is connected to a story from a previous page or column. (Note that you could continue a story on page 1 to page 86, for example—the thread doesn't have to run continuously from one page to the next in sequence). If you click on the handle and drag the windowshade down to reposition the top of the column of text, you would reposition all the text in the text block, as well as in the block to which it is threaded, as shown in Figure 3.1.

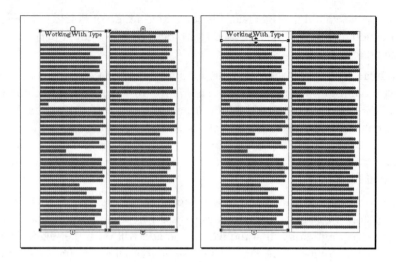

Figure 3.1 *Windowshade handles showing status of threadng in the two columns.*

A plus sign in the bottom handle of a text block means that there is at least one more block of text that follows it. For example, if you had a three-column story, the text block for the story in the middle column would have plus signs in both the top and bottom handles, as shown in the center column in Figure 3.2.

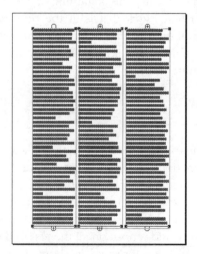

Figure 3.2 *The plus sign in the bottom handle shows how column is threaded.*

❖ A *red arrow* in the bottom handle of a text block means that there is more text to come (the text is stored in a temporary memory area called a *buffer*). Clicking the **arrow** allows you to add, or thread, another text block for this story.

Threading Additional Text

When the bottom windowshade displays a red arrow, indicating there is more text to come, click the **arrow** to thread the text to the next column or page. Here's how:

1. Click the **down arrow** in the windowshade handle, and the pointer tool changes to a loaded-text icon.

2. Place the icon where you want the text block to start, aligning the upper-left corner of the icon with the upper-left corner of the page or column margin.

3. Click the left mouse button. The text block flows down the page as it is transferred from the text block memory buffer. If you have activated the **Autoflow** control, text that would fill more than a full page automatically flows to as many new pages as necessary to empty the memory buffer. If the **Autoflow** control is off, you must move to each page (or insert new pages as necessary) and manually flow the remaining text down each page.

NOTE

Flowing text using a loaded-text icon is essentially the same as placing text using the **Place** command (**File > Place**) described in Chapter 9, "Developing Long Documents."

WARNING

If you decide not to place text using the loaded-text icon, you must cancel the operation correctly or you will lose the text that remains in the text block memory buffer. For example, if you place the text and then delete it, you would not be able to place the text again—there wouldn't be any text in the buffer.

To cancel the loaded-text icon:

1. Without clicking the left mouse button, position the icon anywhere in the boundaries of the toolbox window.
2. Click the left mouse button. The loaded-text icon is canceled without losing the text block(s) that remains in the text block buffer.

To thread the additional text, you can again click the **down arrow** in the text block handle any time after canceling the loaded-text icon.

Threading Text to a Different Page

When the bottom handle indicates that there is more text to come, you are not limited to threading that text on the same page as the selected text block or even the page immediately following it; you can thread the text to any other page in the document. For example, in a newspaper or newsletter, you might wish to continue a story to what is called a *jump page* (all page 1 stories might be jumped to page 14, for example). Here's how to jump a story to another page:

1. Click the **down arrow** in the text block handle. The pointer changes to the loaded-text icon.
2. Without clicking the left mouse button, move the icon to the lower-left corner of the document window and click on the number of the page to which you want to move.
3. Or move the icon up to the pull-down menu bar. The icon changes to the pointer tool. Choose **Layout > Go to Page** (or press **Ctrl+G**) to display the Go to Page dialog box. Type the page number and click **OK** or press **Enter**.
4. When the new page is displayed, position the loaded-text icon where you want to begin flowing the text, aligning the upper-left corner of the icon to the upper-left corner of the page or column margin.
5. Click the left mouse button to flow the threaded text block onto the page.

Even though you may have jumped a continued story from page 1 to page 100 and you have created 98 pages of other stories in multiple-page text blocks, the page 1 story is permanently threaded to page 100, unless you unthread it.

Unthreading Text Blocks

You may wish to unthread a portion of a threaded text block, to use as a separate related story (sometimes called a *sidebar* when it's positioned in a column beside the main story). It's easy to unthread text by following these steps:

1. Select the **Text** tool and highlight the text you want to unthread.

2. Choose the **Edit** pull-down menu and select **Cut** (or press **Alt+E T**). The highlighted text is cut from the body of the text block (the text in the text block reflows to fill the hole).

3. Position the Text tool insertion point where you want to paste the text, and choose **Paste** from the Edit menu.

N O T E   What if you want to unthread a complete text block, instead of just a portion of a text block? That's just as easy. Simply use the **Pointer** tool, instead of the **Text** tool, to select the text block. Cut the selected block and paste it wherever you want.

Rethreading Text Blocks

Rethreading a text block is the opposite of unthreading it. Simply cut the separate text block and paste it inside another text block. Use the **Cut** and **Paste** commands on the Edit menu, or press **Shift+Del** to cut and **Shift+Ins** to paste. The text block readjusts itself, and any affected pages are automatically repaginated.

Making Text Blocks Disappear without Deleting Them

To clear a column of its text block without deleting the text:

1. Select the text block with the **Pointer** tool.

2. Click the bottom windowshade handle and roll the handle up the text block past the top handle. The column looks like the right-hand column in Figure 3.3.

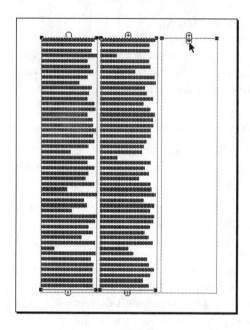

Figure 3.3 *A rolled up text block.*

When you're ready to open the windowshade again, first choose **Select All** from the Edit pull-down menu (or press **Alt+E A**) to highlight all the text blocks on the page. Then click the bottom handle of the hidden text block and pull it down the page.

Selecting Text

You may find selecting text confusing at first, because PageMaker allows you to select text with either the **Pointer** tool or the **Text** tool. In Chapter 2, you learned to select a word or paragraph by double-clicking or triple-clicking the **Text** tool and you learned how to select a text block by clicking with the **Pointer** tool. So which is right?

Choose the tool based on what you want to accomplish. The *Text tool* is generally used to highlight parts of a text block; the *Pointer tool* is used to select an entire text block.

Selecting and Dragging Text

One of the unique features of PageMaker is its ability to allow you to select and drag text blocks and graphic elements anywhere on the page—even off the page onto the pasteboard. You have complete freedom to move text blocks. You can even place them on top of other text blocks or graphic elements, as shown in Figure 3.4.

Figure 3.4 *A drop-shadow box with text, comprised of two graphic elements and a text block stacked on top of one another.*

To drag a text block:

1. Place the **Pointer** tool in the text block you want to move.

2. Click the text block to expose its boundaries. Then hold down the left mouse button. The Pointer tool is replaced by a four-pointed arrow.

3. Continue holding down the left mouse button and drag the text block to its new position on the page. Or drag it off the page onto the pasteboard, for later use.

Although eventually you will want to position text blocks accurately on the pages of your document, you don't have to do so immediately with PageMaker. You can drag a text block off the page onto the pasteboard and leave it there. Save and close the document, exit PageMaker, and when you return you'll find the text block where you left it, waiting to be positioned.

Editing Text

You can easily add, change, or delete words in the document layout window. You may wish to enlarge the view size to make the text easier to read. Then follow these steps:

1. Choose either the **Pointer** or **Text** tool in the toolbox (depending on the kind of editing you want to do; see "Deleting Text" later in this chapter).

2. Then choose an editing option on the Edit menu: **Delete**, **Copy**, **Cut**, or **Paste**.

Deleting Text

You can delete text one character at a time by positioning the **Text** tool insertion point to the right of the letter or word to delete and pressing the **Backspace** key. You can also delete words, sentences, paragraphs, or entire text blocks. Here's how:

❖ To delete a word that will be replaced by another word, select the **Text** tool and highlight the word. Type the replacement word and the word you type replaces the word you highlighted.

❖ To delete words, sentences, or paragraphs within a larger text block, select the **Text** tool, place the insertion point before the beginning of the words you want to delete, and highlight the text. Then press the **Delete** or **Backspace** key or choose the **Edit** pull-down menu and select the **Clear** command. The text is permanently deleted (although, if you immediately change your mind, you can reverse the deletion with the **Undo** command). Any text following the deleted text reflows into the space that was occupied by the text you deleted.

❖ To delete an entire block of text, select the **Pointer** tool and click the text block to select it. Then press the **Delete** or **Backspace** key or choose the **Clear** command on the Edit menu to delete the block. If you delete one text block among several on a page, deleting the text block with the **Pointer** tool leaves the space that the text block occupied; text that follows does not reflow into the blank space.

Remember, the **Text** tool is used to highlight a portion of a text block. The **Pointer** tool is used to select an entire text block.

Cutting, Copying, and Pasting Text

Text is *cut*, rather than deleted, when you want to remove it from its present location and paste it somewhere else. To cut text:

1. Highlight the text you want to cut, using either the **Pointer** tool or the **Text** tool.

2. Choose the **Edit** pull-down menu and choose **Cut** (or press **Shift+Del**). The highlighted text will be deleted from its current position.

When text is cut, it is copied to the Windows Clipboard, where it remains until something else is cut or copied. Place the cut text anywhere by positioning the insertion point where you want the text and choosing **Edit > Paste** (or pressing **Shift+Ins**). The text is pasted into position.

Text is *copied* when you want it to remain where it is but also to use it somewhere else. Do the following to copy text:

1. Highlight the text you want to copy, using either the **Pointer** tool or the **Text** tool.

2. Choose the **Edit** pull-down menu and choose **Copy** (or press **Ctrl+Ins**). The highlighted text is copied and remains highlighted. Click anywhere outside the highlighted text to unselect it.

When you copy text, it is actually copied to the Windows Clipboard, and it replaces anything already in the Clipboard. Place the copied text anywhere by positioning the insertion point where you want the text and choosing **Edit > Paste** (or pressing **Shift+Ins**). The text is pasted into position.

You can paste the contents of the Clipboard as often as you like. For example, let's say you are developing a series of fact sheets for similar products. You could paste your company's name and address on each page of the fact sheet by positioning the insertion point where you want the text to appear and choosing **Paste** from the Edit menu (**Edit > Paste**). The Clipboard contents are copied onto your document each time you select the **Paste** command. Once you cut or copy something else (text or graphics), however, it replaces the contents of the Clipboard.

Text pasted into a text block pushes the existing text to the right of the insertion point forward. The pasted text becomes an integral part of the text block into which it is pasted.

Text pasted into the document, but not in an existing text block, creates its own text block, with the default type and paragraph specifications in effect at the time of the pasting. Normally, the left and right borders of the text block are defined by the page margins. You can define a text block width equal to surrounding text blocks by pasting text with the drag-place method (described next).

Drag-Placing Text

When pasting text from the Clipboard, you may want to define your own line length rather than accepting the line length that PageMaker provides. PageMaker normally uses the width of a column or the width of the page as the default line length. For a narrow measure of text, such as for a byline or photo credit, this makes an abnormally wide text block, as shown in Figure 3.5.

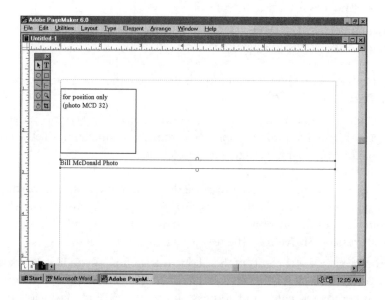

Figure 3.5 *Byline text block naturally seeks the right margin, making an abnormally wide text block.*

To shorten the width of the text block, *drag-paste* the text instead of pasting it. When you drag-paste, you define the width of the new text block. Here's how:

1.   Choose the **Text** tool.

2. Position the insertion point in the upper-left corner of the area where you want to paste the text from the Clipboard.

3. Press and hold down the left mouse button and drag the pointer down and to the right to set the width you want for this text block. As you drag the pointer, a box opens up, defining the size of the text block.

4. When you have established the boundaries for this text block, release the left mouse button, choose **Paste** (**Edit > Paste**) or press **Shift+Ins**, and the text flows into the text block. The text assumes the new line length and wraps at the right-hand boundary. Drag-placed text that has been copied from a wide text block to a narrower one needs more depth. If you see only the beginning of the drag-placed text, click it with the **Pointer** tool and pull the bottom windowshade down to reveal the rest of the text.

You needn't paste anything to drag out your own text block. You can do steps 1 through 3 to create a new empty text block in which to type new text. Simply position the **Text** tool where you want the text block to start and click-drag the tool diagonally until the width (and depth) of the text block is defined. Release the mouse button and start typing.

Power Pasting

Use the *power-pasting* feature when you need to repeatedly paste the same graphic or text in columns or rows across or down the page. For example, let's say you are laying out a form to track hours worked on different projects. Down the left margin are the days of the week. Across the top is **Proj/Hours** repeated in ten columns. Instead of typing the column heading ten times or pasting and aligning nine text blocks, use power pasting to do it automatically. Here's how:

1. Type the first column heading. Highlight it with the **Pointer** tool and copy it by choosing **Edit > Copy**.

2. Hold down the **Ctrl** and **Shift** keys and press **P**. A copy of the text is pasted on top of the text you copied. It will be selected, displaying the text block.

3. Leave the text block selected (don't click the left mouse button), position the pointer on top of the text block, but not over the windowshade handles or sizing handles. Press and hold down the left mouse button, and drag the

text block to the second column heading position. Remember to leave this second text block selected.

4. Power paste the text block again by pressing **Ctrl+Shift+P**. A third copy of the text block is pasted and positioned the same distance from the second text block as you positioned the second one from the first.

5. Continue power pasting across the page to create as many column headings as you need. You can power paste text or graphics across or down the page, as shown in Figure 3.6.

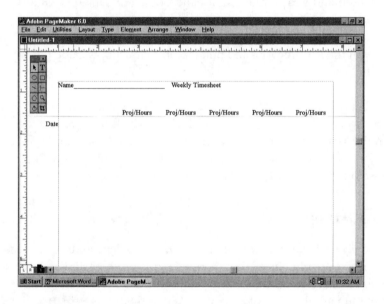

Figure 3.6 *Power pasting text or graphics across or down the page.*

Using Undo and Revert

Whoops! I shouldn't have done that! If you don't utter words to that effect occasionally, you're probably not learning and using all the capabilities of PageMaker. I encourage you to try different capabilities for two reasons: you will often be surprised by the result, and you can almost always back out of a command using either **Undo** or **Revert**. To undo something you've just done:

1. Choose the **Edit** pull-down menu (or press **Alt+E**). Notice the **Undo** command in the Edit menu. If it is dimmed, you can't use it to undo your

last action. If it is highlighted, it lists the action it would undo if you invoked it at this time. For example, if you've just cut some text and you pull down the Edit menu, the **Undo** command says **Undo cut**, meaning it undoes the deletion you just made.

2. Choose **Undo** (or press **Alt+E U** or **Alt+Backspace**) to undo the action you just did.

UNDO COMMAND CONDITIONS

You can use the **Undo** command after:

- ❖ Moving or resizing a text block
- ❖ Deleting text
- ❖ Adding text
- ❖ Deleting a graphic
- ❖ Cropping a graphic
- ❖ Removing pages
- ❖ Inserting pages
- ❖ Editing text with the **Text** tool
- ❖ Using the **Undo**, **Edit**, **Copy**, **Paste**, and **Clear** commands
- ❖ Changing the Page Setup dialog box
- ❖ Moving column guides or guidelines

You cannot use the **Undo** command after:

- ❖ Any commands from the File pull-down menu other than **Docment Setup**
- ❖ Scrolling
- ❖ Changing the Page View size
- ❖ Selecting or canceling a selection
- ❖ Changing line and fill specifications from the Element pull-down menu
- ❖ Any commands from the Type pull-down menu
- ❖ Pasting after cutting or copying with the **Pointer** tool
- ❖ Changing style definition or selection
- ❖ Changing color definition or selection
- ❖ Changing text or paragraph attributes

In circumstances where **Undo** won't work, you can fall back on the **Revert** command (see Chapter 1, "Reverting to a Previously Saved Version"). Remember that **Revert** undoes everything you've done since you last saved the document. You can also close your current document without saving it, which does the same thing as using the **Revert** command: anything done since the last time you saved will be lost.

Inserting and Removing Pages

PageMaker gives you complete freedom to add or remove pages. You specify where by moving to a page adjacent to where you want to add a page or to the page you want to delete. Then select the command from the Pages pull-down menu. The pages you add have the page setup parameters you specified for your existing pages and use the master pages you set up in the same way your existing pages do.

Inserting a Page

Here's how to insert a page:

1. Using the **Go To** command (**Layout > Go to Page**), select the page before or after the page you want to add. That is, if you want to add a page after page 27, go to either page 27 or the current page 28.

2. Choose the **Layout** pull-down menu and choose **Insert pages** (or press **Alt+L I**), to display the Insert Pages dialog box, shown in Figure 3.7.

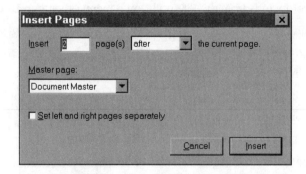

Figure 3.7 *The Insert Pages dialog box.*

3. The insertion point is positioned in the Insert pages text box, which shows a default value of **2**. Enter the number of pages to insert or accept the default value.

4. Click one of the option buttons:

    ❖   **Before current page**. Clicking this option inserts a new page before the page you are on. Your current page number increases by the number of pages you are inserting.

    ❖   **After current page**. Clicking this option adds a new page after the page you're on.

    ❖   **Between current pages**. If you have selected **Double-sided pages** in the Page Setup dialog box for this document, your pages are displayed as two-page spreads. Clicking this option allows you to add pages between the two pages currently displayed. Using this option changes the front and back orientation of the remaining two-page pairs in your document.

5. Choose **Insert** or press **Enter** to return to your document. You can undo the **Insert** command by immediately choosing **Undo** from the Edit pull-down menu (or pressing **Alt+Backspace**).

Removing a Page

It is a good idea to go to the page you want to remove before actually removing it. This way you can confirm that it is indeed the page you want deleted. However, you can remove a specific page or pages from anywhere in the document. To remove a page:

1. Choose the **Layout** pull-down menu and choose **Remove pages** (or press **Alt+L R**), to display the Remove Pages dialog box, shown in Figure 3.8.

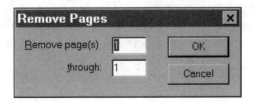

Figure 3.8 *The Remove Pages dialog box.*

2. The insertion point is positioned in the Remove page(s) text box. The Remove and Through text boxes display the page number you are on. Accept the page number or enter the numbers of the pages to remove and press **Tab** to position the insertion point in the Through text box.

3. If you are removing only one page, enter the same page number in both text boxes (for example, if you want to remove page 27, type **27** in both text boxes). If you want to remove more than one page, type the beginning and ending page numbers in the two text boxes (for example, if you want to remove pages **27** through **34**, type those numbers in the two text boxes). Remember, when removing pages, you are entering the actual page numbers of the pages you want deleted. When adding pages you're only dealing with the number of pages you want to add.

4. Click **OK** or press **Enter**. PageMaker displays a dialog box warning that the contents of the pages will be deleted as well. Click **OK** to confirm the removal and return to your document. Click **Cancel** to cancel the deletion.

You can undo the **Remove** command by immediately choosing **Undo** from the Edit pull-down menu (or pressing **Alt+Backspace**).

Adjusting Spacing Between Characters, Words, and Lines

Character, word, and line spacing provide the necessary white space around the words that tell your product's story, communicate your feelings, or create emotion. *Character spacing* is necessary to separate individual letters in words. Some letters— like *M, W, Q,* and *O*—are wider than others, like *I, L, F,* and *J. Letter spacing* in PageMaker is proportional to which letters are being typed and helps to even the spacing of lines of type in justified columns. *Word spacing* determines how many words fit on a given line. Too much spacing between words makes a line difficult to read and gives an unkempt appearance to a page of type. *Line spacing*, or *leading* (pronounced "ledding"), is the space between lines of type. Either too little or too much space makes the lines difficult to read.

Unlike most word processors, PageMaker gives you absolute control over the spacing of characters, words, and lines. You can allow PageMaker to judge the best spacing requirements automatically, or you can manually adjust spacing. The degree of accuracy varies, but in most cases, PageMaker allows you to make extremely fine adjustments. For example, you can set the amount of space text stands off from wrapping around a graphic in 1/1000-inch increments.

NOTE

The 2880 Rule: Though screen resolutions vary greatly, PageMaker always prints pages more accurately than they're displayed. A typical screen resolution may be the equivalent of 96 to 100 dpi. The typical laser printer prints at 300 dpi, and high-resolution imagesetters, like the Linotronic L630, can produce output higher than 3000 dpi. Just remember, regardless of how a page may look on the screen, it prints with an accuracy of 1/2880th of an inch.

Adjusting Spacing

Nothing improves the professional quality of a publication more than establishing proper spacing between letters. Incorrect spacing (usually too much), is a shrieking sign of amateurish work. Overspacing letters is most obvious in large type sizes—as type increases in size, letter spacing should be proportionally reduced. Spacing in PageMaker is controlled through kerning, tracking, and leading.

KERNING

Change the *kerning* of a pair of letters, and you change the amount of space between the letters. Long ago, before the advent of computers, kerning letters involved trimming the vertical sides of lead type to make certain letter combinations fit closer together and look more natural. Now PageMaker does the trimming, but the principle is the same—some pairs of letters (called *kerned pairs* of letters) need closer spacing than other pairs. For example, in Figure 3.9, the letters *A* and *V* on the left should be kerned closer, while the same kerned letters on the right look more natural and pleasing.

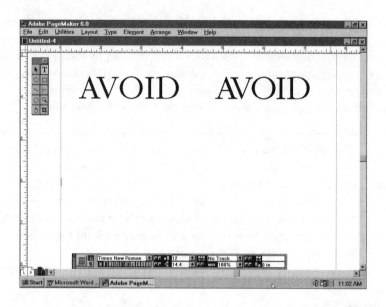

Figure 3.9 *Kerning the space between the letters A and V resulted in a more pleasant-looking word on the right.*

Each PostScript font has a built-in table that determines which letter combinations will be kerned and the optimal amount of kerning. PageMaker kerns these letter-pairs above a certain size, which you set in the Spacing Attributes dialog box.

In some cases, automatic kerning is not enough to attractively display type, especially in larger type sizes—the larger the letter, the more space, proportionally, is allowed on either side of the letter. PageMaker kerns away some of that space, but often not enough. In these situations PageMaker offers two additional ways of adjusting the spacing: track kerning and manual kerning. Let's look first at setting up automatic kerning for a specific type size:

1. To set a different kerning size threshold for selected text, highlight the text with the **Text** tool. To change the default size threshold for the entire document, do not highlight any text.

2. Choose the **Type** pull-down menu and choose **Paragraph** (or press **Ctrl+M**) to display the Paragraph Specifications dialog box.

3. Click the **Spacing** button to display the Spacing Attributes dialog box, shown in Figure 3.10. Use this dialog box to turn kerning on and off and to set a size threshold above which kerning will take place.

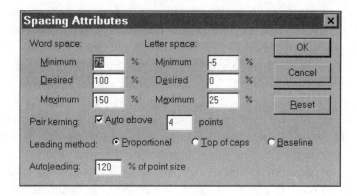

Figure 3.10 *The Spacing Attributes dialog box.*

4. By default, kerning is on (the **Pair Kerning Auto Above** check box is marked with an **X**), meaning that all type above the default **12** point size shown in the Points text box will automatically be kerned. To turn kerning off, click the **Auto above** box to remove the **X**.

Just as the need to kern increases as the type size increases, so the need to kern is reduced as type gets smaller. In fact, in sizes below 10 points, kerning may make the type more difficult to read. The unequivocal exception to this rule is the font Times Roman, which is more than likely resident in your laser printer. Times is not a particularly attractive font and it is made worse by the fact that it has much too much letter spacing. If you must use Times, I suggest setting the **Pair Kerning Auto Above** limit low enough to include all sizes of the font you will use in your documents.

5. Enter a size value in the Auto above text box to tell PageMaker the size type above which to kern. If you want all type, regardless of size, to be kerned, enter a value smaller than the smallest type you use in your document. If you want only headlines kerned, enter a size just below the headline size (for example, if the heads will be 36 points, enter **30 pt** in the text box).

6. Click **OK** or press **Enter** to return to the Paragraph Specifications dialog box, and click **OK** or press **Enter** again to return to your document.

When you are in a series of nested dialog boxes, such as the Spacing Attributes dialog box mentioned earlier, you can return immediately to your document, without having to click **OK** in each successive dialog box. Simply hold down the **Shift** key and click **OK**. You bypass the other dialog boxes and move directly back to your document.

As I have already mentioned, only certain letter-pair combinations are automatically kerned. Those combinations are embedded in the PostScript font and can't be changed in PageMaker. You may find you don't like the amount of kerning applied to a particular pair of letters kerned automatically by PageMaker or you might have a pair of letters not part of the font's kerning table that you want to kern. You may also want to drastically kern two letters for visual effect as part of a logo or design. For whatever reason, you can manually kern letters with PageMaker. Here's how:

1. Position the **Text** tool insertion point between the two letters you want to kern.

2. Press **Ctrl+Shift+Backspace** to increase the space between the two letters in 1/25-inch increments. To decrease the amount of space the same amount, press **Ctrl+Backspace**.

3. Optionally, you can use the numeric keypad: press **Ctrl+Plus** (+) to increase space or **Ctrl+Minus** (-) to decrease space.

4. For really fine work, you can adjust kerning in 1/100-inch increments. On the numeric keypad, press **Ctrl+Shift+Plus** to increase space or **Ctrl+Shift+Minus** to decrease space. You may find it easier to work in such fine adjustments by first increasing the Page view size to 200% or 400%.

5. If you wish to cancel whatever kerning adjustments you've made, press **Ctrl+Shift+0** (use the zero key on the keyboard, not on the numeric keypad). If you manually change the kerning of a pair of letters, it only changes the kerning in that instance, not throughout the document.

TRACKING

Adjusting the *tracking* of a word or group of words gives much more control over the spacing of letters and words. You can set tracking at values from very loose all the way to very tight. Tracking is adjusted from the Tracking submenu or in the Type Specifications dialog box.

PageMaker sets the default tracking to **None**, but it can be changed at any time for an entire story or for highlighted text. Here's how:

1. Choose the **Type** pull-down menu and choose **Expert Tracking** (or press **Alt+T R**) to display the Tracking submenu, shown in Figure 3.11.

Figure 3.11 *The Tracking submenu.*

2. Select the amount of tracking you want by clicking the tracking option. **Normal** tracking can improve the appearance of letter spacing by increasing it in small type and decreasing it in larger type. The other tracking options increase or decrease tracking by more drastic amounts, like these examples.

Avid mimes don't mind	No track
Avid mimes don't mind	Very Loose
Avid mimes don't mind	Loose
Avid mimes don't mind	Normal
Avid mimes don't mind	Tight
Avid mimes don't mind	Very Tight

Adjusting Leading

The *leading* measurement is the height of the line of type, measured from baseline to baseline. It includes the height of the type itself and the space above the type. The size of the line's leading must accommodate the height of the capital letters and ascenders like the stem of a lowercase *d*, as well as the depth of the descenders like the leg of a lowercase *p*. The space that accommodates ascenders and descenders is called the *slug* of the line, as highlighted in Figure 3.12. The slug must be high enough that ascenders and descenders don't touch, and it must allow enough white space between the lines so that type can be read comfortably. When you highlight a line of type with the **Text** tool, the type and the line's slug are highlighted, as shown in Figure 3.12.

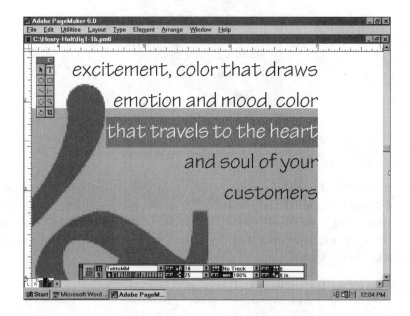

Figure 3.12 *When highlighting a line of type with the Text tool, the type and the line's slug are highlighted.*

PageMaker can set leading automatically, or you can specify any leading value you wish. Automatic leading is about 120% of the type size, although this can be adjusted. For example, if the type is 12 points high, automatic leading would give it about 14.5 points of white space, or 120% of 12. Manual and automatic leading are specified with the Leading submenu, shown in Figure 3.13, or in the Type Specifications dialog box.

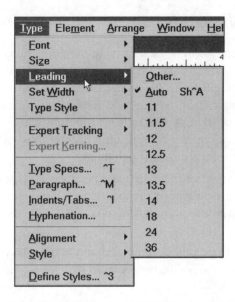

Figure 3.13 *The Leading submenu.*

To change the leading of a line of type:

1. Highlight the type whose leading you want to change with the **Text** tool.

2. Choose the **Type** pull-down menu and choose **Leading** (or press **Alt+T L**) to display the Leading submenu.

3. Choose the amount of leading for the line of type by clicking the leading value you want. If you want to set an amount of leading that is not among the choices displayed on the Leading submenu, choose **Other** to display the Other Leading dialog box, shown here, or enter the amount in the Type Specifications dialog box, as described in Chapter 2.

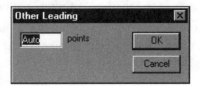

Adjusting Hyphenation

When lines of text are *justified*, neither page margin is ragged—like the lines of text in this book, they are aligned evenly to both the left and right margins. Since words are different lengths, the spacing must be adjusted to make each line the same length. However, some lines would inevitably require more than normal space between one or more words to keep the right margin even. The multiple spaces between words makes for unsightly paragraphs, with what are called *rivers* of white space meandering through them.

To reduce the spacing between words in justified text, PageMaker can hyphenate words that would normally extend past the right margin. Hyphenation is controlled with the Hyphenation dialog box. To change the hyphenation:

1. Choose the **Type** pull-down menu and choose **Hyphenation** (or press **Alt+T H**), to display the Hyphenation dialog box, shown in Figure 3.14.

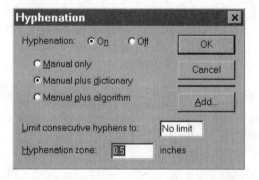

Figure 3.14 *The Hyphenation dialog box.*

2. Use the dialog box to set the parameters for hyphenating the text. Click an option button to select the level of hyphenation you want:

    ❖ **Manual only**. Hyphenates only words you have marked to hyphenate by inserting a discretionary hyphen (hold down the **Ctrl** key and press the **Minus** key) in the word where it would normally break. A *discretionary hyphen* means that PageMaker hyphenates the word (when necessary) where a discretionary hyphen is inserted to justify a line of type that the word falls in. For example, to discretionary-hyphenate the word hyphenate, type **hy(Ctrl+-)phen(Ctrl+-)ate**. You do not see the discretionary hyphens, but if the word extends past the right margin of a justified line, PageMaker breaks the word at one of the two hyphens.

❖ **Manual plus dictionary**. Hyphenates the words to which you've added discretionary hyphens, as well as words hyphenated in the PageMaker dictionary. Any time PageMaker comes to a word that must be split between lines, it checks the dictionary and checks for discretionary hyphens to see how to break the word. If there is a conflict, PageMaker always accepts the way your discretionary hyphen breaks the word.

❖ **Manual plus algorithm**. In addition to using the dictionary, PageMaker uses a mathematical *algorithm* (a set of arithmetic rules that theoretically define how words are hyphenated) and your manually inserted hyphens to break words. Just as there are exceptions to every rule of English grammar, there are exceptions to the rules for hyphenating words. Using the algorithm method may produce incorrect hyphenations, so check PageMaker's work carefully.

3. The Limit consecutive hyphens to text box allows you to tell PageMaker not to stack more than *x* number of hyphenated lines. In typesetting jargon, two or more consecutive lines ending with hyphens is called a *ladder*, and is usually a no-no.

4. The *hyphenation zone* applies only to unjustified lines of text. It is the width of the area in the right margin into which words fall that need to be hyphenated. For example, if you set the hyphenation zone as **.5 inch**, and a word at the end of the unjustified line crosses the zone (extends from .5 inch to the left of the right margin to any amount past the right margin), the word will be hyphenated. The wider the zone, the less hyphenation will appear in a document. The narrower the margin, the more words will be hyphenated.

ADDING WORDS TO THE HYPHENATION DICTIONARY

If you use a number of specialized words in your documents, you may want to add them to the hyphenation dictionary, rather than continually inserting discretionary hyphens. You can also change the hyphenation of words already in the dictionary. Follow these steps:

1. If you are in the Hyphenation dialog box, click the **Add** button. Otherwise, choose **Type > Hyphenation** to display the dialog box, then click the **Add** button to display the Add Word to User Dictionary dialog box, shown in Figure 3.15.

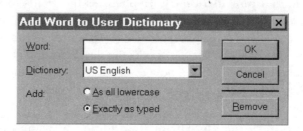

Figure 3.15 Add Word to User Dictioary dialog box.

2. In the Word text box, type the word you want to hyphenate. To add words already in your document, highlight the word with the **Text** tool, then call up the Add Word to User Dictionary dialog box; the word is displayed in the text box.

3. Indicate where PageMaker should hyphenate the word by placing markers at each hyphenation point in the word. The marker is the tilde symbol (~), normally the key to the left of the number 1 key on the keyboard. You can rank the most favorable break in the word by entering one tilde, the second most-favorable break with two tildes, and the third most-favorable break with three tildes. PageMaker will try to honor the most-favorable break, but if the word can't be broken there, it will try the second most-favorable, and so on.

4. To change dictionaries, click the **list box arrow** and choose the dictionary you want to use. You must have loaded the dictionary through the Aldus Setup program for it to be available.

5. To add the word in all lowercase letters, click the **As all lowercase** option button. To add the word exactly as typed in the Word text box, click the **Exactly as typed** option button.

6. To actually add the word, click **OK** or press **Enter**.

7. To remove a word from the dictionary, type the word you want to remove in the Word text box, and click the **Remove** button.

Changing Word and Letter Spacing for Justified Text

Hyphenation helps to ease the burden of unmanageably large gaps between words in justified lines of text. But hyphenation is limited to breaking words at proper hyphen positions, which may still leave a lot of white space between words. To absorb that white space, PageMaker evens out the spacing of words and increases the spacing between letters in words. When done properly, the additional white space is spread out enough so that it's not noticeable. You can adjust the amount of spacing given to words and letters in justified lines with the Spacing Attributes dialog box. Here's how:

1. Choose the **Type** pull-down menu and choose **Paragraph** (or press **Ctrl+M**) to display the Paragraph Specifications dialog box.

2. Click the **Spacing** button to bring up the Spacing Attributes dialog box, shown in Figure 3.16. We will use this box to change the default values to minimum and maximum percentages of word and letter spacing.

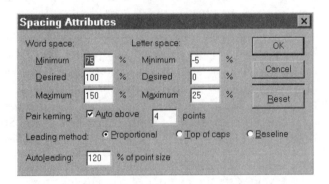

Figure 3.16 *The Spacing Attributes dialog box.*

3. Word space values set the amount of the space band between each word. The *space band* is the amount of space PageMaker moves the Text tool insertion point when you press the **Spacebar**. The space band is different for each font, based on what the font designer determined when the font was developed. To adjust word spacing, change the default values in the Word Space text boxes:

❖ **Minimum**. Enter a percentage of the desired value in the text box that sets the minimum amount of space between words. As PageMaker attempts to even out the word spacing in justified lines, it closes up words to this minimum amount.

❖ **Desired**. Usually this percentage is set at **100**, meaning the proper spacing for the font design's space band. Since the minimum and maximum spacing are based on the desired spacing, entering a different value here affects all spacing in the line. For example, if you want to tighten up the spacing of all words, simply enter a smaller value here, such as **90%** instead of 100. To add spacing across the board, enter a value higher than 100% in this text box

❖ **Maximum**. Enter a percentage of the desired value in the text box that establishes the maximum amount of space between words. The default values in the Word Space text boxes are very broad, allowing PageMaker to adjust spacing from half of the desired size all the way up to twice the desired size. To even out spacing on the page, consider increasing the minimum size to **80%** and the maximum size to **120%** of the desired spacing.

NOTE

While PageMaker makes every effort to honor your spacing requirements in the Spacing Attributes dialog box, it will exceed the values you enter in order to justify the line correctly. PageMaker highlights the areas in which it exceeds spacing values if you request it to do so by checking the **Loose/tight lines** check box in the Show Layout Problems area of the Preferences dialog box (**File > Preferences**).

4. Letter space values set the amount of pen advance for each letter. *Pen advance* is the amount of space bordering the letter, which the font designer determined when the font was developed. To adjust letter spacing, change the default values in the Letter Space text boxes:

❖ **Minimum**. Place in the text box a percentage of the desired value, which PageMaker will subtract to narrow the letter spacing.

❖ **Desired**. Zero means PageMaker will use the pen advance amount specified by the designer. To reduce or widen the overall spacing of all letters in the line, enter a negative or positive value, respectively.

❖ **Maximum**. Place in the text box a percentage of the desired value that PageMaker will add to widen letter spacing.

5. When you are finished changing the spacing values, press **Shift+OK** to return directly to your document.

Adjusting Indents and Tabs

In many word processors, tabs and indents are two different actions: *tab* moves just the first line of a paragraph, and *indent* moves all lines of a paragraph. In PageMaker, both tabs and indents are controlled by pressing the **Tab** key. You define what the **Tab** key does in the Indents/Tabs dialog box. The tool you use to select the Indents/Tabs dialog box determines what text is affected by the changes you make in the dialog box:

❖ Using the **Pointer** tool to select the dialog box means that the changes you make change the default indent/tab structure for the document and affect the next paragraph you type.

❖ Positioning the **Text** tool insertion point in a paragraph means that changes made to the dialog box affect all text in the current paragraph. The tab ruler in the dialog box is aligned to the text block's left edge.

❖ Highlighting text with the **Text** tool means that changes to the dialog box affect all the highlighted text. The tab ruler can be aligned to either the left margin of the page or to the left edge of the highlighted text block. If you want the ruler to be aligned to the text block's left edge, be sure the edge is visible when you invoke the dialog box.

Any of the indent and tab steps that follow, made without opening an existing document or creating a new document, will become the default indent/tab settings for PageMaker.

Setting and Changing Tabs

To set or change tab stop positions:

1. Choose the **Type** pull-down menu and choose **Indents/Tabs** (or press **Ctrl+I**) to display the Indents/Tabs dialog box, shown in Figure 3.17.

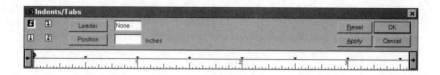

Figure 3.17 *The Indents/Tabs dialog box.*

2. Click on one of the four tab-alignment icons. They define the alignment of text positioned at the tab stop:

❖ **Left alignment**. Text begins at the tab position and flows to the right side of the column.

❖ **Right alignment**. The last character of the text positioned to the right-alignment tab is aligned on the tab stop.

❖ **Center alignment**. Text is centered under the tab stop.

❖ **Decimal alignment**. Text, or more usually numbers, are centered by typing a period for the decimal aligned to this tab stop.

3. Once you have selected the alignment for the tab, position the arrow over the ruler where you want the tab and click the left mouse button.

4. Optionally, you can use the **Position** button to do any of the following:

❖ **Add tab**. Enter an exact tab stop value in the Tab Action text box and choose **Add** to add a tab at that position. Or you can add a tab by clicking the pointer at the position you want.

❖ **Delete tab**. Click on the tab to delete it, or enter the exact position in the Tab Action text box and then press **Delete** to delete the tab. Or grab the tab by positioning the pointer over the tab icon, hold down the left mouse button, and drag the tab icon off the ruler.

❖ **Move tab**. Enter the value for a new position for an existing tab stop. Highlight the tab and choose **Move**. The tab moves to the new position. Or you can grab the tab by positioning the pointer over the tab icon, holding down the left mouse button, and dragging the tab icon to a new position.

❖ **Repeat tab**. Set a tab stop the distance from the zero point on the rule you want for repeatedly positioning other tabs. Highlight the tab and choose **Repeat**. The tab is repeated the same distance from the highlighted tab. For example, if you want a tab every two inches, highlight a tab stop at the two-inch mark on the ruler and choose **Repeat**. You'll see a new tab at the four-inch mark. Choose **Repeat** again and you'll see a tab at the six-inch mark, and so on.

Setting and Changing Indents

To set or change indents:

1. Choose the **Type** pull-down menu and choose **Indents/Tabs** (or press **Ctrl+I**) to display the Indents/Tabs dialog box. The left indent icons are the top and bottom half of a right arrow on the left side of the rule. The top half sets the first line paragraph indent. The bottom half indents all lines of the paragraph to the left.

2. To change the first line indent, click the **top arrow** and drag it to the right. The current position is displayed in the Position text box.

3. To indent the left edge of all lines in a paragraph, click and drag both halves of the **arrow** to the right.

4. To create a hanging indent, in which the second and subsequent lines of a paragraph are indented more than the first line, click and drag the **bottom arrow** more to the right than the top half.

5. To indent the right edge of a paragraph, click and drag the **left arrow**, on the right side of the ruler, to the left.

Setting the Leader Style

Leaders are special characters, often periods, that separate text from referencing numbers or other text on the same line. Leaders are handy in typing page numbers across from table of contents entries or prices across the page from menu items. When you have selected a leader, tabbing across the page will produce a row of the characters you selected as the leader style. To choose the leader style:

1. Choose the **Type** pull-down menu and choose **Indents/Tabs** (or press **Ctrl+I**) to display the Indents/Tabs dialog box.

2. Highlight the tab to which you want to assign a leader style.

3. Click the **Set Leader** button and choose the leader character, or choose **Custom** and select your own character. The leader you select is displayed

in the text box beside the list of leader styles. If you select **Custom**, the insertion point moves to the text box. Type the character you want for your leader.

Resetting the Tab Ruler

You can reset any changes you've made to the ruler tab positions by choosing the **Cancel** button or by clicking the **Reset** button. The tab stops in effect when you invoked the Indents/Tabs dialog box are reset.

To adjust the zero point of the Indents/Tabs ruler, click the **left** or **right arrow** button to scroll the ruler's measurement numbers either lower or higher, respectively. Alternately, you can click one of the **tab stop** icons and drag it in the direction you want, off the ruler's left or right edge. The ruler scrolls in the direction you dragged the icon once it's off the edge of the ruler.

To Sum Up

In this chapter you've seen how versatile PageMaker is in restructuring story text blocks. You can thread or unthread text blocks at will, giving you complete control of page layout. PageMaker's threading feature also allows you to roll up text blocks, temporarily removing them from the page without deleting them.

You've also seen how easy it is to drag and reposition text on the page or to drag it off the page onto the pasteboard. It's just as simple to add and delete pages in PageMaker. You can change the number of pages in your document at any time.

You've also looked at how carefully PageMaker defines and adjusts the spacing of characters, words, and lines of text, giving you complete control over the look of your typography and the image you're creating.

In the next chapter we'll cover the most important addition you can make to your documents: graphics.

CHAPTER 4

Adding Design Elements

❖ Adding graphics to your documents

❖ Changing PageMaker options

❖ Creating graphics in PageMaker

❖ Importing graphics into PageMaker

❖ To sum up

The most important design element you can add to your page is visual relief from the printed word. Column upon column of text may serve to communicate factual information, but it doesn't help the reader process the information, and it can look boring. Visual relief comes in many forms; it can be as simple as one or two graphic lines to break up the text or as complex as a four-color photograph. You may not think of white space as a design element, but it is perhaps the most important design element. A page with nice wide margins frames the text within the margins, drawing the eye to it, asking to be read. A text line with a shorter length, or *measure*, is more inviting, easier to read.

The careful placement and judicial use of graphic elements gives the page a professionally produced look. The elements help to emphasize and organize the page. PageMaker has a number of easy-to-use tools that can draw different types of circles, boxes, and lines. Boxes and circles can be filled with any of a number of *screens* (shades of gray) or fill patterns. Lines can be any number of different *weights* (thicknesses), and several patterns of broken lines are available. Any text or graphic element can be rotated or skewed to any of 360 degrees. Finally, PageMaker makes it easy to import graphics created in other graphics programs, scanned photographs, and drawings.

A word of caution: keep your work simple. A little goes a long way in designing a sophisticated page. Boxes, circles, drop shadows, or reverse type can add or detract from the overall look of your document. The title page shown on the left side of Figure 4.1 uses too many drop-shadow boxes, segmenting the title page and giving the impression that the proposal itself is confusing and disjointed. Furthermore, the text in the screened box on this page is difficult to read, and the page lacks consistency in the weight and style of lines. The page shown on the right side of Figure 4.1 uses a vertical rule to separate the report's title from its subtitle. The center text block is set in italics, giving it the look of an invitation. The dingbat following the italics is used to separate the two sales messages from the title. The vertical screened boxes continue the theme of the vertical rule above.

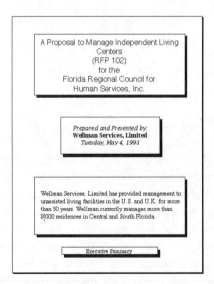

Figure 4.1 *Two examples of a title page. The one on the left is confusing and distracting, with too many design gimmicks; the one on the right is simple and straight forward.*

Adding Graphics to Your Document

You can add graphics anywhere in your document by drawing a graphic with one or more of PageMaker's drawing tools, importing a graphic that you developed in another program, or importing a clip art image or scanned photograph. As you learned in Chapter 2, PageMaker's tools can draw perpendicular and diagonal lines, boxes with either square or rounded corners, and circles and ovals. PageMaker's Rotating tool can rotate anything you draw, clockwise or counter-clockwise, to any degree of rotation.

To use any of the drawing tools:

1. Click the tool you want to use. For this example, let's click the **Constrained Line** tool.

2. When you move the Pointer tool outside the toolbox, it changes to a crossbar icon.

3. Place the crossbar where you want to begin drawing the line.

4. Press and hold down the left mouse button and drag the crossbar to where you want the line to end. Release the mouse button. You will see your line, highlighted with sizing handles, as shown in Figure 4.2.

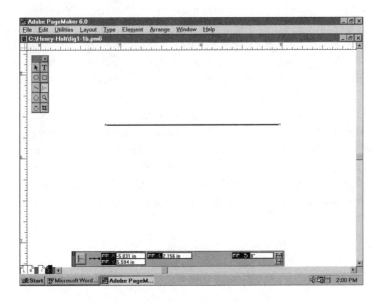

Figure 4.2 *A line drawn using the Constrained Line tool.*

To resize the line, choose the **Pointer** tool and click anywhere on the line, highlighting it. Click a sizing handle and drag it to shorten or lengthen the line.

To move the line (or any other graphic), choose the **Pointer** tool and click anywhere in the line (or graphic) to highlight it. When you click anywhere on the line except a sizing handle, a four-pointed arrow cursor is displayed. Use it to drag the line to a new position.

Adding Lines

Lines or rules are useful in breaking up large blocks of text. You can add lines as part of a paragraph specification or as graphic elements. In Chapter 2, you learned that PageMaker can predefine paragraphs with lines above, below, or both. Now let's look at adding lines as graphic elements.

With lines, as with any graphic element, a little goes a long way. Lines can help to emphasize important information and direct the reader to information that should be remembered. However, if used in excess, lines can be distracting. You should also consider using lines to balance the "weight" of the page. By this I mean the contrast between black and white—text and paper—on the page. To judge balance, choose a small view of the page that greeks the body text (or hold the printed page at arm's length and squint). You may find that you've got too much text that is throwing off the balance. If so, you might use a line to help offset the out-of-balance area. Finally, beware of intersections; be careful of crossing lines that draw the eyes like a magnet. If you must have vertical and horizontal lines on the same page, it's a good idea to keep invisible extensions of the lines from crossing each other. Lines added to master pages do, of course, display on all pages of the document (as long as you activate the **Display Master Items** command on the Layout menu). For some documents, adding recurring lines can be helpful in organizing the page. For example, let's say you've given your text a narrow measure by setting up a two-column format using columns of unequal width. A vertical line added to the narrow column's left margin adds balance to the lopsided column's width, as shown in Figure 4.3.

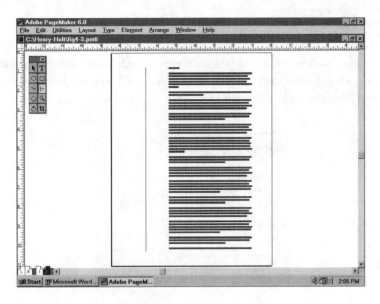

Figure 4.3 *A vertical line added to balance the page.*

Lines that set off page headers and footers can be useful, as shown in Figure 4.4. Adding lines to headers and footers is explained later in this chapter.

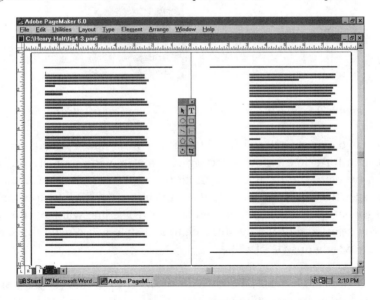

Figure 4.4 *Lines have been added to set off the headers and borders.*

CHANGING LINE SPECIFICATIONS

PageMaker has a wide range of possibilities for lines. The weight can range from none (the line is invisible) to 12 points. Styles include single lines, combinations of weights, and dashes and other types of broken lines. All line specifications are chosen from the Line submenu (**Element > Line**), shown in Figure 4.5.

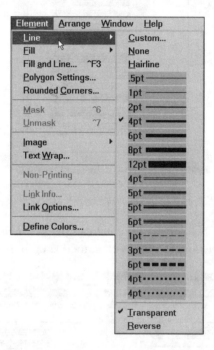

Figure 4.5 *The line submenu, showing some of the possible choices.*

There are two ways to select a weight and style for a line. You can change the specification for a line before selecting the line drawing tool. If you do, the selection becomes the default specification for this and all other lines drawn until the specification is changed. Or you can choose the drawing tool, and then select a weight or style for the selected line only. The line will have the specification you selected, but the default weight and style will remain the same. To change the weight or style of a line:

1.   Choose the **Element** pull-down menu and choose **Line** (or press **Alt+M L**) to display the Line submenu.

2. Hold down the left mouse button and move the pointer down the list to select the weight you want. Release the mouse button at the correct weight.

Use the same steps to select a different style for a line. Choose the **Line** submenu and move the mouse pointer down the list of styles to select the one you want.

You can change the weight or style of any line at any time. Simply choose the **Pointer** tool and click the line to select it. Choose the **Line** submenu and select a different weight or style.

Adding Shapes

In PageMaker you can draw square- and round-cornered boxes, circles, and ovals of any dimension. If you hold down the **Shift** key while you draw, PageMaker gives you perfect squares and circles. But be frugal in adding graphics to your pages. You can add shapes to a document's master pages to have a repeating graphic on every page, and, as with lines, you can draw shapes off the page, on the pasteboard, and either drag or paste them into your document later.

CHANGING SHAPE SPECIFICATIONS

PageMaker lets you modify both the weight and style of the border denoting the shape and change the *fill*, or color, of the shape itself. To adjust the lined border of the shape, select the shape with the Pointer tool. Then open the Line submenu and select the appropriate line weight or style. Figure 4.6 shows some options.

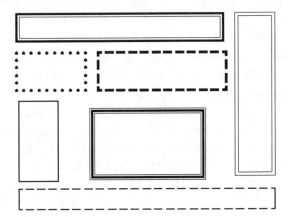

Figure 4.6 *Different weight and style borders for rectangles can be selected from the line submenu.*

To change the fill specifications of a shape:

1. Select the shape by clicking its border with the Pointer tool.

2. Choose the **Element** pull-down menu and choose **Fill** (or press **Alt+M F**) to display the Fill submenu, shown in Figure 4.7.

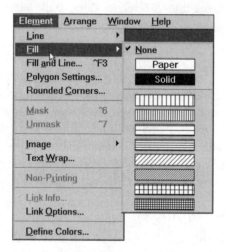

Figure 4.7 *The Fill submenu, showing some of the possible choices.*

3. Select the fill you want by moving the pointer down the Fill submenu. When you release the mouse button, PageMaker fills your shape with one of the following:

    ❖ **None**—Choosing **None** means that the shape will be transparent; that is, whatever is underneath it shows through.

    ❖ **Solid fill color**—Choose **Paper** if you want your shape to be the same color as the paper on which you are printing. Normally, the paper color is white, although you can define a specific color for the paper in the Define Colors dialog box (explained in Chapter 8, "Adding Color"). If you position text inside a shape and plan on adding another shape underneath in a different color, you must choose **Paper**. Choose **Solid** if you want a solid black color for the shape.

    ❖ **Lined fill pattern**—The eight lined choices offer different patterns to fill shapes.

CHANGING LINE AND FILL SPECIFICATIONS TOGETHER

Sometimes you may find it helpful to make line and fill changes at the same time. The Fill and Line dialog box lets you do just that. Follow these steps:

1. Select the shape you want to change with the Pointer tool.

2. Open the Element pull-down menu and choose the **Fill and Line** command (or press **Alt+M A**) to display the Fill and Line dialog box, shown in Figure 4.8.

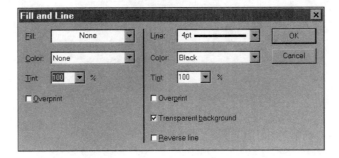

Figure 4.8 *The Fill and Line dialog box.*

3. Choose the fill pattern you want by clicking on the **Fill** list box arrow. You can assign a color to the fill by clicking the color you want in the Color list.

4. To change the line specification, click the **Line** list box arrow and choose the line you want. Again, you can change the color of the line by choosing a different color from the Color list.

5. To force the fill or line to overprint on top of anything underneath the shape (instead of knocking out the object underneath) click the **Overprint** check box for the fill or the line. (Knockouts and overprinting are explained in detail in Chapter 8, "Adding Color.")

CHANGING ROUND CORNERS

Depending on the needs of your design and layout, you may want to round the corners of square or rectangular boxes. To do so, first draw the box in the dimensions you want; then use the **Rounded Corners** command on the Element menu to change the corners. Here are the steps:

1. Select the box you wish to edit. If no object is selected, you will change the default corner radius for all boxes drawn in the future in the current document.

2. Choose the **Element** pull-down menu and choose **Rounded Corners** (or press **Alt+M C**) to display the Rounded corners dialog box, shown in Figure 4.9.

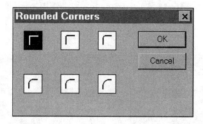

Figure 4.9 *The Rounded Corners dialog box.*

3. You can choose from five styles of rounded corners. Click the corner style you want.

4. Click **OK** or press **Enter** to return to your document.

To change a rounded-corner box back to a square-cornered box, select the box, open the dialog box, and choose the square-cornered icon.

CREATING DROP-SHADOW BOXES

Drop-shadow boxes or circles are actually two boxes or circles, one behind the other, slightly offset and colored black. Drop shadows add a nice graphic touch when used sparingly. To create a drop-shadow box:

1. Select the **Square-Cornered Box** tool and draw a square or rectangle the size you want. When you finish drawing, leave the box selected (so the sizing handles are visible).

2. Choose the **Copy** command from the Edit pull-down menu (**Edit > Copy**) or press **Ctrl+Ins** to copy the rectangle to the Clipboard.

3. Immediately paste the rectangle, by choosing **Paste** from the Edit menu (**Edit > Paste**) or pressing **Shift+Ins**. A copy of the rectangle is pasted over the original rectangle, shifted slightly to the right and down. The copied rectangle becomes the shadow for the rectangle you drew.

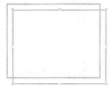

4. While the pasted rectangle is still selected, move it behind the original rectangle by choosing the **Send to back** command from the Element pull-down menu (**Element > Send to back**) or pressing **Ctrl+B**. The pasted rectangle is now behind the original rectangle.

5. Fill in the pasted rectangle with a solid color or with a shade of gray from the Fill submenu (**Element > Fill**). Notice that you can see the pasted rectangle through the original rectangle.

6. To hide most of the pasted rectangle, color the original one. Use the Pointer tool to select the original rectangle. Choose the solid paper color from the Fill submenu (**Element > Fill**).

Now, let's add some text to the drop-shadow box:

1. Use the Text tool to define and open a new text block in the drop-shadow box. Position the insertion point in the upper-left corner of the box, press the left mouse button, and drag to the right and down, defining the text block as the size of the drop-shadow box.

2. Release the mouse button and type some text. Use the Type pull-down menu to change the type specifications and alignment to suit your needs. When you're finished, you'll have a drop-shadow text block.

Changing PageMaker Options

Out of the box, PageMaker is set for a number of default values, as we have seen in earlier chapters. Changing some of these settings can markedly improve your document. Let's take a look.

Adjusting Margins

The *measure* (length of a line of text) is basically defined by the margins you set (and, of course, the overall size of the page and the type). An excessively long measure makes for difficult reading. A line set in 11-point type with PageMaker's default margin setting is too long for an 8.5-by-11 inch page size. Most 6-by-9-inch books use a 26- or 27-pica measure and 10- or 11-point type. Newsletters and magazines typically use a larger page, multiple columns, and a shorter measure—perhaps 18 picas—in a two-column format. PageMaker defaults to an 8.5-by-11-inch page with a 40-pica measure, which is too long for most purposes. You will probably wish to change it, depending on your type size and the sort of document you are creating. You can shorten the measure in a number of ways, the easiest being to widen the left and right margins, squeezing the text between them. To change the default margin setting:

1. If PageMaker is up and running, save and close the document you're working on. With the program window visible but with no document window open, changes made to PageMaker's margins become the new default settings.

2. Choose the **File** pull-down menu and choose **Document Setup** (or press **Alt+F M**) to display the Document Setup dialog box.

3. In the Margins area of the dialog box, enter larger measurements for the left (inside) and right (outside) margins. Left and right margins of 2 inches each give you a line measure of 27 picas, which is better than the default measure of 40.5 picas. If your document will have multiple pages printed on one side only and bound on the left edge, you can add a little more width to the left, or inside margin (the side that will be bound) because the pages will have to bend or fold open at the binding.

Setting and Adjusting Columns

When you are working with larger page sizes and still need a reasonable line measure, you can split the page into columns. The default 8.5-by-11-inch page size with the default margins, if split into two columns, gives you a satisfactory measure of about 19 picas. A tabloid page size (11 by 17 inches), if divided into three columns, gives you a measure of almost 18 picas. Clearly, columns are a handy way to establish a readable line length. To set up more than one column on a page:

1. To set all pages with the same columns, open the master pages by clicking the **Master Page** icon in the lower-left corner of the document window. To set columns on one page only, move to that page.

2. Choose the **Layout** pull-down menu and select **Column Guides** (or press **Alt+L C**), to display the Column Guides dialog box, shown in Figure 4.10.

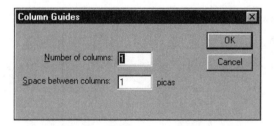

Figure 4.10 *The Column Guide dialog box.*

3. Enter the number of columns you want for this document or page in the Number of columns text box. The default number of columns is **1** (PageMaker sees the default page as a one-column document).

4. Enter the width of the gutter (the area between the columns) in the Space between columns text box. The larger the value here, the wider the gutter and the more white space on your page. However, the wider the gutter, the narrower the columns will be. One pica is a normal gutter width. If you are working in inches instead of picas, 1 pica equals .167 inches.

SETTING UNEQUAL COLUMN WIDTHS

On a smaller page, more than one column creates an unusually short line measure. One way to solve this problem is to create unequal column widths. Here are the steps:

1. Display the Column Guides dialog box (**Layout > Column Guides**).

2. Enter **2** as the number of columns and leave the gutter setting as **1 pica** or **.167 inches**.

3. Click **OK** or press **Enter** to return to your document.

4. Select the **Pointer** tool from the toolbox.

5. Click and drag the column marker to either the right or left, creating a wide and a narrow column, as shown in Figure 4.11. Even with smaller page sizes, the wider column should be 18 to 24 picas, for a readable measure.

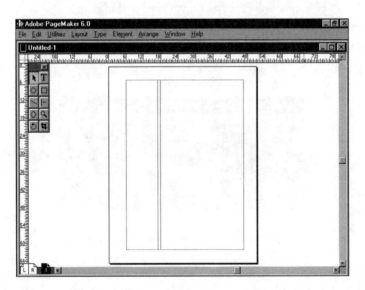

Figure 4.11 *Setting unequal column widths.*

If you were to look at the Column Guides dialog box again, you would see that the Number of columns text box now contains the word **Custom**, meaning that you have customized the column guide position.

If you wish to set unequal column widths for all the pages in your publication, add the columns to the master pages, as described earlier. For facing pages, the narrow column usually goes on the inside, close to the bound edge of the page (the left side of right-hand pages and the right side of left-hand pages).

N O T E

An excellent use for the narrow column, besides giving text in the wider column a more readable line measure, is to hold margin notes. Use it to add small graphics, notes, warnings, or other text that relates to the text in the wider column across from it.

Creating Headers and Footers

Headers and *footers* are text or graphics located above and below the top and bottom margins, respectively. Generally speaking, headers and footers are used to display continuing information about the page, such as the chapter title and page number, the date and time of publication, or the revision level of the document. To add a header or footer to your document:

1. Click the **Master Page** icon to open the master pages for your document. If you have checked the **Facing pages** check box in the Page Setup dialog box, you will see two master pages (as reflected in the dual-page Master Page icon), representing a two-page spread. If you did not set up your document with facing pages, you'll see a single master page, as shown by the single-page Master Page icon.

2. To create a header, move to the top of the master page and drag a guideline out of the top ruler to position the header line.

3. Position the guideline above the top margin. Reset the ruler's zero points, if necessary, to precisely position the text for the header.

4. Format your text in the desired typeface, size, and style, using the Type Specifications dialog box. Enter the text and add lines, shading, color, or any graphic element you would like to have repeated on each page, as shown in Figure 4.12.

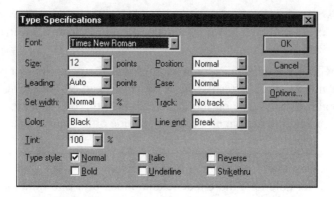

Figure 4.12 *The Type Specification dialog box.*

5. To add a page number, position the Text tool insertion point where you want the page number to appear and press **Ctrl+Shift+3**. A repeating page number marker is inserted. If you are working with facing pages, you must add a page number marker to both pages. The marker you add to the left page displays *LM*, indicating Left Marker. The marker you add to the right page displays *RM*, or Right Marker. If you are not working with facing pages, the repeating page marker always displays RM.

N O T E Automatic page numbering begins based on the starting page number you enter in the Document Setup dialog box. If you have facing master pages, you can create alternating left and right headers or footers. Whatever you enter on the left-hand master page is repeated on each left page of your document. Likewise, whatever is entered on the right-hand master page is repeated on each right page of your document.

If you find that you need a different header or footer on a page or two of your document or if you wish to change the header or footer on two facing pages, you can simply click **Display Master Items** in the Layout pull-down menu. This toggles off the **Display Master Items** command, and any header or footer you see will be hidden on both facing pages. You can then enter new text or graphics in place of the master page items. If you wish to change the header or footer on a single page of a two-page spread (when you set up your document with facing pages, for example), you must first cover the master page text or graphic with a solid paper-colored box, then add your own text or graphics over the box. Here's how:

1. Select the **Rectangle** tool and position the crossbar in the area of the page containing the master page item you want to hide.

2. Click the crossbar above and to the left of the master page item and drag diagonally, creating a box that borders the item. You can see the item underneath the box because the default fill color is **None** (meaning that you can see through the box).

3. Choose the **Element** pull-down menu and choose **Fill** (or press **Alt+M F**) to display the Fill submenu.

4. Click **Paper** to give the box a solid color the same as the paper. The master page item is now covered by a white (paper-colored) box, edged in a black-lined border. Let's remove the border.

5. Choose the **Element** pull-down menu and choose **Line** (or press **Alt+M L**) to display the Line submenu.

6. Click **No Line** to delete the line around the box. Now the master page item is completely covered by the white-colored box, over which you can enter new text or graphics. To see an outline of the box, click along the edge with the Pointer tool. You will see the box's sizing handles.

TIP

If you can't find the edge of the box because it is no longer visible, select the **Pointer** tool and choose **Select All** from the Edit pull-down menu (**Edit > Select All**). All text blocks and graphic elements are selected, and you will be able to see the outline of the "invisible" box.

Creating Graphics in PageMaker

While PageMaker doesn't pretend to match the artistic capabilities of drawing programs like Adobe Illustrator, you can, with a little thought and imagination, produce some workable graphics with PageMaker. For example, you can rotate and skew text and graphic elements in any of 360 degrees of rotation in as small as .01-degree increments. You can also combine lines, boxes, or circles with text to create unique designs.

Combining Graphic Elements to Create Logos

While you will probably want to use a drawing program to finalize a design you sketch together, starting in PageMaker can help you visualize how a logo will look as part of a letterhead or a business card. Let's add some elements together to create a rough logo for a high-rise construction firm called Advanced Construction, Inc. Follow these steps:

1. Select the **Text** tool and create a text block in a new document page at the top-left corner.

2. Select an interesting typeface. Bold typefaces, like Imago Extra Bold, are often used for logos, since they add weight to the name of the company and are very readable in the smaller sizes you would use for a letter-head. (If you don't have Imago, you can substitute Times Roman Bold.) Type the company name in a reasonable size. Try 18 points.

Advanced Construction, Inc.

3. Now try the same name stacked, flush left.

Advanced
Construction
Inc.

4. Let's add some stacked lines, aligned to the left slant of the *A* in *Advanced,* to give the impression of a building. If you find that the *A* moves when you place the lines next to it, make sure the **Text Wrap** command on the Element pull-down menu is off.

≡Advanc
Construc

5. Now slant the left ends of the lines by positioning a diagonal line over the ends, aligned evenly with the progressive slant of the lines. Choose the **Line** submenu (**Element > Line**) and select a **6-point** weight for this line. Click the line with the Pointer tool and adjust it so that it just covers the left ends of the horizontal stacked lines.

6. The only thing left to do is color the diagonal line so that it cannot be seen. With the line still selected, choose the **Window** pull-down menu and choose **Color Palette** (or press **Alt+W C**) to display the Color palette. Click **Paper** to hide the diagonal line, coloring it the same color as the paper. Your logo should look like Figure 4.13.

Figure 4.13 *Logo in progress.*

Rotating Text

Rotated text is a quick attention grabber. Vertically rotated text can be especially handy for section or chapter titles, because the titles can be positioned in the left or right margin of the page and not use up valuable text space. Rotation can also be used in developing unique logo designs. To rotate text:

1. Use the **Pointer** tool to select the text block you wish to rotate. In this example, we'll rotate the name of the Vertical Manufacturing Corporation on the letterhead.

2. Select the **Rotating** tool in the toolbox, position the crosshairs of the tool in the center of the text block and press and hold the left mouse button. You will see a small starburst icon displayed over the center of the crosshairs.

3. Now drag the starburst icon out from the center of the text block (marked by the crosshairs). Still holding down the left mouse button, you see a line displayed in the direction you're dragging the starburst icon. The line is called the *rotation lever*—an imaginary arm connected to the fixed point around which the text block rotates. See Figure 4.14.

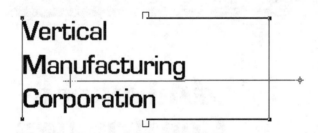

Figure 4.14 *The Rotating tool provides a fixed-point pivot around which the item rotates and a rotation lever to aid in exact rotation.*

4. Still holding down the left mouse button, drag the starburst icon and the rotation lever in the direction you want to rotate the text block. In the example, let's drag the lever up in a counterclockwise movement until the text block is vertical. Now you can release the mouse button.

5. Add some thin vertical lines, and you have a logo for a company that manufactures vertical blinds. See Figure 4.15.

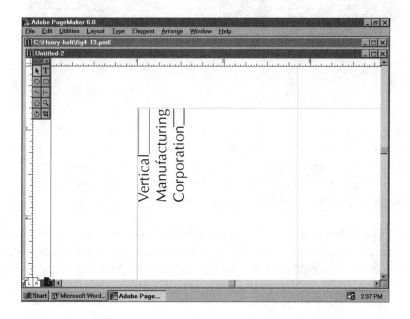

Figure 4.15 *The rotated logo on the page.*

Getting Control with the Control Palette

Some designers working with PageMaker enjoy the freeform approach of the program, which gives you complete freedom in creating a design on the blank page. Others are more precise in detail, perhaps, and want the sort of minute placement control afforded by competing desktop publishing packages (and traditional typesetting). It's a left brain–right brain thing I suppose—I personally enjoy working with PageMaker in the traditional way, but many designers seek more control in the positioning and manipulation of text and graphics. If you fall into this latter category, you'll appreciate PageMaker's Control palette. To display the palette, open the Windows pull-down menu and choose the **Control Palette** command. With an object selected, you'll see the palette shown in Figure 4.16.

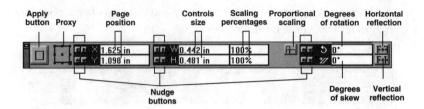

Figure 4.16 *The Control palette.*

The palette changes depending on which tool you choose from the toolbox and what kind of object you select with the tool. For example, if you choose the **Pointer** tool, the **Apply** button on the palette displays the Pointer icon (the button doesn't appear until you have created an object with the tool). Let's look specifically at the parts of the Control palette:

❖ **Apply button**—Use the **Apply** button to apply any alterations you make to values on the palette. For example, if you change the X and Y coordinates of the object, to reposition it on the page, click the **Apply** button to have the new coordinates take affect. Pressing the **Enter** key will do the same thing.

❖ **Proxy**—The Proxy represents the selected object and gives you a reference to affect one specific area of the object, such as a corner dimension or a side sizing handle position. To make changes to only a specific sizing handle, click the represented handle on the Proxy icon.

❖ **Page position**—This position represents the X,Y position of the object's upper-left corner relative to the document page. To move the object on the page, change one or both coordinate positions.

❖ **Size controls**—The size controls determine the size of the object.

❖ **Scaling percentages**—To make scaled changes to the dimensions of the object, enter percentage values in the two scaling percentage text boxes. For example, to reduce the size of the object by half, enter **50%** in each percentage text box.

❖ **Proportional scaling control**—To maintain the original proportion of the object, click the **Proportional Scaling** icon.

❖ **Rotation and skew**—These controls provide precise control over rotating and skewing objects. Click in the appropriate text boxes and enter the degree of rotation or skew you want.

❖ **Nudge buttons**—You can increment the current entry in a text box in minute amounts by repeatedly clicking the associated nudge button. When you click the **Increase** or **Decrease** nudge button, you change the value in the text box by 1/100th of an inch or 1/10th of a degree. If you hold down the **Ctrl** key and click the button, you will make changes to the text box values in 1/10th of an inch or 1 degree.

❖ **Horizontal and vertical reflection controls**—These allow you to create horizontal or vertical reflections of an object.

If you're not sure what value to enter in a text box on the palette but you know the math formula to arrive at the correct value, you can enter the formula in the text box. For example, if you want to add .14 inch to the current value of a text box, click the insertion point in the text box immediately following the current value, type **+.14**, and PageMaker calculates the correct sum when you press the **Enter** key or click the **Apply** button. You can add using the plus (**+**) key, subtract using the minus (**-**)key, multiply using the asterisk key (*****), or divide using the forward slash key (**/**).

SKEWING AND MIRRORING OBJECTS WITH THE CONTROL PALETTE

Skewing and mirroring change the plane of an object. Both can be done in PageMaker for Windows. Each orientation moves the object in essentially a third dimension, forward or backward out of the vertical plane of the page. To skew an object, say the letter *A*, follow these steps:

1. Select the letter text block and open the Control palette from the Window pull-down menu.

2. Enter the degrees of skew in the Skew text box, or use the skew nudge buttons to scroll to the amount of skew you want. A positive angle of skew leans the letter backward; a negative amount of skew leans the letter forward.

3. Click the **Apply** button to apply the skew angle to the text box. The results might look like Figure 4.17, which shows the results of 75 degrees of skew.

Figure 4.17 *The letter A with a positive skew of 75 degrees.*

Mirroring is similar to skewing. It also rotates the object out of the vertical or horizontal plane, depending on which mirror control you choose. As with skewing, select the object you want to mirror, and follow these steps

1. Usually a mirrored object also contains the object in the original plane, so that one can see the reflection of the original. To leave the original object where it is, first make a copy of the object and paste it directly over the original.

2. With the pasted copy still selected, open the Control palette and click the **Mirror** button, just to the right of the Skew text box. The selected text will now look like a reflection of the original text you copied.

David

DЗДИ

MAKING TYPOGRAPHIC CHANGES WITH THE CONTROL PALETTE

When you choose the **Text** tool and highlight text in a text block, the Control palette changes to reflect the many typographic options you have through the Type pull-down menu, like Figure 4.18.

Figure 4.18 *The Character view of the control palette.*

The palette in Figure 4.18 is the Character view of the Control palette. If you click the **Paragraph View** button, you'll see a different palette with paragraph formatting controls, like Figure 4.19.

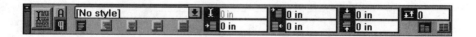

Figure 4.19 *The Paragraph view of the Control palette.*

Importing Graphics into PageMaker

Based on the import filters you choose, you can import most standard graphics formats into PageMaker, including encapsulated PostScript files (files with the extension **.EPS**) created in programs like Adobe Illustrator; tagged-image file format (**.TIF**) files of captured screen images or scanned black-and-white or color photos; Macintosh MacPaint files (**.PNT**); Windows metafiles (**.WMF**); Computer Graphics metafiles (**.CGM**); Windows Paintbrush (**.BMP** and **.PCX**) files; and many others.

Placing Graphics

You import graphics with the **Place** command (**File > Place**). To import a graphic:

1. Select the **Pointer** tool from the toolbox.
2. Choose the **File** pull-down menu and choose **Place** to display the Place dialog box, shown in Figure 4.20.

Figure 4.20 *The Place dialog box.*

3.   Scroll through the list box of file names to find the graphics file you want to place or type the file name in the Name text box.

4.   Choose **Open** or press **Enter** to return to your document. The Pointer tool changes to one of a number of Place graphic icons, depending on the format of the graphic you're placing.

5.   Position the upper-left corner of the icon where you want the graphic and click the left mouse button.

Placing In-Line Graphics

PageMaker normally considers graphics to be independent objects on the page. If, however, the graphic relates directly to text in a specific line or paragraph, you should anchor the graphic to that text by placing an *in-line graphic*. When an in-line graphic is placed, it becomes an integral part of the text block—if text is inserted before the paragraph in which the in-line graphic is located, the paragraph and the graphic are pushed down the page together.

An in-line graphic is placed in the same way as an independent graphic, except that you must select the **Text** tool first and click it in the text where you want the graphic to appear. Open the Place dialog box and enter the name of the graphics file to place. Then choose **Open** or press **Enter** to start the importing process.

CONVERTING AN INDEPENDENT GRAPHIC TO AN IN-LINE GRAPHIC

If you've placed an independent graphic only to find that you'd like it to be anchored to the text as an in-line graphic, here's what to do:

1.   Select the graphic with the Pointer tool. Choose **Cut** from the Edit pull-down menu (or press **Shift+Del**) to cut the graphic from its current position and copy it to the Clipboard.

2.   Choose the **Text** tool and position the insertion point in the text block where you want the graphic.

3.   Choose **Paste** from the Edit pull-down menu (or press **Shift+Ins**) to paste the graphic from the Clipboard to the insertion point position. The graphic is pasted as an in-line graphic.

Aligning In-Line Graphics

When you place an in-line graphic, it assumes the alignment characteristics of the surrounding text. That is, if the text is left-aligned, the graphic will be left-aligned. To change the alignment, highlight the in-line graphic with the Text tool and choose the **Type** pull-down menu, then the **Alignment** submenu to select a different alignment orientation for the graphic.

Sizing Graphics

Independent graphics are sized the same way you size shapes or lines. Click the graphic with the Pointer tool and grab one of the sizing handles to stretch or shrink the graphic in the direction of the arrow. Corner sizing handles effectively enlarge or reduce the overall size of the graphic. To enlarge or reduce the graphic proportionately (resizing the width and height by the same amount), press the **Shift** key, then click the corner handle and drag.

If you resized a graphic incorrectly, simply choose **Undo** from the Edit menu (or press **Alt+Backspace**) while the graphic is still selected. To resize an in-line graphic, select the graphic with the Pointer tool, click a sizing handle, and resize accordingly.

Cropping Graphics

Cropping trims away a portion of the graphic, rather than reducing the size of the graphic. In Figure 4.21, one of the tutorial graphic files has been cropped.

Figure 4.21 *The lower graphic has been cropped with the Cropping tool.*

To crop a graphic:

1.   Select the **Cropping** tool from the toolbox.
2.   Click the graphic to select it and display the sizing handles.
3.   Position the Cropping tool over the necessary side or corner sizing handle. For example, if you want to trim some of the bottom of the graphic, click the bottom sizing handle. If you want to trim both the bottom and the left side, click the lower-left corner handle. Hold down the left mouse button; the Cropping tool changes to an arrow.
4.   Drag the arrow side(s) you are cropping in toward the center of the graphic.

You can uncrop any side you have already cropped, but only back to the original size of the graphic.

Object Linking and Embedding

A step beyond cutting and pasting, and more exacting than using PageMaker's import filters, object linking and embedding is a powerful feature of Windows that PageMaker takes advantage of. Called *OLE* (pronounced o-lay) for short, Object Linking and Embedding lets you link or embed the actual data from other applications directly in your PageMaker documents. For example, instead of importing a Word 7 document into PageMaker, you could link or embed the document. Why bother when PageMaker can import most of the Word formatting? Because when you link or embed the document, you can make interactive changes to the document inside PageMaker. Simply double-click on the Word text and the Word application automatically starts, enabling you to instantly change the document.

There is a basic difference between OLE linking and OLE embedding: when you *link* the work of another application—it could be a spreadsheet from Excel, a document from WordPerfect or Word, an image from PaintBrush, or a photo from Picture Publisher—you are actually pasting a copy of the original in your PageMaker document. When you change the work in the application that created it (called the source) the linked object in PageMaker is automatically changed as well. When you *embed* the source document in your PageMaker document, you're adding the original work, not a copy, and it contains everything needed for you to make changes to the work.

SETTING UP AN OLE LINKED OBJECT

The steps to add a linked object are simple. Create the object in the source application, save the object in the source application, then copy it to the Clipboard. In PageMaker, choose **Paste Special** from the Edit menu to paste the object just as you would paste anything else. Let's take a closer look:

1. Open an OLE server application like Excel. *Server applications* are OLE applications that create the object and provide it to—or serve it to—the OLE client application. *Clients* are those applications, like PageMaker, that can receive an object but not serve them to other applications.

2. In Excel, create a spreadsheet and save it as an Excel file. Now copy the entire spreadsheet or just the range of cells you want to add to your PageMaker document, using Excel's **Copy** command.

3. Now move back to your PageMaker document and choose the **Paste Special** command on the Edit pull-down menu. In a second, the spreadsheet or portion of the spreadsheet you just copied appears in your document.

4. Now the neat part: double-click on the spreadsheet in your PageMaker document. You will see Excel and the Excel **.XLS** file you just created. Make changes to the file, and the changes immediately become apparent in your PageMaker document.

EMBEDDING AN OLE OBJECT

To embed an OLE object, follow these steps:

1. Open the Edit pull-down menu and choose the **Insert Object** command. You will see the Insert Object dialog box, shown in Figure 4.22. The dialog box displays all the OLE server applications available on your system.

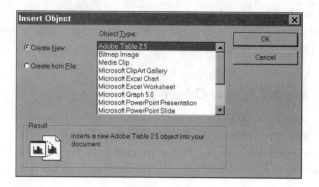

Figure 4.22 *The Insert Object dialog box.*

2. Scroll down the list of applications and double-click on the application you want to use to create the embedded object. For example, if you want to embed a scanned photograph in your document, you might click on **Adobe Photoshop**.

3. You will see the application you selected in the dialog box start, and it present a new, blank window. Create the object you want or use the **Open** command to open the file you want.

4. When you are ready to embed the object, simply double-click in the application's Control-menu box to close the application. The application presents a dialog box asking if you want to update the document. Click **Yes**.

5. You will again see the PageMaker document window, with the object you just created embedded in the PageMaker document. If you want to make changes to the object, double-click it and the server application immediately restarts.

To Sum Up

In this chapter, you've learned how easy it is to add graphics to your documents. You've seen the steps needed to import a wide variety of graphic formats and you've learned that moving, sizing, cropping, and copying graphics are typically straightforward in PageMaker, as is linking or embedding OLE objects.

In the next chapter, you will practice setting up templates for a number of useful documents that serve as master publications you can use over and over.

CHAPTER 5

Setting Up Templates

- ❖ Setting up master page templates
- ❖ Creating a newsletter templates
- ❖ Creating a fact sheet templates
- ❖ Creating templates from existing documents
- ❖ To sum up

Templates save you time with the mundane tasks of desktop publishing. The more time you save doing the everyday chores of preparing a publication design, the more creative time you'll have to add the spark of brilliance that makes your publication stand out. The real power PageMaker gives you is the ability to try before you buy: walk around in the publication for a while, see how it fits, test the look and feel. Take a tuck here, let a little out there, and suddenly it works. If it doesn't, you've lost very little time. Open a new file and start again.

As easy as PageMaker is to get those initial design steps out of the way, by making a template, you'll have to take those steps only once for each type of document. *Templates* are like master plans for your documents. They are created in exactly the same way as documents, using the same commands and options. Just as the Master Pages feature gives you uniformity of design, templates offer a standardized set of designs: Large companies can use templates to ensure that forms, memos, procedural and technical manuals, and letterhead adhere to strict design standards. In a networked environment, templates invite uniformity in creating departmental documents.

Setting Up Master Page Templates

In Chapters 2 and 3, we touched on using master pages to anchor the format of all interior pages of a document. Now let's look at the Master Pages feature again and find out exactly how it can help you prepare a document. Master pages are an invisible formatting area that holds design elements and text to be displayed on all document pages.

For example, if you were developing a twelve-page brochure and you wanted the company name centered at the top of every page, you could either:

❖ Move to the top of each page of your document; reset the rulers' zero points to measure from the top margin; pull down guidelines to set the baseline for the text; open a text block with the Text tool; specify the typeface, style, alignment, size, and leading; type the text; make some fine adjustments; add a line underneath the text for emphasis; and repeat all this eleven more times.

❖ Do all of that once on each master page and forget it.

You can create new templates from scratch, or you can save as a template any document you have already created.

Clearly, adding repeating design elements or guidelines to master pages can save an enormous amount of time when laying out the individual pages of a document. If you preformat the master pages and save the work as a template, you'll save even more time developing similar documents in the future. To set up a master page template:

1. Open a new document. In the Document Setup dialog box (**File > Document Setup**), decide whether the document will be printed on both sides and thus have facing pages or printed on one side only. Click the appropriate option boxes and click **OK** or press **Enter**.

2. Move to the master pages by clicking the **Master Page** icon in the lower-left corner of the screen.

3. Open the Layout menu, choose the **Guides and Rulers** submenu, and turn on **Show Guides**, **Snap to Guides**, and **Show Rulers** by clicking the commands.

4. Choose the **File** menu and open the Preferences dialog box to select the measurement system you want for this document.

5. Choose a page view based on what you want to do. If you want to add guidelines, use the Fit in Window view (**Ctrl+0**) to get a look at the overall layout of the page. If you want to add text, move up to a closer view of the page to align the type accurately.

6. Create whatever items you want on the master pages. If you want page numbers, add a page-number marker by pressing **Ctrl+Shift+3** on each master page.

7. When you have finished with the master pages, you might want to lock the guidelines (**Layout > Guides and Rulers > Lock Guides**). Click a page number to move back to the document, and check the position and look of the items you added to the master pages.

8. If all looks well, save the file as a template (**File > Save**) by clicking the **Save as Type** menu and choosing **Template** in the Save Publication dialog box. Give the file a unique file name, but don't add any extension (PageMaker adds the extension **.PT6** to the file name).

NOTE

PageMaker file names ending in **.PM6** are documents, those ending in **.PT6** are templates.

Creating Custom Page Sizes

There are several default page size options in the Document Setup dialog box. But there may be times when you need to work with an odd page size. For example:

❖   If you work with magazines, you know that most are a standardized size, slightly smaller than the default 8.5 by 11 inches. They generally measure 49 picas by 64 picas and 9 points.

❖ If you want to bleed a graphic (a graphic *bleeds* when it is butted right against the edge of the page, covering the margin) printed on a laser printer, you'll need to set up a page size smaller than the standard 8.5 by 11 inches to account for the unprintable margins that almost all laser printers have.

❖ If you are developing manuals that use a 5.5-by-8.5-inch format or books (like this one) in a 6-by-9-inch format.

❖ If you are producing visual aids—35mm slides or 7-by-9 inch view foils—for a presentation.

In these examples, having a template already formatted with the correct page size, and perhaps guidelines in position, can be a real time saver. To create custom page-size templates:

1. Use the Document Setup dialog box to enter the custom page specifications for each template.

2. Position basic design guidelines on the templates' master pages.

3. Save each template with a descriptive, unique file name.

Creating Custom Borders

If you have a continuing need to add jazzy borders around the pages of special documents—diplomas, forms, certificates, or invitations—adding the border to the master pages of a certificate template will save you from having to re-create the border time and again. To create a custom border:

1. Since the border will be positioned outside the text margins, be sure to set the margins wide enough in the Document Setup dialog box.

2. Choose the master page for the document and select the Fit in Window view.

3. Choose the **Rectangle** tool and draw a border, evenly spaced around the outside of the page margins.

4. With the border selected, choose a line weight or style from the Line submenu (**Element > Line**).

5. To make a fancier border, copy the border by selecting it with the Pointer tool and choosing **Edit > Copy** (or press **Ctrl+Ins**). Then paste the copied border on top of the one you just drew by choosing **Edit > Paste** (or press **Shift+Ins**).

6. Stretch the second border by clicking on the corner sizing handles and enlarging the border slightly more than the first. While the border is still selected, give it a novel style using the Line submenu.

The result could look something like Figure 5.1, in which a frame was made using a dotted-line border with a double-line border on either side of it.

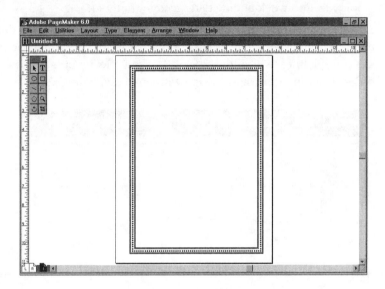

Figure 5.1 *A custom border.*

Creating Custom Forms

Although PageMaker was not developed specifically for designing forms, it's quite versatile. In fact, I know of at least one business, in the Orlando area, that does nothing but design and produce custom forms with PageMaker. The great thing about doing forms in PageMaker is that you're not limited in any way—you have complete freedom of design.

Guidelines are the key to professional-looking forms: They help you to align the many lines and small text blocks that always seem to appear on forms. Use the master pages to hold guidelines and standardized text. With one form template, for example, you can set up different forms for timesheets, invoices, and purchase orders. Here's how:

1. Position the company logo, name, and address in the upper-left corner of the master page.

2. Add guidelines in the top center of the page to designate an area for the form's title.

3. Pull down three guidelines to mark off an area in the upper-right corner for the date, name of department/client/buyer, name of supervisor/ employee, and week ending date/account number.

4. Add enough horizontal and vertical guidelines to accommodate the employee timesheet, which has the most lines of the three forms. The same guidelines will allow you to lay out the invoice and purchase order. The top of the master page will look like Figure 5.2.

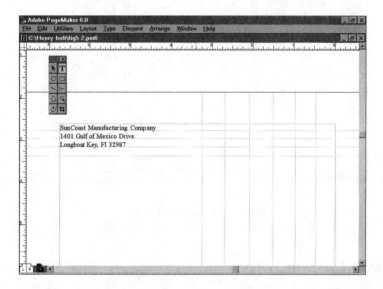

Figure 5.2 *The top of the master page showing guidelines for invoice and purchase order.*

5. In the bottom margin of the master page, designate an area with guidelines for the form number and add the text **Form #** in front of the area.

6. Save the template with a unique file name. Now you're ready to create an employee time sheet on page 1, a company invoice on page 2, and a company purchase order on page 3. Open the template as a document and get started. The results could look like the following Figures 5.3 through 5.5.

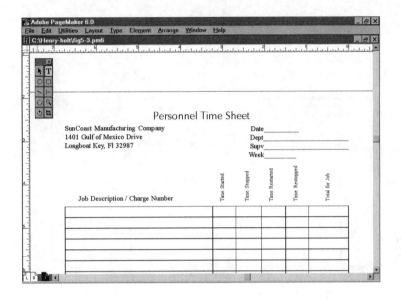

Figure 5.3 *An employee time sheet.*

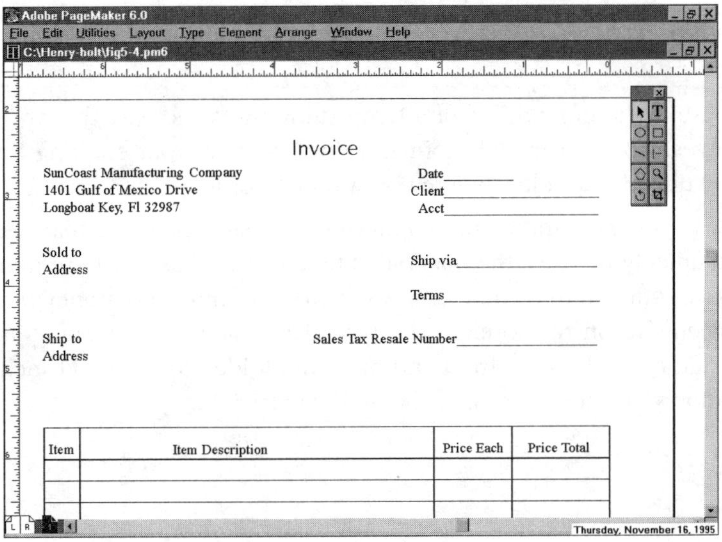

Figure 5.4 *A company invoice.*

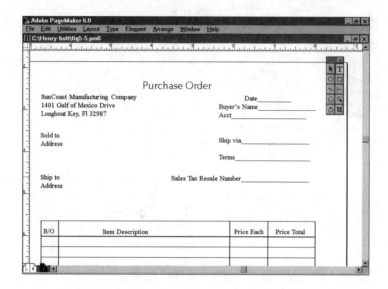

Figure 5.5 *A company purchase order.*

Creating a Newsletter Template

You can use the interior pages of a template in the same way that you use the master pages. You can literally format a document without entering a word of text, by putting placeholders where you want text or graphics to go.

In my experience, there are two kinds of newsletters: those that need to be produced quickly because the material is timely, and those that are more sales- and marketing-driven that you can spend a world of time and money producing. We'll concentrate on the former. The typical newsletter is generally an 11-by-17-inch page printed on the front and back and folded to 8.5 by 11 inches. This configuration yields four pages, as shown in Figure 5.6.

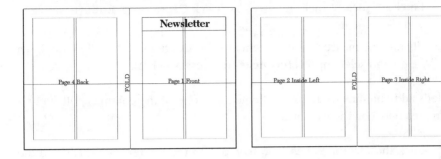

Figure 5.6 *Thumbnails of the front and back of a four-page 8.5-by-11-inch newsletter.*

To add two more pages, print an 8.5-by-11-inch page on the front and back and insert it inside the fold. To add four additional pages, print another 11-by-17-inch page on the front and back, and so on. If you will have a PostScript service bureau output your finished work on a high-resolution phototypesetter that can handle 11-by-17-inch paper, you can configure your PageMaker file for 11 by 17 and print proof copies on your laser printer reduced 77% (to give you about 8.5 by 11 inches). If your final mechanical will be produced by your laser printer (which probably can't handle paper as large as 11 by 17), then configure your page size as 8.5 by 11 inches in the Document Setup dialog box and check the **Double-sided** and **Facing** pages option boxes. You will have to do a little paste-up work to set up the pages to print on 11-by-17-inch paper, but you'll save money in doing the setup for your commercial printer.

Setting Up an 11-by-17 Inch Format

Setting up the newsletter template as the actual size of the page is handy because your commercial printer doesn't have to paste up any pages to shoot negatives; the work is camera-ready. The only tricky part is adding an extra column, which will simulate the fold between pages and the inside margins on either side of the fold. Here's how to do it:

1. Choose the **File** pull-down menu and choose **New** document (or press **Alt+F N**) to display the Document Setup dialog box.

2. Select **Tabloid** in the Page list box (or enter the values **17** and **11** in the Page Dimensions text boxes) and click the **Wide** check box.

3. Enter a **6 pica** (1 inch) margin size. Click **OK** or press **Enter** to move to your document.

4. Change the measurement system to picas by choosing the **File** pull-down menu and selecting **Preferences** (or press **Alt+F R**).

Now let's add columns to the page. Remember, one of the columns will act as a margin area between the two pages.

1. Click the **Master Pages** icon to move to the master pages. Choose the **Layout** pull-down menu and select **Column Guides** (or press **Alt+L C**) to display the Column Guides dialog box.

2. Enter **5** as the number of columns. Leave the default spacing between columns set to 1 pica. Click **OK** or press **Enter** to return to your document.

The page is now formatted with five equally spaced columns (defined by the left page margin, four column guides that we'll number 1 through 4 from left to right, and the right page margin). What we want to do next is to drag the four column guides to establish four equally spaced columns, which will squeeze the middle column to act as an inside margin for each page of the two-page spread that we're simulating. Do the following:

1. Working from left to right across the page, first establish a zero point at the left page margin by clicking in the ruler junction box and dragging the vertical ruler's zero point to align with the left margin.

2. Drag the number 1 column guide to the right, aligning the left edge of the first column guide with the 18 pica mark on the ruler (the line measure for all columns will be 18 picas). Now, reposition the vertical ruler's zero mark to align on the right edge of the number 1 column guide (to give an accurate measurement of the number 2 column's width).

3. Move the pointer over to the number 2 column guide and drag the guide to align the left edge of the column guide with the 18 pica mark on the ruler. You now have two equal columns for one of the two pages.

4. Drag the vertical ruler's zero point all the way across the page to the right page margin.

5. Drag the number 4 column guide to the left to line up the right edge of the column guide with the 18 pica mark on the ruler. Reposition the vertical ruler's zero mark to align to the left edge of the number 4 column guide.

6. Drag the number 3 column guide to line up the right edge of the column guide with the 18 pica mark on the ruler.

Now you have four equally spaced columns on the two-page spread and a narrow column in the middle. All you have to do is find the middle of the narrow column and mark the middle with a guideline. To do this:

1. Realign the vertical ruler's zero point with the right edge of the number 2 column guide (the left side of the narrow, middle column). The left edge of the number 3 column guide (the right side of the narrow column) will be resting on the 14 pica mark on the ruler. Just take half of the measurement, which is 7 picas.

2. Drag a guideline out of the vertical ruler and align it on the 7 pica mark on the ruler. This guideline is the fold mark for your two-page spread, as shown in Figure 5.7.

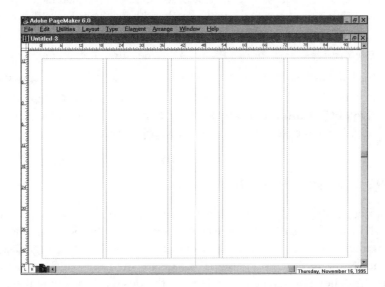

Figure 5.7 *Completed column guides for Template.*

Now that you've done it the hard way, here's an easier way to adjust the column guides. After you initially set up your five columns, position the vertical ruler's zero point on the left page margin. Then set the columns on your master pages to the following positions:

❖   Set the left edge of the first column guide at 18 picas.

❖   Set the left edge of the second column guide at 37 picas.

❖   Set the center guideline at 45 picas.

❖   Set the left edge of the third column guide at 52 picas.

❖   Set the left edge of the fourth column guide at 71 picas.

I walked you through the longer process first to give you some practice realigning the ruler and measuring with the ruler.

Setting Up an 8.5-by-11-Inch Format

To set up your newsletter template in an 8.5-by-11-inch format:

1. Choose **New** document from the File pull-down menu (**File > New**).

2. In the Document Setup dialog box, set up 8.5-by-11-inch facing pages, to be printed front and back, with equal width inside and outside margins.

3. Let's work in picas here, too. Open the Preferences dialog box (**File > Preferences**) and choose **Picas** as the measurement system.

4. Click the **Master Pages** icon to move to the master pages of your document.

5. Format the document in two columns by choosing **Column Guides** (**Layout > Column Guides**). Enter **2** in the Number of Columns text box. Leave the default Space between columns alone.

Setting Up the Front Page

The front page of your newsletter sets the tone for the publication. Is it serious or casual? Witty or strictly informative? Conservative or brassy? The impression made by the newsletter will also spill over to the company or organization it represents. Some of the design considerations for the front page include developing the masthead or nameplate, balancing the design, and setting the column width. Let's look at each of these separately.

DEVELOPING THE MASTHEAD

The most prominent element on the front page of any newsletter is the newsletter's title, sometimes called the *masthead* or *nameplate*. The masthead can be composed of a *logotype*, meaning the type characters making up the masthead name have the look of a logo—through either originally designed type or characters altered to give a proprietary look. Adobe Type Align, Adobe Illustrator, Ares FontMonger, and ZSoft SoftType are just some of the Windows programs capable of altering the shape and baseline of type characters for a masthead logotype. You can also do a lot with PageMaker simply by adjusting the leading, tracking, and width of characters. The logotype for the masthead should be bold enough to support the size of any border that is around it. If not, the characters wind up looking anemic, as shown in the top example in Figure 5.8. In the bottom example, the same word is shown in a much better format.

Figure 5.8 *Helvetica 60 point type isn't strong enough to fill the border for this newsletter's masthead. In the bottom example, Helvetica Black is set in 72 points at 110 percent width, which nicely fills the space.*

To add a traditional masthead border and logotype to your front page:

1. Move to the first page of your document, not the master page. Choose a page view so that you can easily see its full width.

2. Select the **Square-Cornered Drawing** tool from the toolbox. Position the crosshairs in the upper-left corner of the page margin and drag out a box the width of the margins and several inches deep.

3. Select the **Text** tool from the toolbox. Position the insertion point in the upper-left corner of the box and drag open a text block almost as large as the border you just created.

4. Select an appropriate typeface for the masthead logotype, using the Type specifications dialog box (**Type > Type Specs**).

5. Once the masthead name is typed in the box, use the Type Specifications dialog box to alter the type to your satisfaction.

BALANCING THE DESIGN

Not only does the masthead logotype need to be large enough to fill the border around it, the border itself needs to be sized to balance the rest of the page. Figure 5.9 shows what a difference a properly sized masthead can make.

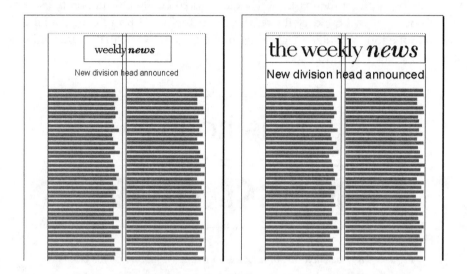

Figure 5.9 *The larger, bolder masthead and headline in the right-hand example demand attention and help to balance the page.*

To quickly change the weight, style, leading, or other specifications of the logotype or headlines:

1. Highlight the text with the Text tool.

2. Use the PageMaker shortcut **Ctrl+T** to display the Type Specifications dialog box. Try changing one of the specifications—for example, the type style—and click **OK** or press **Enter**.

3. The changes made in. the dialog box are reflected in the type, which remains highlighted. To make additional changes, simply press **Ctrl+T** to redisplay the Type Specifications dialog box and try other modifications.

SETTING THE COLUMN WIDTH

A typical newsletter consists of two equally spaced columns. The easiest way to dress up this kind of page would be to move a column guide, giving the page with uneven-width columns. Use the wide column to add prominence to the lead story. Use the narrow column to hold recurring items, like a table of contents, a meeting place box, a guest speaker box, a list of officers box, or what have you. To create unequal-width columns:

1. Move to the first page of your document.

2. Select the **Pointer** tool from the toolbox and grab the column guide.

3. Drag the guide to the left 6 picas, giving you a left column 12 picas wide and a right column 24 picas wide.

In this kind of format, the left column is usually the narrow one. Your page should resemble Figure 5.10.

Figure 5.10 *The column guide has been moved to create one narrow and one wide column.*

ADDING A RECURRING INITIAL DROP CAP

Any recurring item in your newsletter can be added to the newsletter template. In fact, the more you add to the template, the less work you'll have to do when you create each issue. So let's add an initial drop cap to the first character of the page one story. Here's how:

1. Place a column of text on the page to fill the right column (**File > Place**). You can use any text or nonsense text supplied by PageMaker (look for the file **text.txt** in the **\pm5\tutorial\lesson1** subdirectory).

2. Use the Text tool to highlight the first letter of the story (it doesn't matter what the letter is, since you're going to change it in each issue).

3. Cut the letter from the text. Move to an area in the left column and *drag-paste* the letter—hold down the left mouse button and drag open a text box. Release the left mouse button and press **Shift+Ins** to paste the letter.

4. Highlight the letter with the Text tool and increase its size to 48 points (**Type > Type Specs**).

5. Select the letter with the Pointer tool and narrow the text block until it is only slightly wider than the letter (click the lower-right sizing handle and drag to the left until it is almost even with the right edge of the letter).

6. Drag the letter into position on top of the text in the right column and align the top of the letter with the top of the text, as shown here.

New division head
announce

Imsep pretu tempu revol bileg rokam revoc tephe rosve etepe
Inov sindu turqu brevt elliu repar tiuve tamia queso utage udulc
humus fallo 25deu Anetn bisre freun carmi avire ingen
umque miher muner veris adest duner veris adest iteru quevi escit
billo isput tatqu aliqu diams bipos itopu 50sta Isant oscul bifid
mquec cumen berra etmii pyren nsomn anoct reern oncit quqar
anofe ventm hipec oramo uetfu orets nitus sacer tusag teliu ipsev
75tvi Eonei elaur plica oscri eseli sipse enitu ammih mensl quidi
aptat rinar uacae ierqu vagas ubesc rpore ibere perqu umbra
perqu antra erorp netra 100at mihif napat ntint riora intui urque
nimus otoqu cagat rolym oecfu iunto ulosa tarac ecame suidt
mande onatd stent spiri usore idpar thaec abies 125sa Imsep pretu

7. Press **Ctrl+W** to choose the Fit in Window view. Click the column of text with the Pointer tool to select it. Click the bottom windowshade handle and drag it up to cover the top windowshade handle.

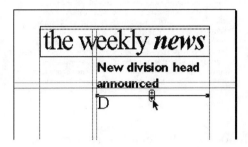

8. Click the **Down Arrow** in the bottom windowshade handle and drag-place a new text block, butting up to the right edge of the initial cap and as deep as the cap.

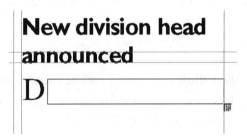

9. Pull down a guideline from the top ruler and align it to the bottom of the windowshade.

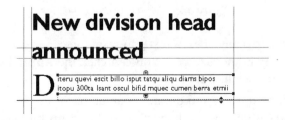

10. Click the bottom windowshade handle and drag-place the remaining text so that it is even with the left and right margins.

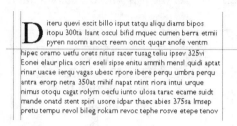

When you're ready to open the template as a document and start your first issue, use the **Replace Entire Story** option in the Replace File dialog box (see "Replacing Template Stories" later in this chapter).

USING THE DROP CAP PLUG-IN

Now that you've learned the hard way to create an initial drop cap, here's how to do it the quick and easy way. Use PageMaker's Drop Cap plug-in:

1. Click the **Text** tool anywhere in the paragraph to which you want to add an initial drop cap.

2. Click open the **Utilities** menu and choose **PageMaker Plug-ins**.

3. In the Plug-in submenu, choose the **Drop Cap** command to open the Drop Cap dialog box, shown in Figure 5.11.

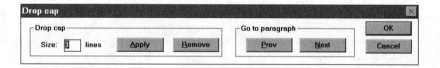

Figure 5.11 *Drop Cap dialog box.*

4. Choose how many lines of text you want the cap to drop into and enter the number in the Size box. You can click the **Apply** button to try out the size and see how it looks.

5. To add the drop cap to the next paragraph or the previous paragraph from the current one, click the **Next** or **Previous** button.

6. When you are finished defining drop caps, click **OK** to save the settings and return to your document.

ADDING AN EVENTS CALENDAR

An events calendar doesn't have to be elaborate; it can simply consist of some events and dates set up in the narrow left column. To make an events calendar:

1. Select the **Square-** or **Round-Cornered Drawing** tool.

2. Position the crosshairs in the upper-left corner of the narrow column. Click and drag the crosshairs to draw a box margin to margin, several inches deep.

3. Select the **Text** tool, click the tool in the upper-left corner of the box, and drag open a text block.

4. Press **Ctrl+T** to choose a typeface and type style for the events calendar. A sans serif font like Helvetica is easier to read in small type sizes.

5. Set up a right-aligned tab at the right edge of the box by choosing the **Type** pull-down menu and selecting **Indents/Tabs** (or press **Alt+T I**) to display the Indents/tabs dialog box. Click the **right-align tab** icon and click its position on the ruler. Click **OK** or press **Enter** to move back to your document.

6. Give the box a title. Highlight the title with the Text tool and use the PageMaker shortcut **Ctrl+Shift+C** to center the title on the line.

7. Press **Return** to move down a line, then type an event. Press **Tab** to move to the right-aligned tab stop, then type the date. Notice that the date fills to the left. Add as many events and dates as you need.

When you open the template as a document to produce an issue of the newsletter, use the Text tool to highlight an event and date you want to change, and type the new event and date.

You can also add a date and an issue and volume number to your newsletter template. The number of years a newsletter has been in publication is its volume number. That is, all issues in the first year of publication are part of Volume 1, those in the second year are Volume 2, and so on. The issue is determined by the number of newsletters published in that year. For example, if the newsletter is produced monthly, the January issue is Number 1, the December issue is Number 12. If the newsletter is biweekly, the last publication in December is

Number 26. To change the date, volume number, or issue number for each issue of your newsletter:

1. Use the Text tool to highlight the information you wish to replace.

Volume IV, Issue 1
January, 1993

2. Type the new information.

Setting Up Interior Pages

The inside pages are set up in the template in the same way as the front page. Add text or graphics as placeholders for real text or graphics. If you have recurring headings in each issue—different departments, perhaps—set up the heads in the template. If you regularly devote a page to employee photos, set up the borders for the photos in the template. Then when you place the pictures, you can size or crop them to fit the borders.

Creating a Fact Sheet Template

Simple two-color fact sheets, printed front and back, are the mainstay of many marketing efforts. Some fact sheets include photos, some don't, depending on the production budget. Whether they have photos or not, fact sheets generally share a common structure, which makes them good candidates for templates. Regardless of the specifics, most fact sheets will contain the following:

❖ Company name and address, product name, product model number

❖ Overall introduction to the product: what does it do, how it does it

❖ Sales rationale for buying the product

❖ Specific advantages of this product

❖ Technical details

❖ Specifications such as weight, size, and voltage

You may not know yet how much room each of these areas will require—or even if you'll include all of these areas—but we can still lay out a basic template.

Adding the Product Name

Let's start with the product name header:

1. Open a new document. Set the page size at 8.5 by 11 inches with moderate margins all around.

2. Move to the right master page (the front page of the fact sheet). Open the Column Guides dialog box and give the template a two-column format.

3. Move to the top of the page, pull down a guideline from the top ruler, and position it about a half inch under the top margin. This area will hold the product name.

4. To preformat the name, select the **Text** tool and drag open a text block in the upper-left corner, right above the guideline you just positioned.

5. Press **Ctrl+T** to open the Type Specifications dialog box. Select a 36-point bold typeface for the product name (chances are you'll be changing these specs when you open this template to create a real fact sheet).

6. Type **Product Name** in the text block.

7. Open a similar text block on the same guideline near the right margin. Choose the same typeface and style, but select **18 points** for the type size.

8. Type **Model No.** or **Version No.** on the guideline. The top of your fact sheet template should look something like Figure 5.12.

Figure 5.12 *The product name and model number*
added to the top of the fact sheet template.

Before you do anything else, choose the **Select All** command from the Edit pull-down menu to select everything you've just done. Now copy it to the Clipboard, move the Text tool insertion point above the page onto the pasteboard, and click once. Choose **Paste** to paste a copy of the header above the page. You'll see why in a minute.

Adding the Introduction and Features Area

The next steps designate areas on page 1 (the front of the fact sheet) for a product introduction and a general discussion of the product's features:

1. Add a horizontal guideline about a third of the way down the page. The area between the line under the product name and this line will be for a product introduction. The area below the line will contain product features.

2. Choose the **Square-Cornered Drawing** tool and position the crosshairs in the upper-left corner of the area above the guideline you just added. Draw a border around the area, as shown in Figure 5.13.

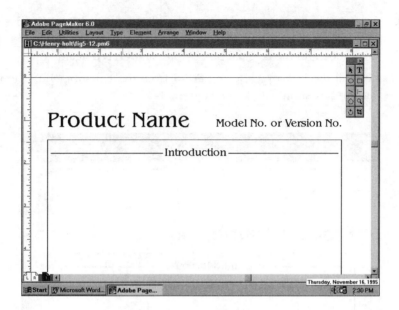

Figure 5.13 *An example of formatting for the introduction area of the fact sheet template.*

3. Choose the **Text** tool and drag open a text block at the top of the introduction area.

4. Press **Ctrl+T** to display the Type specifications dialog box and format the
   type for the word *Introduction*. In the example, I selected an 18-point
   typeface with loose tracking.

5. Draw a box around the word. Choose **No Line** from the Line submenu
   and **Paper** from the Fill submenu. Move the box behind the word by
   pressing **Ctrl+B**.

6. Add a 1-point line across the width of the box and through the middle of
   the word *Introduction*. Move the line behind it and the box by selecting
   the line with the Pointer tool and pressing **Ctrl+B**. Your page should
   look like Figure 5.13.

7. Let's add a drop shadow to the box. Choose the **Pointer** tool and select
   the box by clicking on it. Fill in the box by selecting **Paper** from the Fill
   submenu.

8. The white-filled box has covered the word *Introduction*. While the box
   is still selected, move the filled box behind the type by pressing **Ctrl+B**.
   Now the type is displayed.

9. Choose **Copy** to copy the box to the Clipboard and **Paste** to paste the copy on top of the original (it will be offset a bit down and to the right). Move it behind the original box by pressing **Ctrl+B** again.

10. Now fill the box by choosing **Solid** from the Fill submenu. The introduction box should look like Figure 5.14.

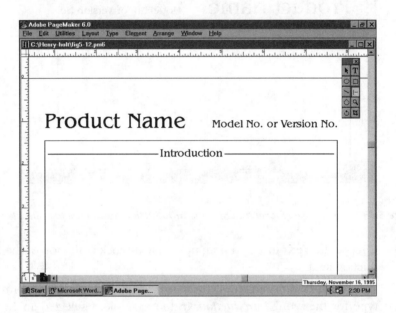

Figure 5.14 *A drop shadow added to the introduction box.*

Follow the same steps to add a second box starting just below the introduction and ending just above the bottom margin. Add a drop shadow to the second box, and the headline features in the same type specifications as the introduction headline. Your page should look similar to Figure 5.15.

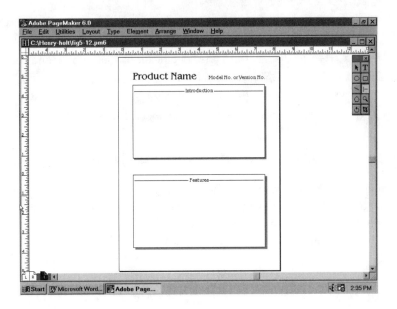

Figure 5.15 *The completed front page of a fact sheet template.*

Adding the Specifications Area

Designating the back of the fact sheet as the area for detailed specifications is useful for two reasons. Those wanting only a cursory glance at the fact sheet needn't wade through a lot of technical jargon to figure out what the product does. They can simply read the introduction or features material on the front. Giving the whole back page over to technical specifications allows all the room you will probably need to provide a detailed technical description. To add a specifications area:

1. Click the left **Master Page** icon (the back of the fact sheet).

2. Choose **Select All** to select all of the header above the page on the pasteboard. Using the Pointer tool, click on the line outside the area of one of the sizing handles. The pointer will change to a four-pointed arrow. When everything is selected with the **Select All** command, dragging any one component moves all the selected components. Drag the whole header down onto the page, aligning it to the left and right margins and the top page margin.

3. Choose the **Square-Cornered Drawing** tool and draw a box the width and height of the margins.

4. Press **Ctrl+T** to display the Type specifications dialog box, and format the type for the word *Specifications.* In the example, I selected an 18-point typeface in small caps with wide tracking.

5. Add the word to the top center of the specifications box.

Adding the Company Name/Address Area

The company name and address can fit easily below the bottom margin. Remember to include the mailing address and a telephone number. You could also include a general disclaimer stating that specifications are subject to change without notice. Finally, you may want to include a copyright notice.

Creating Templates from Existing Documents

As mentioned earlier in this chapter, you can create a template from an existing document by saving the document as a template (**File > Save As**). Simply choose the **Save as template** option button in the Save Publication as dialog box. PageMaker then saves a copy of your document as a new template. The template contains every element of the original document, including the same number of pages, the same font selections and type styles, and the same guidelines. Having saved the document as a template, you can now open the template as a new document and customize it for your needs. Say, for example, that you have completed the first issue of a twelve-page newsletter (named **nwsltr1.pm6**) and saved the file as a template (named **nwsltr1.pt6**). Next month, when you want to produce issue number two, simply open the template as a file and save it as **nwsltr2.pm6**.

Replacing Template Stories

Once saved as a template, it's very easy to swap existing stories and graphics with new stories and graphics needed for the new publication. Here's how:

1. Using the Pointer tool, select the first story you want to replace.

2. Choose the **File** pull-down menu and choose **Place** (or press **Alt+F P**) to display the Place dialog box, shown in Figure 5.16.

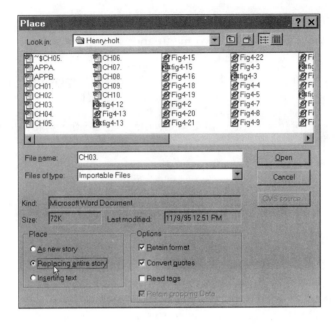

Figure 5.16 *The Place dialog box.*

3. Click the file name for the new story and click the **Replacing entire story** option button.

4. Click the **Retain format** check box if you want to retain the character and paragraph formatting and any style sheets assigned to the text in your word processor. If you do not check the **Retain format** check box, PageMaker imports the text and assigns the default type font and style to the text.

5. Click **OK** or press **Enter** to return to your document.

The entire story will be replaced by the new story you selected in the Place dialog box. If the original story was longer than one page, even if it wasn't selected on additional pages, all the pages of the story will be replaced.

Replacing Template Graphics

You can do the same thing when replacing a graphic:

1. Using the Pointer tool, select the graphic you want to replace.

2. Choose the **File** pull-down menu and choose **Place** (or press **Alt+F P**) to display the Place dialog box.

3. Click the file name for the graphic and click the **Replacing entire graphic** option button. Click **OK** or press **Enter** to return to your document.

The original graphic will be replaced by the graphic file you selected in the Place dialog box.

To replace the original headlines, bylines, photo credit lines, and other small text blocks, highlight the text block with the Text tool and type in the new text. When you begin typing, all the highlighted text will be deleted, but the text you enter will retain all of the type specifications of the original type.

Creating Additional Master Pages

One of the most powerful features of this latest version of PageMaker is its ability to create as many master pages as you need to support the design of your document. In many cases, one master page is enough, but sometimes it's nice to assign different page, section, or chapter designs to different master pages. For example, in a magazine, you can now create one master page for editorial content, a separate master page for full-page ads, yet another master page for front matter, and a fourth master page for classified ads in the back of the publication. To create additional master pages:

1. Click open the Window menu and choose the **Master Pages** command.

2. PageMaker will display the Master Pages palette, shown in Figure 5.17. The master page listed in the palette is the original master page for your document.

Figure 5.17 *The Master Pages palette.*

3. Click the **right-facing arrow** to open the Master Page menu, shown in Figure 5.18.

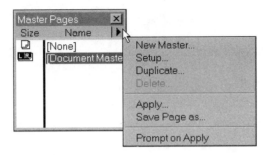

Figure 5.18 *The Master Page menu.*

4. Choose the **New Master** command to open the Create New Master Page dialog box, shown in Figure 5.19.

Figure 5.19 *The Create New Master Page dialog box.*

5. Name the master page, configure its margins and/or columns, and click **OK** to create the new master page. The newly named master page will be added to the list in the palette (Figure 5.20). To go to it or any other master page, click it in the palette, then click on the **Master Page** icon at the bottom of the screen.

Figure 5.20 *The newly added master page is added to the list in the palette.*

To Sum Up

In this chapter, you've learned how to use templates to save time and effort in developing recurring documents. You've seen how to set up multiple-form templates, and you've had a close-up look developing a fact sheet template.

In the next chapter, you'll learn about another important PageMaker time-saver: styles.

CHAPTER 6

Setting Up Custom Styles

- ❖ Defining styles
- ❖ Applying styles to text
- ❖ To sum up

A *style* is simply a way to automate the formatting of text so that if you decide to change the formatting, you need only change the style, not each occurrence of the text in that style. Say, for example, that you compose a multiple-page document in PageMaker and decide you want to change the typeface of the body text. Without using a style, you would have to highlight each paragraph individually, invoke the Type Specifications dialog box, choose the new typeface, and click **OK** to return to the document. This could get downright tiresome after about the third paragraph. If you had used a style called *Body Copy*, you could simply change the typeface portion of the style specification—all the text marked with the Body Copy style would automatically change.

But styles don't apply only to body copy; they can be applied to any sort of characters on the page:

- ❖ **Headline or heading styles.** Set up each level of headline or each heading as an individual style so that you can make documentwide changes to the headings.

- ❖ **Logotype or special name styles**. Using a style for a product or company logotype means you don't have to finalize the type before using it in the document. If you (or your client) decide on a different look for the logotype, all you have to do is change the style.

- ❖ **Header and footer styles**. Header and footer styles ensure consistency. You can set up other styles within a header or footer style: a page number style and a book title style, for example.

- ❖ **Bullet styles for lists**. Bullets are not simply round spots anymore. You can use a style to format square or diamond-shaped bullets, in dropshadow or outline, perhaps.

- ❖ **Text in bulleted or numbered lists**. Often, the text in a list is formatted differently from normal body copy. For example, body copy might be left aligned to give a ragged-right margin, but the text in lists might be justified. Applying a style to list text means there's one less thing you have to remember in formatting your document.

- ❖ **Drop cap or initial cap styles**. Setting up a drop cap as a style means you won't find yourself thinking, "Was that a 37-point cap or a 59-point cap the last time? I'd better check." And again, one change to the style changes all drop caps in the document.

- ❖ **Byline styles**. Bylines may seem like a trivial matter, but in a large publication finding and changing them all to some other specification is not a trivial task.

- ❖ **Jump page callouts, photo credits, figure captions, footnotes, tables of contents, and index entries**. All should be formatted as styles rather than as individual text.

As you can see, there should be no characters in a lengthy document that are not assigned a style. The reason is threefold. First, it takes less time to format a style for a group of characters than to format the characters themselves. Second, when every group of characters is in a style, you won't miss anything when it comes time to change the type specifications. Third, when sending your completed document to a service bureau for high-resolution output, you will need to tell them all the fonts used in the publication. It's a lot easier to look through your styles to see the different fonts than to search through your document manually.

Defining Styles

PageMaker styles are an integral part of the document for which they're created. When you copy a document, you automatically copy the styles. You can't see the styles without the accompanying document, but there is a way to copy the styles of one document to use as the basis for the styles of another.

PageMaker comes with six styles already defined and ready to use: headlines, two levels of subheads, body text, and captions. Any time you create a new document, these styles are available for your immediate use. Or you can alter the default styles and create new ones to customize certain publications. To create a new style, or alter an existing one, choose the **Type** pull-down menu and choose **Define Styles** (or press **Alt+T D**). You will see the Define Styles dialog box, as shown in Figure 6.1.

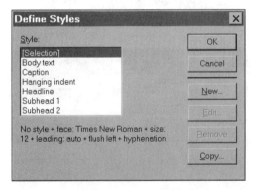

Figure 6.1 *The Define Styles dialog box.*

Use the Define Styles dialog box to create, change, and delete styles. Notice the six PageMaker default styles. The dialog box leads you to the following functions:

❖ **New.** Choose this button to display the Edit Styles dialog box, allowing you to create a new style for this document.

❖ **Edit.** Click one of the existing styles and choose this button to display the Edit Styles dialog box. You'll be able to change the individual specifications tied to this style.

❖ **Remove.** Click on one of the existing styles and choose this button to remove it from this document. Removing a default style from the current document does not erase it from new documents you create in the future.

❖ **Copy.** Click this button to display the Copy Styles dialog box. Choose the document that contains the style(s) you want to add to the current document and click **OK** to copy the styles.

Creating New Styles

Let's set up a new style for a newsletter. We'll create a headline style using the Define Styles dialog box. Here's how:

1. Choose the **Type** pull-down menu and choose **Define Styles** (or press **Alt+T D**).

2. In the Define Styles dialog box, click the **New** button to display the Edit Styles dialog box, shown in Figure 6.2.

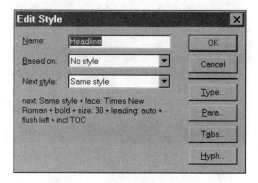

Figure 6.2 *The Edit Styles dialog box.*

3. Enter a descriptive name for the style—up to 17 characters—in the Name text box.

4. If you want to base the new style on an existing style in this document, click the **Based on** list box arrow and select the style name. The attributes

of the style you select will be applied to the new style. You can then change any of the attributes to make the new style different. Otherwise, click the **Based on** list box arrow and choose **No style**, indicating that the new style will not be based on an existing style.

5. For this example, let's base the style on the existing headline style. Open the list box by clicking the **arrow** and double-clicking **Headline**.

6. Click the **Next style** list box arrow. You have three options with this list box:

   ❖ If you want the style you are creating to always be followed by a certain style, choose the name of that style from the list. For example, if you want the body text style to always follow the headline style, choose **Body text**. Then, in your document, whenever you format a headline in the headline style and press **Enter**, the text that follows will be in the body text style.

   ❖ If you don't want a style to always follow the current style, choose **No style** from the list. After typing text formatted in this style and pressing **Enter**, the text that follows will not be formatted in a style.

   ❖ If you want the paragraph that follows the current style to be formatted the same (as with body copy, for example), choose **Same style** from the list.

7. Now decide what formatting specifications you want to add to this style. Choose:

   ❖ **Type**—Click the **Type** button to display the Type specifications dialog box. Configure the typeface, type size, leading, style, width, tracking, case, and so forth for this type in this style. Then choose the **Options** dialog box, if you wish, to change type option values, such as the size and position of subscript or superscript type. Click **OK** or press **Enter** to accept the specifications and return to the Edit Style dialog box.

   ❖ **Para**—Click this button to display the Paragraph Specifications dialog box. Set up the paragraph indents, spacing, alignment, and options for this style. You can also move to the Rules dialog box and the Spacing dialog box to further define how paragraphs in this style will be formatted. Click **OK** or press **Enter** to accept the specifications and return to the Edit Style dialog box. If you are creating styles for a publication that will have a table of contents, click the **Include in Table of Contents** check box for all heading and sub-heading styles to automatically generate table of contents entries.

❖ **Tabs**—Click the **Tabs** button to display the Indents/Tabs dialog box. Set up tab stops, choose tab alignments, and add leader tabs, if you wish. Click **OK** or press **Enter** to accept the specifications and return to the Edit Style dialog box.

❖ **Hyph**—Click the **Hyphenation** button to display the Hyphenation dialog box. Set up hyphenation parameters for this style, if pertinent. Click **OK** or press **Enter** to accept the parameters and return to the Edit Style dialog box.

8. For the style specifications to take effect, you must click **OK** or press **Enter** to leave the Edit Styles dialog box. To leave the dialog box without saving the style, choose **Cancel**.

9. Now that you're back in the Edit Styles dialog box, click **OK** or press **Enter** to return to your document.

You can accept the Edit Styles dialog box and move immediately back to your document by using the PageMaker shortcut **Alt+OK** (hold down the **Alt** key and click **OK**).

Editing Styles

Editing styles is done in exactly the same manner as creating styles. Open the Define Styles dialog box, select the style you want to edit from the Style list box, and click the **Edit** button (it will be dimmed until you select a style). PageMaker displays the Edit Style dialog box. Choose from among the **Type**, **Para**, **Tabs**, or **Hyph** buttons to change whichever style specifications you want. Click **OK** or press **Enter** when you're finished.

REMOVING STYLES

The **Remove** button does just what it says. There's no additional dialog box, and no warning that you're about to remove a style. To remove a style:

1. Choose the **Type** pull-down menu and select **Define styles**.

2. In the Define Styles dialog box, select the style you want to remove.

3. Click the **Remove** button. The style will be deleted from the Style list box and removed from your document.

Any text that had already been formatted with the removed style will retain the formatting but will now be marked *No style*. Any styles that were based on the style you removed will now be based on No style. In addition, any style that had been set up so that the removed style followed it (defined as the Next style) will now be followed by No style.

Removing one of the default styles from a particular publication does not remove it from the PageMaker default style sheet in future documents.

N O T E

COPYING STYLES

You can use any style you've created in document by copying that document's styles into the current document. Here's how:

1. Choose the **Type** pull-down menu and choose **Define Styles**.

2. Click the **Copy** button to display the Copy styles dialog box, shown in Figure 6.3.

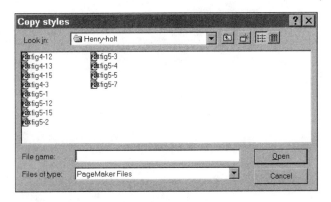

Figure 6.3 *The Copy Styles dialog box.*

3. Choose the PageMaker document that contains the style(s) you want to copy into the current document. Select the document from the Look in list box or double-click a drive letter to move to a different drive. If you know the path and file name, enter them in the Filename text box.

4. Click **OK** or press **Enter** to return to the Define Styles dialog box. The styles in the document you just selected will be added to the styles in the Style list box. Click **OK** or press **Enter** to return to your document.

Applying Styles to Text

There are two ways to apply styles to your text: by using the Styles palette or by selecting the style from the Style submenu. To use the palette, choose the **Window** pull-down menu and choose the **Styles** palette. The palette will be displayed, as shown in Figure 6.4. To display the Style submenu, open the Type pull-down menu and choose **Style** to display the submenu.

Figure 6.4 *The Style submenu and the Styles palette.*

To apply a style to a paragraph of text:

1. Select the **Text** tool and click the insertion point anywhere in the text you want to mark with a particular style.
2. Choose the style you want from the Styles palette or the Style submenu.

I find it a lot easier to use the Styles palette than the Style submenu. When the Styles palette is displayed in the document window, the style of the paragraph that your insertion point is in will always be highlighted in the palette, as shown in Figure 6.5.

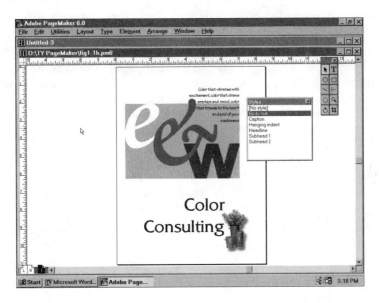

Figure 6.5 *Palette displays style of text block by clicking on insertion point in the block.*

Changing Styles

You can change styles for a given paragraph at any time by simply selecting the text and choosing a different style. To do this:

1. Position the insertion point in the text that has the style you want to change.
2. Click another style in the Styles palette. The text will be changed to the style you selected.

Modifying Styled Text

Just because you have marked a paragraph with a given style doesn't mean you can't change the specifications for that paragraph. Just be aware that you are deviating from the style and that other text marked with the style won't contain the modifications. If the modifications are important, consider modifying the style or creating a new style for the text.

When text marked as a style has been modified, a plus sign (+) is displayed after the style name in the Styles palette. For example, let's say that in a paragraph marked with the default body text style, you selected a word and italicized it with the PageMaker shortcut **Ctrl+Shift+I**. If you position the insertion point in the copy next to the italics, the Styles palette indicates **Body Text**. If you click the insertion point in the italicized word, the Styles palette says **Body Text+**.

To Sum Up

A *style* is a set of formatting specifications for a *paragraph*, which is defined as anything preceding a carriage return. Styles standardize the formatting of similar paragraphs (for example, all paragraphs of body text are set in 12-point Helvetica, left-aligned, with 18 points of space between paragraphs). You can have as many styles as you need for a particular document. Styles allow you to make global changes to type, paragraph, and hyphenation specifications.

Styles are tied to the documents in which they are created; they stay with the document when it is copied. You can copy the styles of one document into another document. You can remove styles from a document. However, removing a default PageMaker style from one document does not affect future documents.

In the next chapter, you'll learn how to print what you've so carefully designed and laid out

CHAPTER 7

Printing

- ❖ Targeting the right printer
- ❖ Printing your documents
- ❖ Working with service bureaus
- ❖ To sum up

Nowhere is the importance of desktop publishing more evident than on a sheet of paper reeling out of a laser printer. Fonts in virtually any size are sharp and black; pages contain boxes, circles, diagonal lines—elements that just a few years ago were practically impossible to either create or print. It is the PostScript laser printer and the PostScript page description language that, in large part, account for PageMaker's magic. Before the development of PostScript by Adobe Systems, printing scalable fonts was limited to cumbersome typesetting systems that cost tens of thousands of dollars and used proprietary codes that only highly trained operators could understand. A decade ago, the state-of-the-art for producing text on a page was to have it typeset by a typesetting service or printed on an IBM SilentWriter impact printer (at the blinding speed of three pages a minute). Today, we drum our fingers on the desk because our laser printer churns out only 16 pages a minute! We have the far-reaching vision of folks at Adobe, Aldus, Apple Computers, and Microsoft to thank for what is so easily taken for granted today.

Fonts are tied to the printers that use them. For example, a dot matrix printer cannot understand PostScript scalable fonts; it only knows to print lines of text in pica or elite, like a typewriter font (although a type manager, like Adobe Type Manager, can create bitmapped files of scaled fonts that the dot matrix printer can print). If the dot matrix printer is a little more sophisticated, it may have a slot to hold font cartridges. These fonts emulate the look of typeset-quality fonts and may offer an italic font, a roman or serif font, and a sans serif font. All PostScript printers come with at least 13 scalable fonts, comprising four font families. But you must print to the PostScript laser printer in order to use them.

The Apple LaserWriter was the first laser printer to understand and print PostScript. Soon after the introduction of the LaserWriter, several companies began offering PostScript laser printers, including NEC, QMS, and Texas Instruments. Today, there are many more brands of PostScript-compatible printers than there are non-PostScript printers. Hewlett-Packard now manufactures laser printers that have a printer description language similar to PostScript, which can print scalable fonts. There are even circuit cards to install in your computer that will make non-PostScript printers, like the early Canon and HP printers, understand and print PostScript fonts.

Printing PageMaker files is especially easy in Windows, because Windows controls the printing with a print spooling program available to PageMaker and all other Windows applications. Because the printer is still the slowest component in any desktop publishing system, the spooler accepts the print-formatted file from the application (in this case, PageMaker) and releases the application to go about its business. The spooler then feeds the pages of the document to the printer at a rate the printer can accept. While the printer is printing your document, you're back in PageMaker doing something productive. Before printing the document, however, be sure you have targeted the right printer.

Targeting the Right Printer

The time to target a printer is when you create a new document, because different printers will change the page format slightly. Almost all laser printers leave
an unprintable margin around the edge of the page, usually about 1/8 inch.
Decide which printer to use early so you won't have to worry about choosing a
different printer with a different unprintable margin, which may affect the layout
of your document. Targeting your printer first means you won't be struggling
with a reformatting problem at the last minute. To see which printer PageMaker
currently has targeted:

1. Choose the **File** pull-down menu and choose **Document Setup** (or press
   Alt+F M) to display the Document Setup dialog box, shown in Figure 7.1.
   Click the **Compose to printer** list box to select the printer you want to
   target this document to.

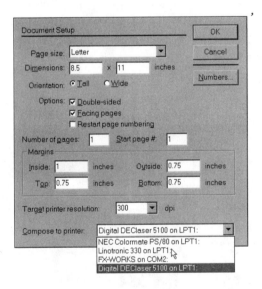

Figure 7.1 *Use the Compose to printer list box to target the printer.*

2. The list box displays the names of all of the printers you've installed in
   Windows. Scroll up or down the list and click the printer you want to use.

3. If you are printing to a higher-resolution laser printer or an imagesetter, you can change the dot-per-inch resolution by clicking the **Target printer resolution** list box and clicking the dpi resolution you want.

4. Click **OK** or press **Enter** to return to your document.

You can change printers in the Print dialog box, but changing the printer there does not change the targeted printer. See "Selecting a Printer in the Print Dialog Box" later in this chapter.

Choosing the Correct PostScript Printer Description File

The printer you target your document to should be the printer that will ultimately print the document. For example, if you will eventually use a PostScript service bureau to produce high-resolution negatives of your document pages, then you should select the Windows printer driver that supports the model imagesetter that the service bureau uses. You should also select a PPD file (PostScript printer description) for the same model imagesetter. For example, let's say that the service bureau uses a Linotronic L330. To ensure accurate reproduction, you should select the **Windows L330** driver in the Document Setup dialog box and the **L330 PPD** in the Print Document dialog box. Here are the steps:

1. Open the File pull-down menu and choose the **Print** command (or press **Alt+F P**) to display the Print Document dialog box, shown in Figure 7.2.

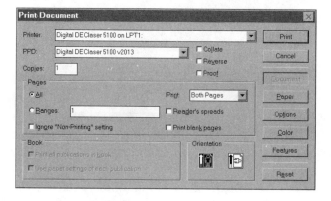

Figure 7.2 *The Print Document dialog box.*

2. Notice that the targeted printer is shown in the Print to list box. Now, click the **Type** list box to display the PPD files you've installed (like the example on the right). Scroll down the list and double-click the PPD for the type of imagesetter used by the service bureau.

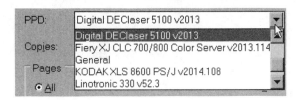

Choosing the Printer Inside PageMaker

As I mentioned, the Compose to printer list box in the Document Setup dialog box sets the ultimate printer that your document is targeted for. However, you may want to print proof copies of the document to lower-resolution printers. To do so, use the Printer list box in the Print Document dialog box. Here's how to change printers:

1. Open the File pull-down menu and choose the **Print** command (or press **Alt+F P**) to display the Print dialog box.

2. Click the **Printer** list box arrow to open the list box (like the example here).

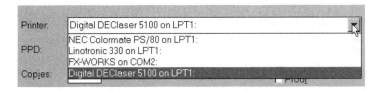

3. Choose the printer from the list of installed Windows printers in the list box by double-clicking. Choose **Print** or press **Enter** to begin printing. If you cancel the print operation, the printer you just selected remains selected the next time you open the Print dialog box.

Changing Printer Emulations

Most PostScript laser printers can emulate a variety of printers, including HP LaserJets and several kinds of impact printers. My DEC PostScript printer, for example, can emulate a LaserJet model 4. Basically, the emulation represents an additional printer on the same port, and both the PostScript printer and its HP emulation are available for use in Windows.

To make use of the emulations in Windows, and particularly to be able to print PageMaker files to either PostScript or LaserJet printers:

1. For each emulated printer you want to use in Windows, install the Windows printer driver for the emulated printer in the Printers dialog box using the New Printer Wizard. In the case of my DEC laser printer, I would have to install the HP LasertJet 4 printer driver.

2. Set up the printer on the same printer port as the physical printer (if the laser printer is cabled to LPT1, then all the emulation printers will be cabled to that port as well).

To switch among the emulated printers while in PageMaker:

1. Check the targeted printer in PageMaker. Choose the **Document Setup** command from the File menu and choose the correct printer.

2. Change the printer emulation on the printer. Most emulations are controlled by buttons on the front panel of the printer. Use the printer's **Change Emulation** feature to set up the same printer you marked as active in Windows. Some laser printers can automatically switch emulations based on the file being sent, in which case you can skip this step.

Printing Your Document

It's a good idea to print proofs of your document as it is being developed. When you finish a page or two, print a proof copy to verify the alignment of all the text elements. As I stated earlier, PageMaker's accuracy is much higher on the printed version of the page than on the screen version (up to 1/2880 inch), so to be absolutely sure of very close alignments, print the page. It's easy to do; here are the steps:

1. Choose the **File** pull-down menu and choose **Print** (or press **Alt+F P**) to display the Print Document dialog box.

2. Use this dialog box to set up the number of pages you want to print, the order that pages pass through the printer, and other conditions. Choose among the following options and features:

   ❖ **Copies**—Choose as many copies of the document as you need. The **Collate** and **Reverse order** option boxes determine the order of printing.

   ❖ **Pages**—Print the entire document or a range of pages.

   ❖ **Book**—Use special features to print the chapter or sections of a book that you've defined with the **Book** command.

   ❖ **Even/Odd Pages**—You can order even or odd pages to print separately. Use this option if you are printing a document on the front and back. Odd pages are normally considered front pages, so print all odd-numbered pages first. Then insert the stack of printed pages back in the paper tray so the back will be printed, and choose **Even pages**.

3. The Print Document dialog box is just the first of four or five dialog boxes that PageMaker uses to define exactly how you want your document printed. To access the remaining dialog boxes, choose one of the command buttons:

   ❖ **Paper**—Includes options for printing thumbnails, setting up tiling, and the paper size. For laser printers that can print duplex (print both sides during one pass of the paper through the printer), like the HP LaserJet IID, you can specify which edge will be bound.

   ❖ **Options**—Allows you to set the degree of graphic resolution to improve printing speed. You can also set up printer's markings and prepare the document to be printed to disk for use in sending to a service bureau.

   ❖ **Color**—Gives you infinite control in printing color pages to a color printer or color laser printer.

❖ **Features**—Use this dialog box (if it's available based on your printer) to make changes in your printer's capabilities. For example, when printing to my DECLaser 5100, I can implement a number of sharpness and contrast controls in the Features dialog box to improve the clarity of my document pages.

4. Make the necessary changes to the dialog boxes and choose **Print** or press **Enter** to print the document.

5. You can cancel the print job while it is being sent to either the printer or the Windows Print Manager by holding down the **Ctrl** key and pressing the **Break** key.

Document-Oriented Print Options

The initial Print Document dialog box gives you a choice of printers and PPDs to choose from. It also lets you configure the order of printing, the page orientation, and how documents that are members of a book grouping will be printed together.

SELECTING THE PRINTING ORDER

Two check boxes in the Print Document dialog box control the order in which pages print with a laser printer. Normally, if more than one copy of a multiple-page document is printed, PageMaker prints all page 1s first, then page 2s, and so on. To print collated sets of the document, click the **Collate** check box to put an **X** in it. Some laser printers print the pages of a document from beginning to end; others print from end to beginning. To reverse the order of printing, click the **Reverse order** check box to put an **X** in it. To include blank pages in the printed documents, click the **Print blank pages** check box (normally, PageMaker does not print blank pages).

SELECTING A RANGE OF PAGES AND THE NUMBER OF COPIES TO PRINT

Normally, PageMaker prints all the pages of a document. If you want to print only certain pages, click the **Ranges** option button. In the text box, enter the inclusive page numbers of the pages you want printed. For example, to print pages 7, 8, 9, and 10 type **7-10** in the text box. If you have a range of pages and specific pages, enter each page number separated by a comma. To add individual pages in our example, type this: **7-10,14,22-26,41,43,44-47**. To print all the pages of a document, just click the **All** option button. You specify the number of complete copies of your document by entering the number in the Copies text box—you can print up to 32,000 copies at one time.

PRINTING PROOF COPIES

Sometimes it's nice to be able to print out a quick copy of a page or document to check some small item, but you don't need to see placed graphics in detail. PagerMaker can do this; they are called *proof copies*. Click the **Proof** check box and you will see gray boxes instead of your graphics. Everything but the graphics will be as you have specified. Clicking the **Proof** check box drastically speeds up the printing of pages containing graphics or scanned photographs.

CHANGING THE PRINTING ORIENTATION

The standard orientation for printing in your laser printer is called the *portrait* orientation: the text is parallel to the short sides of the paper. To change the orientation to what is called *landscape* (in which the text is parallel to the wide sides of the page) click the **Wide Orientation** icon. The orientation you select here should be the same as the tall/wide orientation you selected in the Document Setup dialog box when you first created your document.

PRINTING FILES ASSOCIATED WITH THE BOOK COMMAND

If the document you want to print is a member of a publication list created with the **Book** command, you can print it plus all other members of the publication list by clicking the **Print all publications in book** check box. For example, if you have designated PageMaker documents as the table of contents, the front matter, chapters 1 through 22, the appendix, and the index as belonging to a publication list, clicking the check box prints all 26 documents in the proper order with pages numbered correctly at one time. If you want the page and printing setting you've made in the individual documents to have priority over any setting you make to the current document, click the **Use paper settings of each publication** check box.

Paper-Oriented Print Options

The Print Paper dialog box, shown in Figure 7.3, controls the paper passing through the laser printer and how the image of the PageMaker document page will be produced on the paper. Under normal circumstances, you might only need to adjust the size and source of the paper, although the other options can be very useful. Let's look at them in more detail.

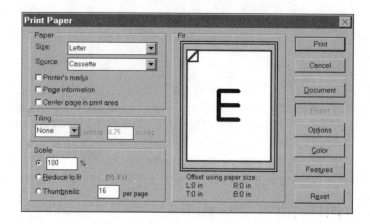

Figure 7.3 *The Print Paper dialog box.*

SETTING PAPER OPTIONS

The paper types listed in the Size list box are presented according to the printer you selected in the previous Print Document dialog box. The size for each paper type is shown to the right in the Fit preview box. Where the printer allows for it, you can also select **Custom** as a paper type and define your own customized page size. (The type and size information is actually stored as a part of the printer PPD.) The source of the paper is also presented according to the printer type you have already selected. If you are printing to a printer that does not center the printing on the page, you can click the **Center page in the print area** check box to do so. However, if you are tiling the page, PageMaker ignores this checked option.

PRINTING OVERSIZE PAGES WITH TILES

PageMaker can display and print type as large as 650 points. What may not be readily apparent is that since PageMaker can enlarge a page up to 1600%, you can actually print type large enough to fit on a billboard. Since no PostScript printer can take paper 8 feet wide, PageMaker has an option on the Print dialog box called **Tile**. *Tiling* breaks up the ultimate size into pieces (like tiles on the floor) that fit the page size specified in the Document Setup dialog box. PageMaker sets an automatic overlap of the tiles that takes into account the unprintable margin around the edge of the page (you can manually set the overlap, if you wish). It also marks each page with alignment marks so that the pages can be arranged correctly. Finally, the tiles are numbered, so that you know what goes where. To create tiles automatically:

1. Choose **Auto** from the Tile menu.

2. Accept the default overlap value or enter a different value in the text box.

3. Choose **Print** or press **Enter** to print the tiles.

To create manual tiles, follow these steps:

1. Choose **Manual** from the Tile menu.

2. Accept the default overlap value or enter a different value in the text box.

3. Choose **Cancel** to return to your document.

4. Choose the **Pointer** tool and click the ruler zero point. Reset the zero point to the area of the page you wish to designate for the first tile.

5. Return to the tile controls in the Print Paper dialog box and choose **Print** or press **Enter** to print the first tile.

6. Repeat steps 4 and 5, resetting the zero point each time to designate the next tile, until all the tiles have been printed.

PRINTING ON BOTH SIDES OF THE PAGE

Some laser printers can print *duplex* (that is, print on both sides of the page during one pass of the paper through the printer). This is a very handy feature if you need to print front and back originals. Choose the **Long edge** option button if the page is in the portrait orientation and you want the left edge to be bound like a book; if the page is in landscape orientation, the **Long edge** option binds along the top like a calendar. Choose the **Sjhort edge** option button if the page is in portrait orientation and you want the top to be bound like a calendar; if the page is in landscape orientation, the short edge would be the left edge (like the bound edge of a book). If you need to print front and back and aren't fortunate enough to own a duplex laser printer, here's how to do it:

1. In the Print Document dialog box choose the **Odd** option button to print all odd pages first.

2. If your laser printer prints multiple documents page by page (all page 1s first, then all page 2s, and so on, click the **Collate** option.

3. Print all odd-numbered pages.

4. To print the back side of the odd pages that have just printed, take the stack out of the discharge tray, still facing down, and put them back in the paper tray with the top of the page still toward the inside of the printer, printed side facing down.

5. Click the **Even** option to print all even-numbered pages. Again, choose **Collate** if necessary. Then print the pages. They come out of the printer printed on the front and back.

PRINTING REDUCTIONS AND ENLARGEMENTS

PageMaker can reduce or enlarge any document by the amount entered into the Scale text box. You can reduce documents as small as 5% of original size or enlarge them to 1600% of original size in increments as small as .1% (Figure 7.4 shows a page reduced to 25% of original). The option is useful when you want to print proofs of spot or process color separations when your page size is 8.5 by 11 inches. Enter a reduction value of 85%, and your spot color overlays print out with crop marks, registration marks, and color labels (or choose the **Reduce to fit** option button). If you scale your document to print larger than original size, you may have to invoke tiling to see the entire printed results.

Figure 7.4 *The printed page reduced to 25% of original size.*

PRINTING THUMBNAILS

Thumbnails are an easy way of looking at all the pages in a document, to see the overall design theme. You can print up to 100 pages of your document on one page. The thumbnails provide a storyboard look at the document. Text can't be read, but the placement of photos, graphics, columns, and headings is readily visible. A thumbnail is useful for showing a client progress on a project. To print thumbnails, click the **Thumbnail** option box and enter the number of thumbnails you want per page, in the Per Page text box. The more thumbnails you request on the page, the smaller each thumbnail will be. For greater page detail, print fewer thumbnails per page. An example of this is shown in Figure 7.5.

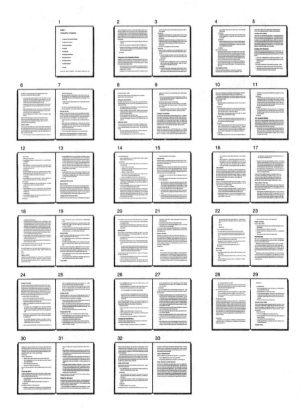

Figure 7.5 *Thumbnails of a document.*

Setting Additional Print Options

By choosing the **Options** button you will see yet another dialog box, shown in Figure 7.6, of choices to further define how you want to print your document. These options help you set the resolution of printed graphics, add bullets and annotations to the page for your commercial printer to use, and define print-to-disk files to send to your service bureau.

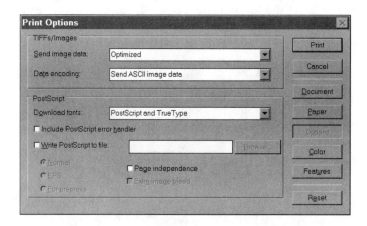

Figure 7.6 *The Print Options dialog box.*

SETTING THE PRINT RESOLUTION OF GRAPHICS

Normally, you will probably be anxious to print your graphic images at their normal resolution, if only to admire how nice they look. But the Print Options dialog box gives you several important choices to control the printed resolution of those graphics. For example, the **Optimized** option is a useful way to speed up the printing of scanned images that have a higher scanned resolution than your printer can reproduce. The higher the scanning resolution, the larger the graphic file, and the printer normally must read the entire file before it can compose the image, regardless of whether it can reproduce the image at the scanned resolution. If you choose **Optimized**, PageMaker only feeds the printer as much of the resolution as it can reproduce, thus significantly speeding up printing the image without any degradation in quality (scanned line art may appear slightly blurred).

Another way to speed up printing is to choose the **Low resolution** option, which sends the printer a low-resolution version of TIFF graphics (between 25 and 72 dpi). The graphic will be recognizable but will lack its original high resolution. If you click **Omit TIFF files**, the TIFFs won't print at all, which is handy if you just want a printout of the text portion of the document.

ADDING PRINTER'S AND PAGE MARKINGS

Click open the Print Paper dialog box and choose the **Printer's marks** check box to see trim marks, registration bullets, and color bars for spot or process colors. If you click the **Page information** check box, PageMaker adds the file name, date and time the file was last saved, and color plate information in very small print in the lower-left corner of the page.

PRINTING DOCUMENTS TO DISK

Generally speaking, PostScript service bureaus do not want you to send them PageMaker **.PM6** files because they are probably not using PageMaker to print the files to their PostScript imagesetters. In most cases, they are printing PostScript files created by a variety of applications. Consequently, they will probably want you to print the file to disk, creating a **.PS** file. They then send the **.PS** file to the PostScript device using either a file downloader (like Adobe's Font Downloader) or the DOS **copy** command.

To print a file to disk:

1. Click open the Print Options dialog box.

2. Click the **Write PostScript to file** check box.

3. Click the **PostScript and TrueType** option in the Download fonts list. This means that any fonts in your system (not resident in your laser printer) that would download if you printed the document will be added to the print-to-disk file. This is an important option; without it you would see Courier substituted for the downloadable fonts unless the service bureau happened to have the same font on hand and took the time to download it to the printer before printing your file.

4. In the text box to the right of the **PostScript** check box, PageMaker will create the name of the file. Click the **Browse** button to look through your folders and drives to find the correct location for this file. Add the proper extension to the name of the file based on the following considerations:

❖ If you click the **Normal** option button, PageMaker will add the **.PS** extension. This is a normal PostScript file.

❖ If you click **EPS** (for *Encapsulated PostScript* file), PageMaker will add the **.EPS** extension. Only single pages can be saved as EPS files, which are used as graphics rather than print-to-disk-files.

❖ If you want to print color separation plates of your document to use in an OPI-based prepress system like Aldus PrePress, click the **For separations** option button. OPI comments are saved along with your separations. PageMaker will add the **.SEP** extension.

Now that you've created a **.PS** file, how do you get it to the printer? Use the DOS **copy** command:

1. Type the following command from DOS:

   ```
   Copy C:\NAME.PS LPT1
   ```

2. Substitute the real path of the file for **C:**, and the real name of the file for **NAME.PS**. For example, if the file were named **BROCHURE.PS** located in **D:\DOCS**, you would type:

   ```
   Copy D:\DOCS\BROCHURE.PS LPT1
   ```

3. Make sure that you add one space between the **copy** command and the file name and one space between the file name and **LPT1**.

4. The file will be copied to the laser printer and, about a moment later, begin to print.

SETTING COLOR PRINTING OPTIONS

The Print Color dialog box, shown in Figure 7.7, gives you precise control over handling color separations and printing color. You can also specify line frequency and line angles for process color separation plates, based on the PPD you have selected.

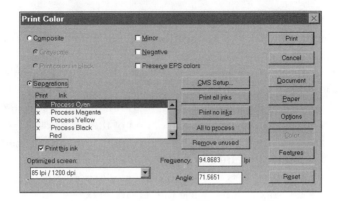

Figure 7.7 *The Print Color dialog box.*

CONTROLLING COMPOSITE PRINTING

Printing a *composite* of a color document is the opposite of printing separations. Instead of the colors being separated, they are printed in place, as either shades of gray (from a laser printer) or as close approximations of the colors (from a color printer). Composites are an important aspect to proofing your color job; it's difficult to visualize having all the correct colors, especially spot colors, unless you run a proof through a color printer. The colors won't be exact, but you'll have a close idea of the finished work. To print colors on a color printer, click the **Grayscale** option button. If you are printing to a laser printer, selecting this option shows the colors in shades of gray. If you click the **Print colors in black** option button, the colors all print in shades of black in the same screened percentages as if you printed process and spot separations.

CREATING MIRROR AND NEGATIVE IMAGES OF YOUR DOCUMENT

Both the **Mirror** and **Negative** check boxes are generally for use with an imagesetter. The **Mirror** option is normally used with the **Negative** option to control on which side the emulsion is for film negatives. If the negatives need to be right reading and you want the emulsion side up, set Mirror to off. Turn Mirror on if you want the emulsion side down. If the film needs to be wrong reading, set Mirror to on if you want the emulsion side up. Set it to off if you want the emulsion side down. Click the **Negative** check box to generate film or paper negatives.

CONTROLLING SEPARATION PRINTING

To print separations, click the **Separations** option button. The Separations list box and command buttons will darken. Notice the list box contains the process colors cyan, magenta, and yellow, plus black, the registration color, and any spot colors you have defined for this document. Scroll down the list box and click the colors whose separations you want to print and click in the **Print this ink** check box to add an **X** in the Print column of the list box—PageMaker only prints separations for the colors with **X**es in the Print column. To mark all colors with **X**es, click the **Print all inks** command button. To remove all the **X**es, click the **Print no ink** button. If you want to convert all spot color separations temporarily to process separations, click the **All to process** button (the process equivalent of the spot color may not be the same tint).

Working with Service Bureaus

There are several things you can do to help process your job at a service bureau and cut down on any possible misunderstandings. When you establish a relationship with a service bureau, give them a list of all the fonts you have (whether or not they are in a particular document). With the list,, include a file with at least a couple of words set in each font. Ask the service bureau to print the file and look for any fonts that have been substituted with Courier. The substitution will indicate that your font and the service bureau's font are different even though they are named the same. There are so many fonts called by similar names that this kind of test is important.

If possible, give the service bureau a copy of the file you have printed on your laser printer. If you request spot color separations from the service bureau, run a set of separations reduced to 85% so the service bureau knows exactly what to expect with your job.

Ask to see an example of the service bureau's exposed film before requesting that your first job be printed on film. The negative film should be free of pin holes (hold the film up to the light to check).

If the service bureau gives you a choice of resolutions (for example, a Linotronic L330 can print at 1270 or 2540 dpi resolution), opt for the lower resolution for text, unless you are working with very fine serif type in very small sizes. The lower resolution costs less per page. If you request spot color or process color separations, be aware of the costs involved—film can cost twice as much as paper, and in creating separations you're producing several pages for each page of your document—the costs can mount rapidly.

Finally, don't expect the service bureau to proof your work, catch misspellings, or make corrections for you. The work should be correct before you give it to the service bureau, and, generally speaking, they do not proofread documents.

A Word of Caution

Printing is not a science, it's an art. Adding PostScript and PageMaker, as accurate as they are, doesn't make printing foolproof. There are many variables, even with PostScript, including:

❖ **Chemistry**—This includes the chemistry of the developer and fixer used in processing film and resin-coated paper in the imagesetter's processing unit; the speed of the material running through the processor, the temperature of the chemicals, and the temperature and humidity of the ambient air. All these variables affect the exposure, developing, and fixing of the photographic paper or film.

❖ **Shelf life of materials**—The freshness of the chemicals, paper, and film plays a direct role in the developing process and the end quality of the printed page. Ideally, service bureau operators should buy supplies in small quantities and replace their inventories of supplies rapidly.

❖ **Exposure**—The exposure settings in the imagesetter are different for film and paper and are affected by chemical and air temperature.

❖ **Fonts**—As crisp as PostScript fonts are, different fonts reproduce differently. The thinner the letters and the more delicate the serifs, the more likely that characters will break up in small sizes. Type in italics can be particularly susceptible to breaking up in small sizes. To keep the letters from breaking, the service bureau operator must expose the type longer to make the serifs stronger. The printer must compensate by exposing the printing plate longer and adding more ink. However, these longer exposures can create other problems. Achieving high quality is a delicate balancing act between the production of the PostScript originals in paper or film and the printed results.

❖ **Paper, ink, dryers, folders, and die cutters**—All of these variables play a part in how good or bad the finished work looks. Different papers accept and hold different quantities of ink; different inks have different properties; dryers make the ink dry faster but can change the quality of the finished print; folders, die cutters, and other machinery that aid in the production of the finished piece can help or hinder a job.

❖ **Knowledge and experience of the operators**—All the computers in the world can't duplicate the knowledge of an experienced and capable service bureau operator and printer. Much of the success lies in their desire to do the job right and in their understanding of how to fine-tune and adjust very delicate machinery.

To Sum Up

Printing is the melody that gives life to the written word. PageMaker awards the designer with boundless freedom in developing the printed page with accuracy as sharp as a tack. You've learned how easily PageMaker handles all the chores of producing a camera-ready printing mechanical.

In the next chapter, you'll see how easy it is to add color to your document.

CHAPTER 8

Adding Color

215

Sometimes even the best choice of words arranged in the best possible layout just can't hold a candle to a touch of color on the page. Color is like a flashing arrow drawing the eye to your words, magnifying their meaning, clarifying the results. Color invokes emotions—think about Christmas without red and green or the Fourth of July without red, white, and blue. Color imbues a document with sharp or subtle moods. It gives the message subconscious appeal— recall the blue of IBM's logotype, for instance, or the broad red stripe of the Coast Guard emblem.

You work with color all the time and probably don't even think about it. Putting black text on a white page still adds color to the page. Black is created by combining all the primary colors (proved to me every time I watch my two-year-old daughter Kathleen mix too many finger paints together; she gets black every time). Normally, one-color printing is black—in part because the toner for laser printers and high-speed photocopiers is black. Unless you can add different-colored toner, your printed output will be black.

Even a one-color black-on-white document can be dressed up by a commercial printer using colored ink and/or paper. For example, you could print medium blue ink on a buff or beige stock, dark gray ink on a light gray stock, or maroon ink on a light gray stock. Suddenly your plain document is starting to look pretty jazzy.

Adding a second color ink can make a tremendous improvement for very little increased cost. You could create the appearance of a second color using a screen of the single-color ink. For example, a 20% screen of black yields light gray; 20% of a dark green makes a very nice shade of light green, and so on. In this case, the second color is free!

PageMaker's color capabilities support all the examples I have just given you. PageMaker can provide your commercial printer with screens of solid colors, color overlays for each color you add to a design, knockouts for printing one color on top of another, and much more.

Using PageMaker's Default Colors

PageMaker's colors are displayed and activated with the Colors palette. Similar in use to the Styles palette, the Colors palette is a small window containing the default colors and any custom colors you define.

Opening the Colors Palette

To open the Colors palette:

1. Choose the **Window** pull-down menu (or press **Alt+W**).
2. Choose **Colors** (or press **C**). The palette will be displayed on the right side of the document window, as shown in Figure 8.1.

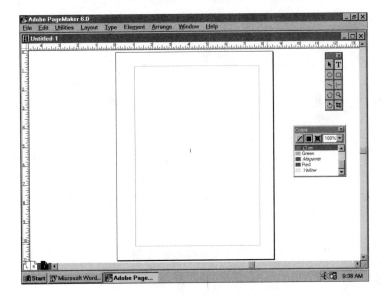

Figure 8.1 *The Colors palette.*

3. Or you could use the PageMaker shortcut **Ctrl+K** to open the Colors palette window.

PageMaker comes configured with three default colors shown in the Colors palette: blue, green, and red. These colors have the following properties:

❖ **Blue** is configured as *Pantone 2685 blue*, composed of 100% cyan and 100% magenta.

❖ **Green** is configured as *Pantone 355 green*, composed of 100% cyan and 100% yellow.

❖ **Red** is configured as *Pantone 1795 red*, composed of 100% magenta and 100% yellow.

"Defining Custom Colors," later in this chapter, covers the different color models and the Pantone Color System.

NOTE

To see colors on your computer, you must have a color monitor. To print color, you must use a color printer such as a color laser, dye sublimation, or inkjet printer.

The default colors are similar to default styles; they are always present when new documents are created. And like styles, changing or removing a default color from a particular document doesn't alter the default colors in future documents.

You can color text that is created in or imported into PageMaker. You can also color any element drawn with one of the drawing tools or any imported graphic. Some graphics, including TIFF files, EPS files, and Windows Metafiles, print in the color you specify, although they will not be displayed in that color.

The Colors palette has several useful tools for coloring items on the page (see Figure 8.2). Let's take a look:

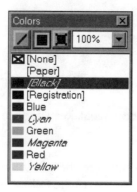

Figure 8.2 Parts of the Color palette.

❖ **Line button**—Click this button to color a line or the lined border of a shape.

❖ **Fill button**—Click this button to color the *fill* (inside) of a closed shape.

❖ **Both button**—Click here to apply a color to both the line and the fill.

❖ **Tint list**—Use the list of percentages to tint a solid color.

❖ **None**—Choose to hide the line and/or fill.

❖ **Color Paper**—Applies the color of the paper on which the document is printed. As opposed to the color **None** (which makes the colored object transparent), coloring something with the paper color means whatever is behind it is hidden. The best example of the paper color is used in creating a drop-shadow behind a box (see "Adding Additional Colors to Shapes" later in this chapter). You cannot modify the paper color.

❖ **Color Black**—This is the standard process black color used in your publications. You cannot modify this color, but you can apply screens of black to create shades of gray.

❖ **Color Registration**—Registration is really not a color; it is an attribute you can apply to a color or anything you want to print on all separation overlays. For example, if you wanted to create your own crop marks, you would mark the marks with the color **Registration** so that the crop marks would appear on all separation plates.

❖ **Colors**—PageMaker's default colors are cyan, yellow, magenta, red, green, and blue. Any additional colors you define are displayed on the palette.

Adding Color to Text

There are a number of reasons you might want to color text. For example, in technical manuals and proposals, coloring headings helps refine the look of the page and breaks up large blocks of text. Adding colored callouts to an illustration helps to show a distinct separation between the figure and its annotation. In brochures and marketing literature, color can add class and emphasis.

There are two methods of coloring text in PageMaker: selecting the color as part of the text specification or marking the text using the Colors palette.

USING THE TEXT SPECIFICATION DIALOG BOX

To color text as part of the text specification:

1. If you're about to type new text, choose the **Text** tool and place the insertion point where you want to start the text. If you want to color text that is already on the page, highlight the text with the Text tool.

2. Choose the **Type** pull-down menu and choose **Type Specs** (or press **Alt+T T**) to display the Type Specifications dialog box, shown in Figure 8.3.

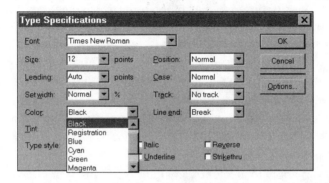

Figure 8.3 *The Type Specifications dialog box.*

3. Click the **Color** list box arrow to open the list box and click one of the choices:

   ❖ **Paper**—Just as it's used in the Fill submenu, **Paper** indicates the color of the paper for this document.

   ❖ **Black**—This color can't be changed in the Define Colors dialog box. All text is initially set to this color.

   ❖ **Registration**—This refers to crop marks and registration marks that PageMaker prints when the **Printer's Marks** option box is checked in the Print dialog box. Text marked as **Registration** prints on every page with color overlay registration marks or page crop marks.

   ❖ **Cyan, Yellow, Magenta, Red, Green, Blue**—Text marked with any of these colors will be displayed in the color on your color monitor. If printed on a color laser or inkjet printer, the marked items will be printed in a similar color to what is displayed on your monitor (an exact match depends on the number of colors your monitor is capable of displaying, the resolution of your monitor, and the color resolution of the color printer). If you select **Spot Color Overlays** in the Print dialog box, PageMaker will print a color overlay for each of these colors used in the document.

4. Click **OK** or press **Enter** to return to your document. If you highlighted text to color, it will now be displayed in the color you selected. If you position the insertion point back in the text, the Color list box in the Type Specifications dialog box will display the color you selected.

Using the Colors Palette

To mark text in a color using the Colors palette:

1. Select the **Text** tool and highlight the text you want to color.
2. In the Colors palette, click the color you want for the highlighted text.

The text is displayed in the color you select. If you position the insertion point back in the text, the Colors palette displays the color you selected. To change the color to another color or back to black, simply highlight the text again and choose the new color.

Adding Colors with the Styles Palette

In longer documents you may find it easier to assign a color to certain text you've already defined as a style. Then, whenever you choose the style, you automatically assign the color. Here's how:

1. Choose the **Type** pull-down menu and choose **Define Styles** (or press **Alt+T D**).
2. In the Define Styles dialog box, select the style to which you want to add a color assignment. Click the **Edit** button.
3. In the Edit Style dialog box, press the **Type** button to move to the Type Specifications dialog box.
4. Choose a color for the type by clicking the **Color** list box arrow and choosing a color from the list.
5. Click **OK** or press **Enter** in all the nested dialog boxes (or use the PageMaker shortcut **Alt+OK**) to return to your document.

Now, whenever you choose the style with the color assignment, you will also color the text in that style.

Working with Color Graphics

Any graphic created with or imported into PageMaker, with the exception of scanned color TIFF files, can be colored. Some graphic formats (including encapsulated PostScript files and Windows Metafiles) can be marked with a color but will not be displayed in the color (they will, however, print in the specified color). To fill a graphic with a color other than black, simply create the graphic shape, choose the color you want from the Colors palette, and choose **Solid** from the Fill submenu. The graphic shape will be filled with the color you selected. Graphics created in PageMaker can also be shaded using the shade percentages in the Fill submenu (see "Screening Text and Graphics" later in this chapter).

Adding Color to a Graphic Shape

You can easily add color to squares, rectangles, ovals, and circles you create in PageMaker. To color a PageMaker graphic shape:

1. Choose the **Rectangle** tool and draw a rectangle on the page.
2. While the border of the rectangle is still selected, choose a color in the Colors palette and click the color. The border of the rectangle will change to that color. Or you can click the **Line** button and click the color you want to add to the line.
3. Again, while the border is still selected, choose the **Element** pull-down menu and choose **Fill** (or press **Alt+M F**) to display the Fill submenu.
4. Choose **Solid** or one of the percentage screens of a solid color and the rectangle will be filled. Then click the color in the Colors palette you want for the fill color. Or click the **Fill** button and select the color of the fill.

Changing the Viewing Resolution of Scanned Images

Even very fast computers will tend to choke on TIFF files displayed at high resolution in PageMaker, especially in the 200 or 400% page views. The images are just so big that it takes a few moments for the screen to redraw as you scroll up or down the page. Full grayscale TIFFs can easily be 500 kilobytes; just a small scanned color photo can exceed several megabytes. To speed up the redraw (or *screen refresh rate*, as it's called), you can change the display of the TIFF file to a lower resolution. The Preferences dialog box is used to set the display resolution of graphics. Follow these steps:

1. Choose the **File** pull-down menu and choose **Preferences** (or press **Alt+F F**) to display the Preferences dialog box, shown in Figure 8.4.

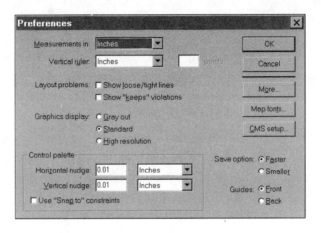

Figure 8.4 *The Preferences dialog box.*

2. In the Graphics Display area of the dialog box, choose the appropriate display resolution:

   ❖ **Gray Out**—Graphics at this display resolution are represented as a gray box. Gray out provides the fastest refresh rate at high page magnifications.

   ❖ **Normal**—This is a good compromise between details and speed. You'll see a pretty good representation of your graphic.

   ❖ **High Resolution**—This gives the highest resolution possible but the slowest redraw.

3. Click the appropriate button for the display resolution you want.

Another way to see an individual graphic in high resolution (if **Normal** or **Gray Out** is in effect) is to press **Alt+Shift** while the graphic is being refreshed (when you move up or down the area of the page that the graphic is in using the scroll bar or when you move to another page containing a graphic).

Defining Custom Colors

If the default colors provided in the Colors palette don't fit the bill for a particular document, you can create a custom color. PageMaker provides three color models (or schemes of color blending) to use in customizing a color. The models are:

❖ **RGB** treats color in much the same way that your color monitor does: it blends percentages of red, green, and blue.

❖ **HLS** (hue, lightness, and saturation model) treats color hues as degrees in a color wheel, increasing or decreasing the lightness and saturation of the hue as percentages of 100 to create the color.

❖ **CMYK** stands for the primary colors of four-color printing: cyan, magenta, yellow, and black. Mixing them in varying percentages of 100 yields different color combinations.

PageMaker also gives you four color-matching libraries and a provision for adding more customized libraries as they become available. The most popular color-matching system is the Pantone Matching System (PMS). It has become the de facto standard to define and mix ink and is used by most commercial printers to reproduce colors. However, PageMaker also provides matching systems from DIC, Munsell, Focoltone, Toyo, and TruMatch.

To define a custom color:

1. Choose the **Element** pull-down menu and choose **Define Colors** (or press **Alt+M D**) to display the Define Colors dialog box, shown in Figure 8.5.

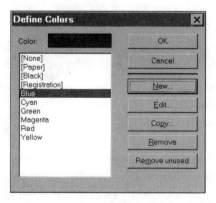

Figure 8.5 *The Define Colors dialog box.*

The Define Colors dialog box lists all the currently available colors defined for this document. It is very similar in use to the Define Styles dialog box (see Chapter 6) in that you can create new colors, edit existing colors, copy custom colors you defined for other documents for use with this document, and remove colors.

2. Click the **New** button to display the Edit Color dialog box.

3. Click the option button for the color model you want or open the **Libraries** list box and choose among the color-matching libraries.

4. For each color model, choose whether you want items in the color to be included on a spot color separation by clicking the **Spot** option, or as a part of the four process separation by clicking the **Process** option.

5. Enter a name for the color in the Name text box. The name you enter here will be displayed on the Colors palette and will print outside the margin on spot color and process color separations (so your commercial printer will know which overlay is which).

You can call your new color whatever you want, but the name should be descriptive of the color. For example, you could call a light green *Light Green*, since there is already a default green on the Colors palette. Or you could call it *Logo Green* if your client uses a particular shade of green for a company logo.

You don't have to actually select a color to create a special name for a color. For example, if you want to print this document on a special brand of paper or print selected pages on different colors of paper, you can itemize the colors of the paper as custom colors. Then, before placing anything on the page, draw a square-cornered box the same size as the overall page size (using the Fit in Window view), mark the box as the special paper type or paper color, choose **Fill Paper** (**Element > Fill**), and choose a color for the paper. Then when you print out your spot color overlays, the specific paper types or paper colors will be automatically specified for the commercial printer. To create a custom paper type, simply enter the name in the Name text box (like **Classic Laid Bone**) and click **OK** or press **Enter**. The name is added to the Colors palette.

Similarly, you can name a custom color *Varnish* if you want your commercial printer to varnish the printed page. *Varnish* is a clear coating applied over the ink to keep the ink from smearing and add gloss to the page. Varnish is treated like a spot color by your commercial printer and needs its own spot separation. For a jazzy effect, varnish only certain areas of the page, such as graphics or photos. By making the varnish a color, it's a simple matter to fill the graphic boxes that will hold photos with the varnish color. To add Varnish to the Colors palette, enter **Varnish** in the Name text box and click **OK** or press **Enter**.

Defining RGB Colors

To create an RGB color:

1. In the Edit Color dialog box, click the **Model** list box and choose **RGB** to select the RGB color model, as shown in Figure 8.6. You will see three color text boxes and slide bars to enter values for red, green, and blue.

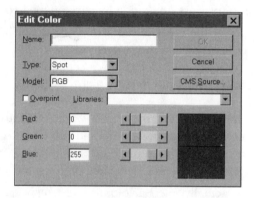

Figure 8.6 *The Edit Color dialog box with the RGB color mixing model.*

2. Position the insertion point in the appropriate text box and type a percentage of 100 for each color or adjust the slide on the slide bar to the value you want. The resulting color mix is displayed in the preview box to the right. (The top half of the box shows the latest color adjustment; the bottom half shows the original color setting.) Entering a higher value results in a higher proportional mix of the color.

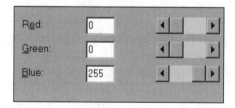

3. When you have defined the color you want, click **OK** or press **Enter** to save the color and return to the Define Colors dialog box. Click **OK** again to return to your document. The name of the color you created is displayed in the Colors palette.

Defining HLS Colors

To create an HLS color:

1. In the Edit Color dialog box, click the **Model** list box and choose **HLS** to select the HLS model, as shown in Figure 8.7. You will see three color text boxes and slide bars to enter specific color values for hue, lightness (sometimes called *lumination* or *brightness*), and saturation.

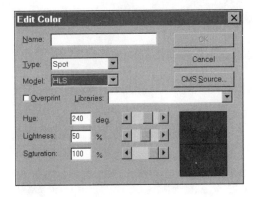

Figure 8.7 *The Edit Color dialog box with the HLS color mixing model.*

2. Position the insertion point in the appropriate text box and type a value or adjust the slide on the slide bar to the value you want. *Hue* is adjusted from 0 to 360 degrees on an imaginary color wheel containing the full color spectrum. Entering a specific degree in the hue scale provides an exact position in the color spectrum. Add *saturation* to intensify the color. Zero percent saturation would be a complete lack of the color, or *white*. One hundred percent saturation of the hue would be the *pure color*. *Lightness* adds a specific level of light intensity to the hue, like increasing the brightness of a light bulb. Zero percent lightness is *black*, no matter what the level of saturation is for the hue, and 100% lightness is *white*.

When all three variables are combined, you create a color. For example, if you select **205** degrees of hue you will be in the blue color spectrum. But without saturation and lightness, you'll see only black in the preview box. Now increase the lightness by moving the slide on the slide bar to the right. As you increase the value, the preview box changes from black to lighter shades of gray to white. Now set the level of lightness at **50%**. We still have no color because saturation is set at zero. Now begin to add saturation, and the preview box changes from a dull gray to a bright medium blue.

3. When you have defined the color you want, click **OK** or press **Enter** to save it and return to the Define Colors dialog box. Click **OK** again to return to your document. The name of the color you created is displayed in the Colors palette.

Defining CMYK Colors

To create a CMYK color:

1. In the Edit Color dialog box, click the **Model** list box and choose **CMYK** to select the CMYK color model, as shown in Figure 8.8. You will see four color text boxes and slide bars to enter values for cyan, magenta, yellow, and black.

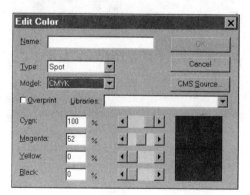

Figure 8.8 *The Edit Color dialog box with the CMYK color mixing model.*

2. Position the insertion point in the appropriate text box and type a value or adjust the slide on the slide bar to the value you want. The CMYK

model of specifying color is the system used most often for printing process color (also called *four-color printing*, because the four colors cyan, magenta, yellow, and black are used to produce all printed colors). Because this color model is used most often in printing process color, the four colors are also known as *process blue* (cyan), *process red* (magenta), *process yellow*, and *process black*. As you adjust the percentages to fine-tune the color you want, keep in mind that the more color you add, the darker and duller the color becomes. Try to keep the total percentage of the cyan, magenta, yellow, and black values below 240%. For example, a dark royal blue that is 100% cyan, 100% magenta, and 40% yellow is a vibrant color. Increasing the yellow to 100% makes the blue almost black. Likewise, be judicious with your use of black; a little goes a long way.

3. When you have defined the color you want, click **OK** or press **Enter** to save the color and return to the Define Colors dialog box. Click **OK** again to return to your document. The name of the color you created is displayed in the Colors palette.

Defining Pantone Colors

To create a Pantone color:

1. In the Edit Color dialog box, click the **Libraries** list box and choose **Pantone** to display the Pantone Color dialog box, shown in Figure 8.9.

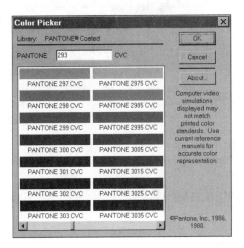

Figure 8.9 *The Pantone Color dialog box.*

2. If you know the Pantone color number, enter it in the text box. Otherwise, scroll down the list of sample colors and select the one you want. The color numbers shown match the *Pantone Matching System Color Formula Guide 747XR*, which is used by printers around the country as a standardized way to mix custom colors of ink (much like custom house-paint colors are mixed).

3. When you have selected the color you want, click **OK** or press **Enter** to save the color and return to the Edit Color dialog box. Click **OK** twice more to move through the nested dialog boxes and return to your document.

The name of the color you created is displayed in the Colors palette. You can choose one of three other color-matching libraries, including a Pantone library of matching process (instead of spot) colors.

Defining Color Tints

A *tint* of a solid color is essentially a screen of the color. You can create screens of solid colors you have already defined by choosing one of the standard screen percentages on the Fill and Line dialog box.

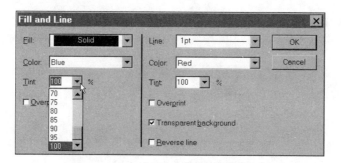

However, if you want a percentage other than those provided on the submenu, you must first define the tint in the Edit Color dialog box. Here are the steps:

1. Click the **Tint** option button to display the tint color controls, shown in Figure 8.10.

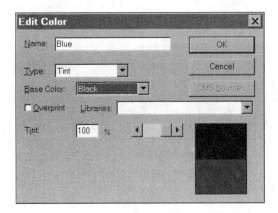

Figure 8.10 *The Edit Color dialog box showing the tint color controls.*

2. Click the **Base color** list box arrow to open the list box and choose the color you want to create a tint of.

3. Click and drag the tint scroll box to the amount of tint you want or enter an exact percentage in the Tint text box.

4. Give the tint a descriptive name and click **OK** or press **Enter**.

Editing, Copying, and Removing Colors

PageMaker allows you to change the values of colors once they're defined. Keep in mind, however, that when a value is changed, all text and graphics marked with that color are also changed.

When you change the name of a specified color, the name is changed automatically in the Colors palette and on spot color overlays. PageMaker gives you an easy way to change color models; a color defined in one model is automatically defined in every other model. For example, if you customize a particular shade of blue in the RGB model, clicking each of the other color model option buttons (or the **Pantone** button) gives you the settings for the same color in the other models. For example, as shown in the following table, if you define an RGB color, PageMaker defines the same color in the other color models.

Color Model	Settings
RGB	100% blue
HLS	240 degrees hue 50 degrees lightness 100% saturation
CMYK	100% cyan 100% magenta
Pantone	Pantone 2685 cv blue

It is equally easy to copy custom colors from other PageMaker documents into the current document or to remove a color you no longer want.

Editing Colors

To edit a color:

1. Choose the **Element** pull-down menu and choose **Define Colors** (or press **Alt+M D**) to display the Define Colors dialog box.

2. Click the color you want to edit. Then click the **Edit** button to display the Edit Color dialog box (this is the same dialog box you used to create the colors).

3. Change the values for the color.

4. If this is a Pantone color or a color from one of the other color-matching libraries, click the **Libraries** list box and choose **Pantone** or the other matching system you want. Click **OK** or press **Enter** to move back to the Edit Color dialog box.

5. Click **OK** or press **Enter** to save the color value changes and return to the Define Colors dialog box. Click **OK** or press **Enter** again to return to your document.

Copying Colors

It's not necessary to create the same custom color for more than one document. Instead, simply copy the colors you created in the first document. Here's how:

1. Choose the **Element** pull-down menu and choose **Define Colors** (or press **Alt+M D**) to display the Define Colors dialog box.

2. . Click the **Copy** button to display the Copy Colors dialog box, shown in Figure 8.11.

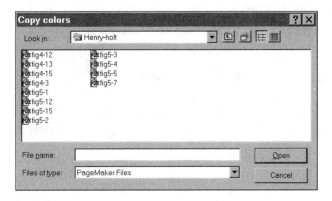

Figure 8.11 *The Copy Colors dialog box.*

3. Type the name of the document with the colors you want to copy in the File name text box. If you're not sure of the file name, use the Folders list box to scroll through the list of files.

4. Click **OK** or press **Enter** to go back to the Define Colors dialog box. The colors in the document you specified are copied to the current document and added to the list of colors in the dialog box. If colors in both documents have been named the same, PageMaker warns you and asks whether you want to replace the existing color with the color of the same name. If you choose **Yes**, the current color name is copied over. If you choose **Cancel**, the color is not copied.

Removing Colors

Custom colors that you define, as well as the PageMaker default colors, can be removed from a document at any time. Simply follow these steps:

1. Choose the **Element** pull-down menu and choose **Define Colors** (or press **Alt+M D**) to display the Define Colors dialog box.

2. Choose the color you want to delete and click the **Remove** button. PageMaker warns you that you are removing the color and that it will change all items in the color to black.

3. Click **OK** or press **Enter**. The color will be deleted from the color list and any items in the color will be changed to black.

Screening Text and Graphics

There are two ways for a commercial printer to print a colored ink on paper: using a custom-mixed spot color ink (as discussed earlier), which coats a printing plate and makes an impression on paper, or by screening one or more process colors to get the correct printing color. Let's talk about screens (halftone and printer's) for a minute.

Photographs that we snap with our cameras and have developed at the drug store are known as *continuous-tone* photos; they can be developed as prints or slides (*transparencies*). If you look at one with a magnifying glass you will see that the colors gradually blend into one another—they are all solid, continuous tones, whether they are light or dark. With one obscure exception, it is impossible to print continuous tones onto paper; they must be converted to halftones.

Halftones are made by photographing the continuous-tone photo through a very fine screen. The screen breaks up the continuous tones into dot patterns—the darker the color, the larger and closer together the dots. The lighter the color, the smaller and fewer the dots. When the photo is printed, a dot of ink appears for each dot created by the screen, and the image is transferred to paper. Take a moment to look at a printed photo with a magnifying glass. Compare it with a photo you've taken. You will see the difference between photographic processing and printing.

Halftone screens are measured in lines per inch—the more lines, the finer the detail and the higher the resolution of the printed photo. Typical screens are 55, 65, 85, 110, 120, and 133 lines per inch. The screen to be used is determined by the type of printing and the type of paper. For example, newspapers typically use *85-line screens* for their photos because newsprint is so coarse and the ink so watery that dots from a finer screen simply run together and blur. High-quality magazines generally use *133-line screens*, and may use *150-* or even *200-line screens*, again depending on the printing press and type of paper.

The screen for a continuous-tone photo, scanned into a TIFF file and placed in PageMaker, can be specified by the Image Control dialog box. In this dialog box you can adjust the brightness and contrast of the photo, indicate the number of lines per inch for the line screen, and specify the angle of the screen (more about this in "Adjusting Scanned Image Screens" later in this chapter).

Printer's screens are measured in percentages of solid colors. The dot-patterned shades on the Fill submenu are percentage screens of black or any color on the Colors palette. Specifying a line or box as a 75% screen in the Fill submenu means that when the screen is turned into a printing plate, only 75% of the color prints through the screen. Therefore, if you color the screen black, you get a second color in the screened area that looks dark gray. If you specify a dark red ink, the color in the screen prints medium red, and so on. If you're already using a solid color on the page, the screen is a way of getting a free second color on the same page.

There are two important considerations concerning screens:

❖ If you are preparing a document for commercial printing and you've included screens to produce screened colors, you must have film negatives for final output from the PostScript imagesetter. The negatives are necessary to make the printing plate. Normally, the printer gets positive paper from customers, which must first be reshot as a negative, and the negative used to generate the plate (the plate needs to be a negative so that when it's inked against paper, the resulting impression will be a positive). If you give the printer a positive mechanical, the screens will not survive the photographic transition to negative. The printer will have to cut out the PageMaker screens and strip new screens into the negative.

❖ The 10% screen on the Fill submenu acts differently based on the resolution of the final output device. It will look fine when proofed on a 300-dpi laser printer. However, when the output is from a PostScript imagesetter at less than about 2500 dpi, the 10% screen may lose most of the screen dots (too much white space appears between each dot for the dots to provide a screen of the ink color). When the screen is output at 2500 dpi or higher, it is again filled in properly to provide 10% of the solid color. Be careful using 10% screens.

Creating Text Screens

Text is screened when you apply a tint percentage of black to the text using the Type Specifications dialog box. Here's how:

1. Highlight the text you want to screen using the Text tool.

2. Press **Ctrl+T** to open the Type Specifications dialog box.

3. Click open the **Tint** menu, shown in Figure 8.12, and choose the percentage from the list. To enter a percentage not shown on the list, type it in the Tint text box.

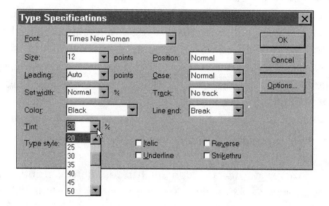

Figure 8.12 *The Type Specifications dialog box with the Tint list box open.*

4. Click **OK** to return to your document.

Creating Graphic Screens

As I have mentioned, any graphic shape created in PageMaker can be screened by using the Fill and Line dialog box. Follow these steps:

1. Draw a shape using one of the drawing tools.

2. While the shape is still selected (displaying its sizing handles), open the Fill and Line dialog box (**Element > Fill and Line**), open the **Tint** list, and select one of the screens. The shape will be filled with the percentage screen you select.

Adjusting Scanned Image Screens

Any scanned photo, placed as a TIFF file in a document, can be refined using PageMaker's Image Control feature. Follow these steps:

1. Select the image with the Pointer tool.

2. Choose the **Element** pull-down menu and choose **Image Control** (or press **Alt+M I**) to display the Image Control dialog box, shown in Figure 8.13.

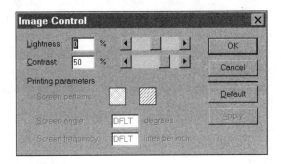

Figure 8.13 *The Image Control dialog box.*

3. Use this dialog box to adjust and control the final printed image. You have the following options:

    ❖ **Lightness**—Use the slide control or enter a percentage value to adjust the lightness of the image. Add more lightness (a higher value) to make the image lighter. Reduce the lightness value to make the image darker.

    ❖ **Contrast**—Use the slide control or enter a percentage value to adjust the contrast of the image to the surrounding background. Entering a higher value increases the contrast. A lower value reduces the contrast.

    ❖ **Screen patterns**—This may seem a little confusing, but bear with me. PageMaker provides two patterns of screens for photographs: screens made up of varying sizes of dots and screens made up of varying thicknesses of lines. The dot screen box (the left box) produces normal photographic screens (based on the number of lines per inch in the Screen Frequency text box). The dot pattern is normally selected when you are working with photos. The right box represents a special effects lined-screen pattern. The pattern uses lines of various thicknesses to provide the details of the photo.

❖ **Screen angle**—The default angle (indicated by *DFLT*) is 45 degrees for most PostScript printers. You can specify your own angle by entering a value here, from 0 to 360 degrees.

❖ **Screen frequency**—This determines the number of lines per inch for the screen. The default setting (indicated by *DFLT*) means that PageMaker assigns the number of lines per inch based on the PostScript device to which you are printing. For example, if you are printing to a 300-dpi laser printer, the maximum lines per inch the printer can handle is 53. PageMaker automatically assigns that frequency to the image. If you print to a higher-resolution device, PageMaker automatically increases the lines per inch accordingly. You can enter any value in the text box from 10 to 300.

4. Choose the **Default** button to reset the default values you changed in the appropriate text boxes.

5. Choose the **Apply** button to see the results of the values you entered on the selected image. You can click on the title bar of the Image Control dialog box and drag it out of the way if it is blocking the image.

6. Click **OK** or press **Enter** to save the values you changed and return to your document.

Adding Special Effects to Images

For TIFF files, PageMaker can not only adjust lightness, contrast, and screen parameters, but it can also add special Photoshop effects. Follow the preceding steps to open the Image submenu and choose **Photoshop Effects**. PageMaker will open the dialog box shown in Figure 8.14. To keep from modifying the original TIFF, PageMaker creates a duplicate for you to apply the effect to. Choose the name offered by PageMaker or enter a different name, perhaps reflecting the effect you apply. Then, pick the effect you want from the list. Click **OK** or press **Enter** to see the results.

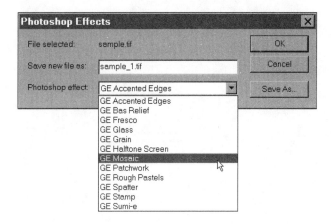

Figure 8.14 *The Photoshop Effects dialog box.*

To Sum Up

In this chapter you learned how easy it is to add color to your document. You've also learned that color really depends on the way the document will be printed: if printed to a color laser printer, virtually any color you create will be replicated when printed. However, if you plan to take the document to a commercial printer, you must specify colors the printer can create. You've learned that except for separating the colors of color photographs, PageMaker offers sophisticated color tools that make it as easy to add, create, and print spot colors as it is to compose the page.

In the next chapter, you will see how easily PageMaker deals with long documents, like books and proposals.

CHAPTER 9

Developing
Long Documents

- ❖ Using the Story Editor
- ❖ Checking your spelling
- ❖ Using the **Find** feature
- ❖ Using the **Change** feature
- ❖ Linking text and graphics
- ❖ Compiling chapters into a book
- ❖ Creating an index
- ❖ Creating a table of contents
- ❖ To sum up

Long documents are multiple-page publications with stories or chapters, possibly containing black- and-white or color photographs or graphic illustrations. Long documents can be magazines and trade publications, professional journals and technical reports, sales presentations and proposals, books (like this one), and catalogs. Long documents are different things to different people. If you are comfortable producing one-page fact sheets, then a twelve-page brochure may seem like a very long document. If you normally work with technical manuals or proposals, then a 200- or 300-page document may not be especially intimidating.

A long document magnifies the multitude of decisions necessary to write, edit, design, lay out, and produce information in the form of a book or manual—your decisions seem to increase exponentially with the number of pages in the document. Consider the problem of changing a proper name. lets say you are producing a proposal for the Parker Active Waste Recycler, and the chairman of the board wants to rename the company after his newborn granddaughter. So now you face changing 342 product name references to Cindilou's Urban Recycling Center. How do you find all those references; how can you be sure you won't miss one or two?

Long documents often involve many writers, editors, designers, graphic artists, managers, reviewers, proofreaders, test readers, and others just wanting to help stir the pot. How can you be sure which is the latest level of revisions to the work? When was the text for Chapter 2 last edited? How can a new chapter be inserted between two chapters? Is there a way of adding a spreadsheet to the text? Is the spreadsheet updated? For computer software manuals and proposals, there's always a new revision needed just around the corner. How do you change the text files without disturbing the layout and pagination of the existing book? Can you edit existing graphics or must they be created from scratch?

It's obvious that long documents require special attention, be they highly stylized color magazines or commercially produced volumes. Whether you are experienced with book-length publishing or not, PageMaker's long-document capabilities make the task a lot easier.

Using the Story Editor

Up to this point, I've suggested you enter text on the page in the document window (what PageMaker calls the *Layout Editor*). The reason for this is that it's a good way to help you learn the software, and typing in the Layout Editor gives you complete WYSIWYG control over the page. However, PageMaker also contains a word processor called the *Story Editor*. Use the Story Editor when writing or editing longer passages of text.

The Story Editor can be a welcome relief from the distractions of working in the page layout. Sometimes the text needs the full attention of a writer or editor who doesn't want to bother with formatting type, aligning graphics, and other layout activities. Using the Story Editor is faster than writing the text in a word processor and then placing the text in PageMaker.

Opening the Story Editor

The Story Editor is not only easy to use, it's easy to access. You'll find yourself switching to the Story Editor often, to make text changes or type new text. Stories that were started on a word processor and placed in PageMaker can be finished or edited in the Story Editor. To open the Story Editor:

1. Choose the **Edit** pull-down menu (or press **Alt+E**).

2. Choose **Edit Story** (or press **E**) to display the story view, shown in Figure 9.1. PageMaker's shortcut for the Story Editor is **Ctrl+E**.

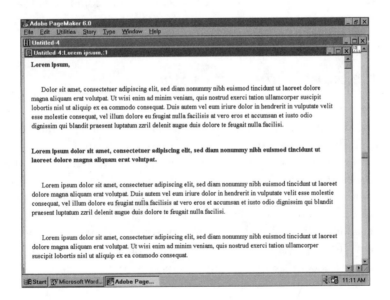

Figure 9.1 *PageMaker's Story Editor Window.*

NOTE

When you're working in the Story Editor, you're seeing the *story view*. When you're in the Layout Editor, you're seeing the *layout view*. To keep from confusing you with these views and the page view size (which is applicable only in the layout view), I will refer to the views as their respective editors.

The Story Editor provides a blank typing area, like a white sheet of paper, to type on. The insertion point is similar to the Text tool insertion point. It marks the position at which characters will be typed or deleted. While you can't use the toolbox tools, if the Styles or Colors palettes were visible in the Layout Editor, they will also be available in the Style Editor, as shown in Figure 9.1 (or, you can open the palettes using the Window pull-down menu). You can mark text in styles and colors the same way you do in the Layout Editor. The colors will not be visible until you switch back to the Layout Editor. Some style changes—namely bold and italics—are shown in the Story Editor. Type size changes are not displayed in the Story Editor, nor are paragraph specification changes (other than indents). The typeface and size displayed in the Story Editor are those specified in the story view area of the Preferences dialog box (**Edit > Preferences**). You may have noticed that some of the commands in the menu bar are different when you are working in the Story Editor. I'll explain the differences in a moment.

How the Story Editor Names Stories

Stories displayed in the Story Editor are named with the first 19 characters of the first sentence of the story. For example, a story beginning "Computers can be grouped according to the type of central processing unit (CPU)" is named **Computers can be gr:1**. The colon and the number 1 indicate that this is the first story with this name (a second story starting with the same first few words would be named with a **:2**, a third story starting with the same words would be named with a **:3,** and so on). Since the Story Editor considers any text block a story, a headline that is in a separate text block would be named by the same convention. If the headline is less than 19 characters long, you will see the whole headline, a colon, and the number 1 as its story name.

Switching between the Story and Layout Editors

There are several ways to move between the Layout Editor and the Story Editor, depending on what you are doing at the moment. For example:

❖ After you access the Story Editor the first time, you can switch between the Story Editor and the Layout Editor using the Window pull-down menu. Although you can open only one document at a time in the Layout Editor, you can open a number of different stories in the Story Editor (based on the amount of memory and free system resources your computer has). The Window pull-down menu, shown in Figure 9.2, was opened while the Layout Editor was active. It shows the opened story in the Story Editor.

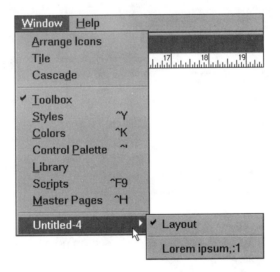

Figure 9.2 *The window pull-down menu shows the story submenu with the stories opened in the current document.*

❖ To move to a different story in the Story Editor, choose the **Window** pull-down menu (or press **Alt+W**) and click the story you want. If you want to move back to the document, click the document file name.

❖ Once you are in the Story Editor, you can move back to the Layout Editor by clicking anywhere in the Layout Editor window. You can move back to the same story in the Story Editor by choosing it from the Window menu (see Figure 9.3).

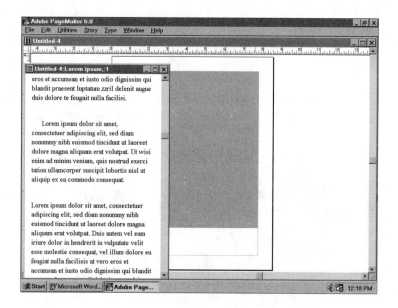

Figure 9.3 *Click the document window to move from the Story Editor to the Layout Editor*

❖ Use the PageMaker shortcut **Ctrl+E** to toggle between the Layout Editor and Story Editor. The position of the insertion point is maintained between the two editors.

❖ Once you are in the Story Editor, click the **Minimize** button to shrink the story window to an icon and reveal the document window (and the Layout Editor) underneath. You can minimize all stories and your document, as shown in Figure 9.4, or double-click on the document or one of the stories to continue work, as shown in Figure 9.5.

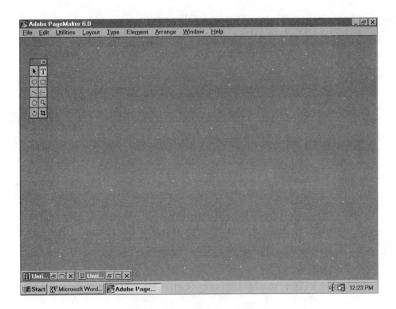

Figure 9.4 *The document and one story minimized in PageMaker.*

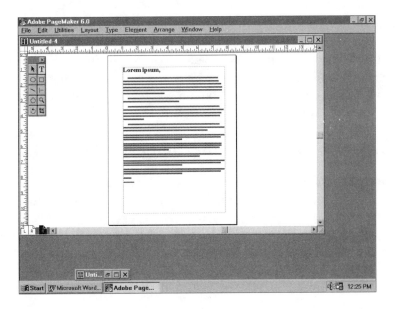

Figure 9.5 *One of the minimized documents is maximized for work.*

Closing the Story Editor and Placing the Story

If you create a new story in the Story Editor, you will want to place the story in the Layout Editor. PageMaker gives you several ways to do this:

❖ Open the File pull-down menu and choose **Place** (or press **Alt+F L**) to place the story. The Story Editor closes and the insertion point changes to a loaded-text icon, indicating that the story is ready to be placed on the page in the Layout Editor.

❖ Close the Story Editor window by double-clicking the **Control-menu** box in the upper-left corner. PageMaker displays an alert dialog box, shown in Figure 9.6, indicating that the story has not been placed.

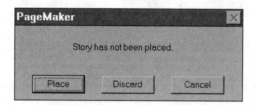

Figure 9.6 *An alert box warns that the story you are closing has not yet been placed.*

To place the story, click the **Place** button. The insertion point changes to a loaded-text icon, indicating that the story is ready to be placed on the page in the Layout Editor. Click the **Discard** button if you want to throw away the story you just finished. Choose **Cancel** to return to the Story Editor.

Differences between the Story and Layout Editors

The most visible difference between the Layout Editor and Story Editor is that in the Story Editor some of the items on the menu bar change, as shown here.

For example, the Story Editor replaces the Layout pull-down menu with the Story menu (shown here), and hides the Element menu (since the Story Editor works only with text, none of the element commands are applicable).

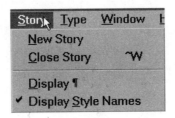

Also, some commands on some of the pull-down menus are not available in the Story Editor. For example:

❖ **File menu**—The **Document Setup** and **Print** commands are dimmed, because you're not working with pages in the Story Editor, just stories. To print what you have done in the Story Editor, first move back to the Layout Editor.

❖ **Utilities menu**—The **Find**, **Find Next**, **Change**, and **Spelling** commands are available in the Story Editor. The first three commands are for searching and replacing text (see "Finding and Changing"), and the **Spelling** command checks spelling (see "Checking Your Spelling"). The menu includes commands for marking words and phrases for an index and for creating an index and a table of contents (see "Creating an Index" and "Creating a Table of Contents").

In the Story Editor, PageMaker defines a story as any single text block. So in a newsletter like the one shown in Figure 9.7, each block of text, including headlines, and bylines, and so on, is considered an individual story in the Story Editor.

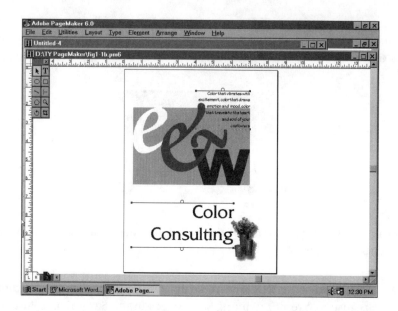

Figure 9.7 *In PageMaker, each block of text, including headlines and bylines, is considered an individual story in the Story Editor*

Text blocks that are threaded together in the Layout Editor comprise the same story in the Story Editor. While a text block may be split among several pages in the Layout Editor, you will see it as a continuous story in the Story Editor.

Although graphics are not displayed in the Story Editor, *in-line graphics* (those that are part of a text block) are shown with the in-line graphic symbol (see below).

Closing the Story Editor

There are several ways to close the Story Editor, including:

❖ Open the Story pull-down menu and choose **Close story** to move back to the Layout Editor. Choose **New story** to open an additional story window to begin typing a new story.

❖ Choose **Place** or **Replace** in the File pull-down menu to close the story, return to the Layout Editor, and place the story you finished in the Story Editor.

❖ Double-click the Control-menu box in the upper-left corner of the Story Editor window to close the window and return to the Layout Editor.

Moving Around the Story

You may have noticed that there are no page number icons at the bottom of the story document windows. That's because stories in the Story Editor aren't related to pages in the Layout Editor. To move up or down the story you can use the scroll bar or one or more of the following keys:

❖ **Page Down** and **Page Up**—Move the insertion point down or up the story screen (if the document window displays 10 lines of text, the insertion point moves down or up the story 10 lines at a time).

❖ **Ctrl+Down Arrow** and **Ctrl+Up Arrow**—Move the insertion point down or up the story a paragraph at a time.

❖ **Ctrl+Page Down**—Moves the insertion point to the end of the story.

❖ **Ctrl+Page Up**—Moves the insertion point to the beginning of the story.

❖ **Left Arrow** and **Right Arrow**—Move the insertion point left or right one character at a time.

❖ **Ctrl+Left Arrow** or **Ctrl+Right Arrow**—Move the insertion point left or right one word at a time.

❖ **Home**—Moves the insertion point left to the beginning of the current line.

❖ **End**—Moves the insertion point right to the end of the line.

Displaying Special Characters

While working in the Story Editor, you may find it helpful to see the hidden marks for spaces, tabs, and paragraphs. When the hidden marks are displayed, you can use the **Find** and **Change** commands to search for the marks and delete them or change them to something else. For example, you could search through the story for tabs and then delete the tabs (see "Using the Find Feature" and "Using the Change Feature").

To display the hidden marks:

1. Choose the **Story** pull-down menu and choose **Display ¶** (or press **Alt+S D**).
2. PageMaker redisplays your story showing the following symbols:

   ❖ **Space markers**—A dot is shown each time the **Spacebar** is pressed.

The·parade·was·

   ❖ **Tab markers**—A tab marker is shown every time the **Tab** key is pressed.

   ❖ **Paragraph marker**—A paragraph marker is shown each time the **Enter** key is pressed.

In addition to the hidden marks, the following symbols are displayed whenever they occur in the text block, regardless of whether or not you are displaying the hidden marks:

   ❖ **In-line graphic marker**—Displayed wherever you have placed an in-line graphic in the text. The graphic itself will not be displayed in the Story Editor.

   ❖ **Page number marker**—Any time you insert a page number marker (**Ctrl+Shift+3**) in the text, a marker symbol, rather than the actual number, is shown in the Story Editor. In the Layout Editor, the actual number is displayed.

   ❖ **Index entry marker**—Shown whenever you have marked a word for inclusion in the publications index.

Displaying Style Names

Style names for each paragraph marked as a style can be displayed in the Story Editor. To display the names, choose the **Display style names** command from the Story pull-down menu. PageMaker adds a left margin to the story window, called a *sidebar*, and displays any style names assigned to paragraphs, as shown in Figure 9.8.

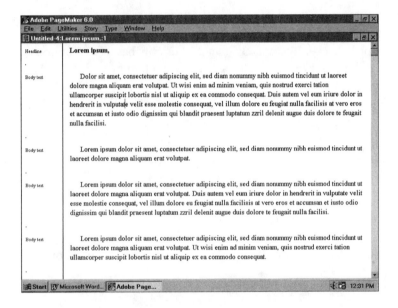

Figure 9.8 *The Story Editor showing the sidebar with style names.*

You will notice some small dots in the sidebar. The dots correspond to each paragraph in the story. Click the dot to highlight the associated paragraph. You can also highlight an entire paragraph by clicking its sidebar style name.

Checking Your Spelling

A speller can be a help or a hindrance, depending on how you use it. A *speller* compares each word in a document with a list of words and calls your attention to any discrepancies. A speller can give you a false sense of confidence that a document is spelled correctly, when it may in fact contain wrong, but correctly spelled, words. For example, the words *principle* and *principal* are both spelled correctly, and the speller does not care which word you use. Nor does a speller help you with words like *it's* and *its*, *bear* and *bare*, or *ware*, *where*, and *wear* (it's up to you to use the correct word). A speller does not understand the correct order of words in a sentence. If, by chance, you transpose two words, the speller will not notice. Similarly, if you type an if where you should have typed an is, the speller will not detect the error.

If you have used earlier versions of PageMaker or if you've used a word processor without spelling capabilities, you know what it's like to dream about having a spell checker. Fortunately, PageMaker now has a full-featured speller that adds a number of related capabilities to its strength in managing long documents. The speller can be used only in the Story Editor.

Starting the Speller

The speller can check any single story in a publication, or all of the stories. To start the speller:

1. Open the Utilities pull-down menu (or press **Alt+U**).

2. Choose **Spelling** (or press **S**) to display the Spelling dialog box, shown in Figure 9.9. For a quick PageMaker shortcut to the speller, press **Ctrl+L**.

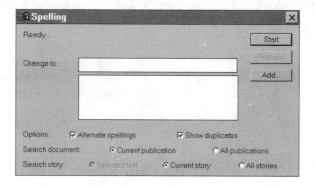

Figure 9.9 *The Spelling dialog box.*

The Spelling dialog box offers the following commands and options:

❖ **Start button**—Click to begin spell checking a story.

❖ **Replace button**—When the speller finds a discrepancy, it highlights the word in the story and displays it in the Change to text box. Edit the word or choose from a list of possible words and press **Replace**. The speller replaces the incorrect word with the one in the text box or with the word you selected from the list.

❖ **Add button**—If the speller comes to a word that isn't in its dictionary, it pauses and highlights the word. If the word is correctly spelled, you may want to add it to the dictionary by clicking the **Add** button.

❖ **Alternate spellings**—The default setting is to have PageMaker suggest alternative spellings to words it does not understand. However, to speed up the spelling program somewhat, you can click this check box to remove the **X** and disable the option.

❖ **Show duplications**—The normal setting for the spelling program is to search for and report duplicate words. Click this check box to remove the **X** if you wish to disable this option.

❖ **Current publication**—You can specify whether you want the speller to check the spelling of the currently displayed publication by clicking the **Current publication** option button or of all open documents by clicking the **All publications** option button.

❖ **Selected text option**—If you have highlighted text with the insertion point and you start the speller, the **Selected text** option button will be marked, indicating only the selected text is checked for spelling.

❖ **Current story option**—If you want to check the spelling of the currently displayed story only, click the **Current story** option button.

❖ **All stories option**—If you want to check the spelling of all stories in the document, click the **All stories** option button.

Positioning the Spelling Dialog Box

If the Spelling dialog box is blocking some text you want to read, click the title bar of the dialog box and drag it to another area of the story window. If you click any-where in the story text while the Spelling dialog box is active, you will move the story window to the foreground, and the Spelling dialog box will move behind it. To activate the speller again, you can either restart it from the Edit pull-down menu or reduce the size of the story window so that you can see and activate it. Simply click on the upper border of the story window (if it is not at the maximum size) and drag it down a bit or click the **minimize** button to reduce the story window to an icon and reveal the Spelling dialog box, as shown in Figure 9.10. Then choose **Start** to begin spell checking. When a misspelled word is located, the story window will automatically maximize, and the word will be highlighted.

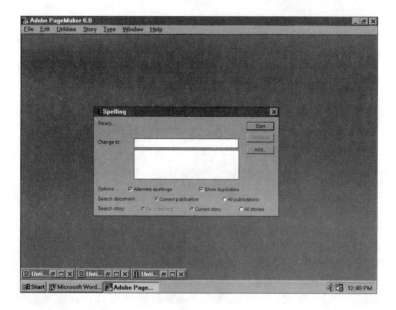

Figure 9.10 A story minimized to reveal the Spelling dialog box underneath it.

Correcting Misspelled Words

To begin the spell checking, click the **Start** button. The speller starts comparing each word in the story with its dictionary from the insertion point position forward to the end of the story. If the speller is started in the middle of a story, when it reaches the end it asks if you want it to go back to the beginning and check the part of the story before the insertion point's location.

At the first spelling discrepancy, the speller pauses to let you know the word doesn't match any of the words in its dictionary, as shown in Figure 9.11.

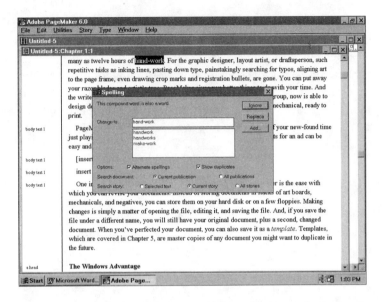

Figure 9.11 *The Speller pauses and highlights a word it doesn't find in its dictionary.*

The misspelled word is displayed in the Change to list box. The speller attempts to identify words in its dictionary that come close to what the misspelled word should be. These words are displayed in a list under the Change to list box. Do one of the following:

❖ If the word is misspelled and the correct word is displayed in the list of possibilities, click the correct word to highlight it and choose **Replace**. The correctly spelled word replaces the misspelled word in the story, and the speller continues spell checking.

❖ If the word is misspelled and the correct word is not displayed in the list of possibilities, position the insertion point in the Change to text box and edit the misspelled word to correct it. Then choose **Replace** to replace the misspelled word with the correctly spelled word in the story. The speller continues spell checking the story.

❖ If the word is misspelled and the speller offers no possible alternatives to choose from, edit the word in the Change to text box and choose **Replace** to replace the misspelled word with the corrected word in the story. The speller continues spell checking the story.

❖ If the word is not misspelled but you don't wish to add it to the spelling dictionary, choose **Ignore**. The speller ignores the word and continues spell checking.

❖ If the word is not misspelled and you want to add it to the spelling dictionary, choose **Add**. The word is added, and from that point on the speller will know how to spell the word. The speller continues spell checking the story. See "Adding Words to Different Dictionaries."

Correcting Duplicate Words

When PageMaker's speller encounters a pair of duplicate words, it stops on the second word, highlights it, and displays *Duplicate word:(name)* in the dialog box, as shown in Figure 9.12.

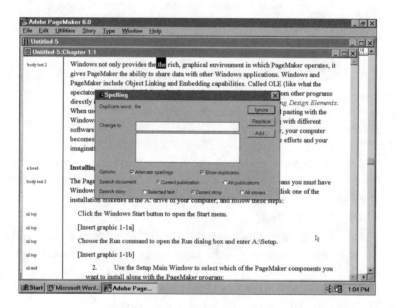

Figure 9.12 *The Speller notifies you of duplicate words.*

If the duplicate words are a typing error, click **Replace** to delete the second occurrence of the word and continue spell checking. If the duplicate words are correct, choose **Ignore** to continue.

Adding Words to the Different Dictionaries

The English language contains a lot of words, more than any other language. There are about 450,000 words defined in *Webster's New International Dictionary*. If you add all the English technical vocabularies (for disciplines like computer science, medicine, engineering, physics, and many others) you will add hundreds of thousands—if not millions—of words. While PageMaker's dictionary is large, you may want to add many technical terms it doesn't contain. Here's how:

1. Start the speller by choosing **Spelling** from the Utilities menu.

2. When the speller encounters a word not currently in its dictionary and you wish to add to your dictionary, choose the **Add** button. The speller displays the Add Word to User Dictionary dialog box, shown in Figure 9.13.

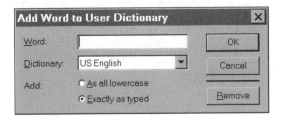

Figure 9.13 *The Add Word to User Dictionary dialog box.*

Use this dialog box to add the highlighted word to the spelling dictionary. This is the same dialog box used to add a hyphenated word to the hyphenation dictionary (see "Adding Words to the Hyphenation Dictionary" in Chapter 3).

3. In the Word text box, change the spelling of the word as you want it to be recorded in the dictionary. Enter tilde marks to indicate the most favorable hyphenation breaks, as explained in Chapter 3.

4. If you have purchased additional dictionaries from Aldus Corporation, click the **Dictionary** list box arrow to open the list of available dictionaries. Choose a different dictionary, if you want.

5. The word will normally be saved in the dictionary in all lowercase letters. If you want the word to be saved as shown in the Word text box, click the **Exactly as typed** option button.

6. To save the word in the dictionary, click **OK** or press **Enter**. To cancel the word, choose **Cancel**. You will return to the Spelling dialog box. Click the **Continue** button to continue spell checking the story.

Removing Words from the Dictionaries

You can remove any word from the spelling and hyphenation dictionaries. To remove a word, type the word in the Word text box and click the **Remove** button. The word is removed. Click **OK** or press **Enter** to return to the Spelling dialog box.

Closing the Speller

When the speller finishes checking the document, it reports *No spelling errors* detected in the dialog box. Close the dialog box by clicking the **Close** button. Likewise, you can close the speller at any time while you are spell checking a document by using the **Close** button.

Using the Find Feature

In long documents, corrections are often multiplied by the number of pages involved. For example, if a model number changes, there may be many references to the old model number in the document. Each reference must be ferreted out and changed; there can be no old model numbers remaining. PageMaker's **Find** feature is capable of finding all instances of the theoretical old model number, and, when used with the **Change** feature, can change the old number to the new one automatically.

Like the speller, the **Find** feature has some limitations. It's very literal and finds *exactly* what you request. For example, if you ask PageMaker to find all occurrences of the word *men*, it finds the word, but it also finds any words with *men* in the word, such as *women, elements, cumbersomeness, gentlemen,* and *immense*. The reason for this is simple: you didn't tell PageMaker to look for complete words. If you had added a space before and after the word, PageMaker would have located only the exact matches you were looking for. The lesson here is to be careful and literal when you want to either find or change something.

Searching for Words

There are any number of reasons why you might want to search for a word in a document, from outright changing the word to altering the type specifications to simply moving to an area of the story where you know the word is located. To access the **Find** feature and search for a word:

1. Position the insertion point where you want to begin the search.

2. Open the Utilities pull-down menu and choose **Find** (or press **Alt+U F**) to display the Find dialog box, shown in Figure 9.14. Or Use PageMaker's shortcut, **Ctrl+F**.

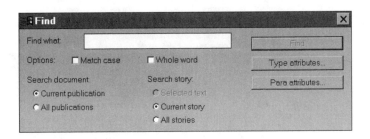

Figure 9.14 *The Find dialog box.*

3. Type the word you wish to search for in the Find what text box. Enter the word *exactly* as you want PageMaker to search for it. For example, if you were searching for figure references in this chapter to check the sequence of figure numbering, you might enter the word **figure**. PageMaker would not only find the figure references, but any in-text references to the figures as well. By entering **Figure 9**, Find takes you only to numbered figure references, in order. By entering **Figure 9.9**, PageMaker takes you to that exact figure reference.

4. Choose **Find** to find the first instance of the word you entered. PageMaker searches from the insertion point forward to locate the first occurrence of the word. The word is highlighted when found, as shown in Figure 9.15.

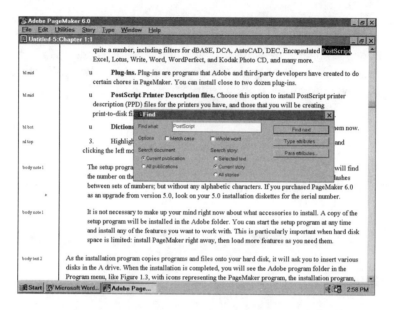

Figure 9.15 *A word found with the* **Find** *command*

5. To search for the next occurrence of the word, click the **Find next** button (after finding the first occurrence of the word or phrase, the **Find** button changes to the **Find next** button).

   If you began your search in the middle of the story, when PageMaker reaches the end of the story you'll be asked if the search should continue from the beginning.

6. To close the Find dialog box, click the **Close** button.

Using Find Next

Once you have located your first occurrence of the word or phrase with the Find dialog box and closed the box, you can use the **Find next** command to search again for the same word or phrase. There is no dialog box. **Find next** simply highlights the word or phrase when found, or reports that there are no more occurrences of the word or phrase.

Positioning the Find Dialog Box

If the Find dialog box is in the way of some text you want to read, click the title bar of the dialog box and drag it out of the way. You can place the dialog box anywhere on the page, even tuck some of it under the bottom border of the Story editor's window, as shown in Figure 9.16 (just leave enough showing so that you can still click the **Find** button).

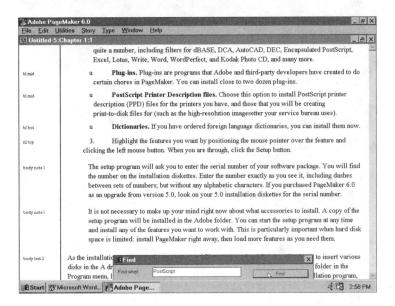

Figure 9.16 *Position the Find dialog box to make it accessible
even when the story window is at its maximum size.*

If you click anywhere in the story text while the Find dialog box is active, you will move the story window to the foreground and the Find dialog box behind it. To activate the Find dialog box again, you can restart it from the Edit pull-down menu, or by reducing the size of the story window, you can see and activate it. Simply click on the upper border of the story window (if it is not at the maximum size) and drag it down a bit. If the story window is maximized, click the **Minimize** button to reduce the story window to an icon and reveal the Find dialog box beneath it, as shown in Figure 9.17. Then choose **Find** to search for the word entered in the Find what text box, or type in a different word. When the word is located, the story window automatically maximizes, and the word is highlighted.

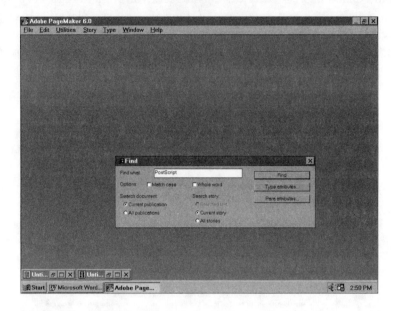

Figure 9.17 *Minimize the story window to an icon to see the Find dialog box.*

Matching the Case of Words

Normally, the **Find** feature looks for both lowercase and uppercase versions of the word you are searching for. If you want PageMaker to match the uppercase and lowercase letters exactly as typed in the Find what text box, click the **Match** option box to add a check in the box. Then, if you enter a proper name or a word with an unusual case structure (like **LaserJet**), PageMaker will find it but not lowercase versions of the word.

Matching Only Whole Words

If you are looking, for example, for all references of the word *ion* and you don't wish to find every word ending in *tion*, click the **Whole word** option box to add a check mark. Then PageMaker will find only the whole word you entered in the Find what text box.

Defining the Search Pattern

If you have highlighted text to search, the **Selected text** option button will be checked. If it's not, the **Current story** option button will be checked. If you want to search all the stories in the current document, click the **All stories** option button. To look through the current story only, leave the **Current publi- cation** option button checked. To look through all open publications, click the **All publications** option button.

Searching with Wildcard Characters

Wildcard is a software term that has come to mean a special character or charac- ters that represent any other character. In PageMaker, the wildcard is the caret symbol (**Shift + 6** on the keyboard) together with the question mark. A wildcard is useful when you are searching for a word and are not entirely sure how you spelled the word. For example, you want to find the word *rendezvous*, but you can't remember if you spelled it correctly or if you changed the *ez* to *is*. To ensure that PageMaker finds the word regardless of the two letters in question, you could replace the two letters with wildcards. In the Find what text box, you would type **rend^?^?vous.** PageMaker would search for the word without regard to the two letters between the *d* and the *v*, and find each occurrence of the word.

Searching for Phrases

You can enter a phrase or individual words in the Find what dialog box. Just be sure of the order and spelling of the words, and use wildcards where you are not sure. To enter a phrase, simply type the words you want in the text box (you can enter as long a string of words as you want). Use the **Right** and **Left Arrow** keys to move through the phrase. Use the **Del** or **Backspace** key to delete words. Or highlight the word and type the correction. When you are finished entering the phrase in the text box click the **Find** button to search for the string of words.

Searching for Type Attributes

PageMaker can find not only words, but also words with specific type attributes. For example, PageMaker can find instances of the word *IBM-PC* when used in the Caption style and when specified in 9-point Helvetica Narrow italic. Or it could identify all uses of the word *PageMaker* in second-order headlines, when specified in 24-point bold Palatino. To identify the special attributes you want to search for:

1. Click the **Attributes** button in the Find dialog box to display the Find Type Attributes dialog box, shown in Figure 9.18.

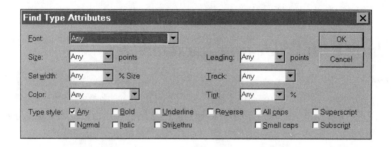

Figure 9.18 *The Find Type Attributes dialog box.*

2. Use this dialog box to set up specific attributes for the word or phrase you want to find. Choose among the following options:

    ❖ **Font**—Click the list box arrow to display PageMaker's list of fonts. The list box defaults to **Any**, meaning that all fonts currently used in the document are eligible for searching. You may select a font to be included in the search criteria.

    ❖ **Size**—Click the list box arrow to display a list of type sizes. The list box defaults to **Any**, meaning all sizes of type are eligible for searching. You may select a specific size to be included in the search criteria.

    ❖ **Set width**—Click open the list box and select the width of type you want to search for. The list box defaults to **Any**, meaning all widths will be included in the search.

    ❖ **Type style**—All of the styles are available to select as a part of the criteria for your search. **Any** means that all styles will be included in the search you define. Click the appropriate box to select the styles you want.

❖ **Leading**—You can search for type with specific size leading. Enter the leading value in the box. Choose **Any** to include all leading sizes as a part of the criteria for your search.

❖ **Track**—Choose the amount of tracking assigned to the type you want to find.

❖ **Color/Tint**—You can search for type in any color and any percentage of tint. Leave the text boxes defined as **Any** to include all colors and all tints in your search criteria.

3. When you have selected the attributes you want for this search criteria, click **OK** or press **Enter** to return to the Find dialog box. Click the **Find** button to begin the search.

In addition to locating type-related criteria, PageMaker can search for specific styles. Click the **Para attributes** button in the Find dialog box. PageMaker will open the Find Paragraph Attributes dialog box.

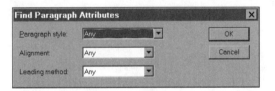

Then, click open the **Paragraph Style** list box and select the style you want to search for. You can also search for text that has a specific alignment or text with leading aligned by PageMaker's different methods.

Searching for Special Characters

PageMaker can find not only specific styles and type attributes, it can also locate a multitude of special characters, many of them hidden characters or codes. The following table provides a complete list of special characters and the sequence to type in the Find What text box in order to search for them:

To search for this special character:	Enter this in text box:
Beginning "curly" quotation marks (")	^{
Ending "curly" quotation marks (")	^}
Beginning single "curly" quotation mark (')	^[
Ending single "curly" quotation mark (')	^]
Embedded page numbers (RM LM)	^3
Bullet	^8
Registered trademark symbol	^r
Copyright symbol	^2
Paragraph symbol (¶)	^7
Section symbol (§)	^6
Index entry	^;
In-line graphic marker	^g
Em space	^m
En space	^>
Thin space	^<
Nonbreaking space	^s
Nonbreaking hyphen	^~
Discretionary or soft hyphen	^-
Em dash	**^+Shift+-**
En dash	^=
Nonbreaking slash	^/
Tab	^t
Soft return	^n
End of paragraph or hard return	^p

When the special characters are used in conjunction with the **Change** command, you can find (and change) literally any character in any format, as well as many of PageMaker's hidden codes.

Searching for Bookmarks

Although PageMaker doesn't have a bookmark feature, bookmarks are very useful in marking your place in a long document. It's easy enough to make a "bookmark". The key to a bookmark is using the **Find** command to take you back to it. Here's how:

1. Place a "bookmark" in the text where you are currently working. The bookmark can be any letter or symbol, but it's a good idea to make it unique to the document (using the dollar sign, for example, isn't a good idea because you might use dollar signs in the text as well). I use two question marks as a bookmark, but anything not ordinarily used in text will do nicely.

2. To find the bookmark, simply choose **Find** from the Edit menu, enter the bookmark in the Find what text box, and click the **Find** button. PageMaker takes you to your bookmark. Remember to delete the bookmark before continuing.

It's easy to set up multiple bookmarks in the same document by numbering them. For example, the first bookmark is *??1*, the second bookmark is *??2*, and so forth.

It's a good idea, before printing, to check your stories for bookmarks you may have failed to delete. you'll see how in the next section.

Using the Change Feature

The **Change** feature is often the next step after finding something—you want to change it to something else—that's why **Change** incorporates the **Find** command with the **Change** command in one dialog box. An easy example of using the **Change** command is to replace the two hard returns often added between paragraphs in text with one hard return. Simply invoke the **Change** command, search for double hard returns (by using ^^**p**), and replace with one ^**p**. In a long document, you will save a great deal of time and manual changing.

Replacing Text

The **Change** command can also be used to replace multiple occurrences of one word with another word. For example, it would be an easy matter to replace all occurrences of the word **PageMaker** in this book with **Adobe PageMaker 6** by using the **Change** command. Just enter **PageMaker** as the word to search for, and **Adobe PageMaker 6** as the text with which to replace the word. The **Change** command is very similar in use to the **Find** command. Follow these steps:

1. Since you will be making changes to your story, save the document first by choosing **Save** from the File menu (or press **Ctrl+S**). Then, if you change something incorrectly, use the **Revert** command to go back to the version of the document before you started these steps.

2. Open the Utilities pull-down menu and choose **Change** (or press **Alt+U H**) to display the Change dialog box, shown in Figure 9.19. PageMaker's shortcut to the Change dialog box is **Ctrl+H**.

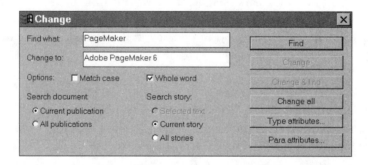

Figure 9.19 *The Change dialog box.*

3. Enter the word or words you want to search for in the Find what text box.

4. Enter the replacement word or words in the Change to text box.

5. Now define how word or phrase matches will take place:

   ❖ To match the exact uppercase or lowercase letters in a word or phrase, click the **Match case** check box.

   ❖ If the search will not be case-sensitive, leave the **Match case** option box unchecked.

   ❖ If you want the text in the Find what text box to match the whole word, click the **Whole word** check box.

❖ If you want partial matches of the text in the Find what text box (so that searching, for example, for *add* would also find *addition*), leave the **Match case** option box unchecked.

6. If you have selected text in the story to be searched, the **Selected text** option button will be checked. If not, the **Current story** option button will be checked. If you want to search all stories in the current document, click the **All stories** option button.

Once you have defined what you are searching for and with what you are replacing the text, you have the following choices.

❖ Click the **Find** button to find the first occurrence of the text you entered in the Find what text box. PageMaker begins searching from the insertion point forward and highlights the first instance of the searched-for word or phrase. If you want to change this occurrence, click the **Change** button. If not, continue searching by clicking the **Find next** button.

❖ Click the **Change** button to change only this occurrence of the searched-for word or phrase. Click the **Find next** button to find the next occurrence.

❖ Clicking the **Change & find** button is the same as clicking the **Change** button and then the **Find next** button. **Change & find** changes the currently found occurrence of the word or phrase and searches for the next occurrence.

❖ Click the **Change all** button to find and change all occurrences of the searched-for word or phrase. Take care in using this option, as it can result in strange, unexpected combinations of words.

Replacing Type Attributes

Attributes can be assigned to both the searched-for text and the replacement text. The steps are easy:

1. Click the **Type attributes** button in the Change dialog box to display the Change Type Attributes dialog box, shown in Figure 9.20.

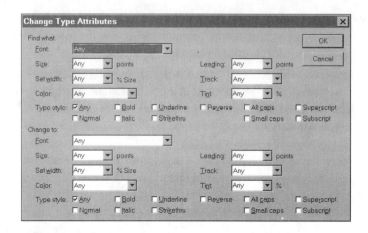

Figure 9.20 *The Change Type Attributes dialog box.*

2. Use this dialog box to set up specific attributes for the searched-for word or phrase. Then select the attributes you want to assign to the replacement word or phrase. Choose among the following options:

❖ **Font**—Click the list box arrow to display PageMaker's list of fonts. The list box defaults to **Any**, meaning that all fonts currently used in the document are eligible for changing. You may select a font to be included in the criteria.

❖ **Size**—Click the list box arrow to display a list of type sizes. The list box defaults to **Any**, meaning all sizes of type are eligible for changing. You may select a specific size to be included in the criteria.

❖ **Set width**—Click open the list box and select the width of type you want to change. The list box defaults to **Any**, meaning all widths will be included.

❖ **Type style**—All of the styles are available to select as a part of the criteria. **Any** means that all styles will be included in what you define. Click the appropriate box to select the styles you want.

❖ **Leading**—You can change type with any specific leading. Enter the leading value in the box. Choose **Any** to include all leading sizes as a part of the criteria.

❖ **Track**—Choose the amount of tracking assigned to type that you want to change.

❖   **Color/Tint**—You can change type in any color and any percentage of tint. Leave the text boxes defined as Any to include all colors and all tints in your criteria.

3.   When you have selected the attributes you want for the search and replacement criteria, click **OK** or press **Enter** to return to the Change dialog box.

Linking Text and Graphics

Whenever text and graphics are imported or placed into a document, PageMaker links the file automatically. The *link* is an invisible connection between the application that created the file (called the *external application*) and the copy of the application's files used in the PageMaker document (called the *linked text element* or the *linked graphic element*). The link is fluid. As the external application makes changes to the file, the linked element is changed whenever the PageMaker document is opened or whenever you manually update the link.

With text and graphics linked to a PageMaker document, many people can continue refining their parts of a document, while the document itself is designed, formatted, and composed in PageMaker. For example, in developing a large proposal in PageMaker, the engineering department can continue editing and amending the technical sections written in WordPerfect files that are linked to the PageMaker proposal. The art department can continue altering graphics files of drawings made in Micrografx Designer that are also linked to the PageMaker document. And the financial wizards can continue recalculating material costs and milestone payments in Microsoft Excel spreadsheets linked to the same PageMaker document. While the changes are being made, the internal linked text and graphic elements are updated so that when the proposal is printed for reviews, it is current.

Any application's files that can be imported or placed in PageMaker are linked (PageMaker will even link other PageMaker documents). However, the application's files must be accessible to PageMaker, either on a floppy or hard disk of the computer or on the file server in a recognized search drive of a network. It is important to keep in mind that the link is a one-way street; updates go from the external file to the linked element, but changes you make in PageMaker to the linked element don't update the external application's file.

Checking the Status of Links

The status of all links in a document are available at any time through the Links dialog box, shown in Figure 9.21. Open the dialog box by choosing the **Links** command from the File pull-down menu (**File > Links**).

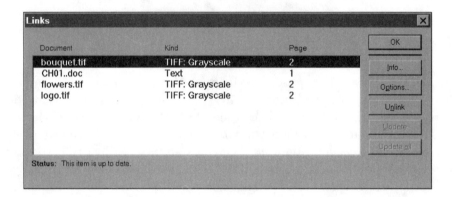

Figure 9.21 The Links dialog box.

Currently linked files are displayed in this dialog box, indicating the file name, the kind of file, and the page of the document. Choose a file by clicking it, and the status of the file is described in the Status line.

Link Status Codes

Status marks next to the file name show the current status of the linked file. You will see one of the following codes:

❖ **A question mark (?)** means the internal element's external file cannot be found. To locate the external file, click the file displaying the question mark and choose the **Link Info** button to display the Link Info dialog box.

❖ **NA** means the item in question has no link. Instead it was pasted as an OLE embedded object.

❖ **A plus sign (+)** next to a file name means that the external file has been updated since the file was placed or imported, and the internal element needs to be updated. Choose the **Update** or **Update all** button to manually update the file. If you have set up automatic updating for the document in the Link options dialog box, the internal element is updated automatically when the document is opened or printed.

❖ **A minus sign (-)** next to a file name also means that the external file has been updated and the internal element has not. But the minus sign also indicates that automatic updating has not been chosen for the file and that you must choose **Update** or **Update all** to update the internal element.

❖ **An exclamation point (!)** next to a file name means that not only the external file, but also the internal linked element, has been updated.

❖ **A diamond (♦)** means that the internal copy of the item has been modified.

❖ **No status indicator** means that everything is up to date with the file and no updates are required.

The type of file is listed under the Kind heading in the dialog box. Word processing files are listed as text, and graphics files are listed by the type of graphic (draw or image).

The Page column notes on which page the linked element was placed:

❖ A number in the Page column represents the page number where a file was placed, even if the file extends to more pages.

❖ **UN**—PageMaker doesn't know the location of the element. It's still in the Story Editor and hasn't been placed.

❖ **LM**—The element is placed on the left master page.

❖ **RM**—The element is placed on the right master page.

❖ **PB**—The element currently resides on the pasteboard.

❖ **OV**—Stands for *overset text*; it means that an in-line graphic is part of a text block that hasn't been placed on a page, or has been only partially placed.

Displaying Link Information

To display file information about the linked element, choose the **Link Info** button in the Link dialog box, shown in Figure 9.22, or double-click the file whose link information you want to see. In the Layout Editor, you can also position the insertion point in the linked text and choose **Link info** from the Elements pull-down menu (**Elements > Link info**).

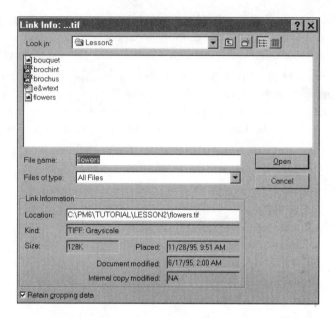

Figure 9.22 *The Link Info dialog box*

The dialog box gives the following information about the linked element:

- ❖ **Path**—The current path to the external file.
- ❖ **Name**—The current name of the linked element.
- ❖ **Location**—The name of the external file.
- ❖ **Kind**—The type of file this is, as described in the Links dialog box.
- ❖ **Size**—The current size of the external file.
- ❖ **Placed**—The date and time that the file was placed in PageMaker.
- ❖ **Original Modified**—The date and time of the last modification to the external file.
- ❖ **Internal Copy Modified**—The date and time of the last modification to the linked element.

To replace the current linked element with another external file, choose the file from the Directories list box or type the path and file name in the File name text box. Then choose the **Link** button.

Linking Files Versus Pasting Files

As stated earlier, any file that is physically accessible can be linked to a PageMaker document. However, when you paste text from the Clipboard into a document, it is not linked and will not be listed in the Link dialog box because PageMaker must establish a direct connection from the linked element to the original file created by another application.

The Clipboard can paste embedded linked elements. You can cut linked text from one PageMaker document and paste it into another PageMaker document, and the link will transfer to the new document.

Setting Link Options

The **Link** feature has certain options for text and graphic files that determine how linked elements are updated and how elements are stored (an important consideration with very large graphic files). Choose one of the following ways of displaying the Link options dialog box:

❖   To set up or change default link options that will be in effect for all future links in PageMaker documents, without opening a document window, choose the **Link options** command from the Element menu (**Element > Link Options**). You will see the Link Options: Defaults dialog box, shown in Figure 9.23. Use this dialog box to determine for both text and graphics how the linked element will be stored, whether the element will be updated automatically, and whether you will be alerted before updating. Click the appropriate option boxes.

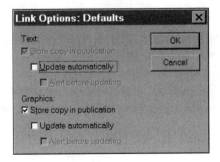

Figure 9.23 *The Links Options: Defaults dialog box.*

❖ When a document has been opened or you have selected a text block, choose **Link Options** from the Element menu to display the Link Options dialog box, shown in Figure 9.24. This window is either the text or graphics half of the default dialog box, depending on what you have selected. While you cannot change where the linked element is stored, you can request automatic updates.

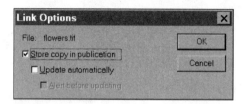

Figure 9.24 *The Link Options dialog box.*

❖ If you have selected a linked element in the Links dialog box, click the **Link Options** button to display the Link Options dialog box. The same options are available.

Click **OK** or press **Enter** to save the options and return to either the document or the Links dialog box.

Compiling Chapters into a Book

The **Book** command essentially takes the idea of linking one step further and links all the chapters of a book together—there is no single large document. You still work with the chapters individually, but your individual documents become parts of a book. If you have ten chapters, two appendices, a glossary, and an introduction—each a separate PageMaker document—the **Book** command links them together in the right order, and even straightens out page numbering. And it compiles the book without ever creating a document of the combined files. So you're not forced to work with a large cumbersome document that is slow to use, save, and move around in. Keep in mind that what PageMaker calls a **book** can be any large document that you write in smaller sections. A magazine could just as easily be the "book" with individual stories and ads comprising the "chapters."

Preparing the Book

Plan a little before rushing ahead with the creation of a book, manual, or proposal. How do you want to present information: topically or functionally? Who is the audience for this publication? How many chapters will cover the subject without discouraging the reader? What will be the unified look of the chapter layout? All of these questions, and many more, must be answered before the idea can be developed effectively.

Use the tools that PageMaker provides to help you produce a professional-looking publication. Chapters should have a uniform look, develop a chapter template for the page size, margins, headers, and footers. The book should have an understandable hierarchy of headings so that the reader will always know the relationship of the section being read to the preceding sections and the sections to come. Set up your headings as styles to make them consistent. Make each chapter a separate document. Make the introduction, preface, foreword, and each appendix a separate document. You can even create empty documents for the table of contents and the index—you'll need them eventually. When you have done all this (and finished the writing), you are ready to combine all the separate documents into one book.

Combining the Chapters

To create the book:

1. Open the first document for the book (perhaps the introduction or table of contents).

2. Open the Utilities pull-down menu and choose **Book** (or press **Alt+U B**) to display the Book Publication List dialog box, shown in Figure 9.25.

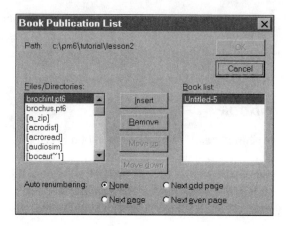

Figure 9.25 *The Book Publication List dialog box.*

3. Use the Book Publication List dialog box to select each part of the book (chapters, index, glossary, introduction, and so on) and insert them in order into the publication list.

4. Use the Files/Directories list box to display the document names you want. Scroll up or down the list or double-click on a different directory to change to that directory. Click a different drive letter to change to that drive.

5. When the document names are displayed, click each document name and then the **Insert** button to add the name to the Book list box.

6. Add to the book list all of the document names that comprise the book. To change the order of the list, click a document name and click the **Move up** or **Move down** button to move the name up or down one position. To remove a document name from the book list, click the **Remove** button.

7. When you're finished, click **OK** or press **Enter** to return to your document.

To perform book-oriented tasks such as building the index and table of contents and printing the book, you must repeat steps 1 through 7 in each document you have just added to the book list in the dialog box. Or you can use this easy shortcut:

1. Choose the **Book** command again (if you are no longer working in the document to which you have added the first book list, open that document and then choose the **Book** command).

2. Before clicking the **Book** command, hold down the **Ctrl** key. Instead of displaying the Book Publications List dialog box again, this opens a message box that shows the book list being copied to each of the documents in the list.

That's all there is to it! The book list is added to each document in the list. Before leaving the Book Publications List dialog box, let's talk about page numbering.

WARNING

If you change the external file names or the document names of the internally linked files of any of the documents in the book list, those documents will no longer be associated with the book list. You must add the new document names to the book list using the Book Publications List dialog box and recopy the book list to each document in the list.

Numbering Pages

Do not attempt to add page numbers manually to the pages of your document. As I have explained earlier in this book, simply add the page number marker (**Ctrl+Shift+3**) to the master page(s)—PageMaker takes care of the rest. But what happens when the individual chapters of a book, each of which already has page number markers, are combined using the **Book** command? You choose among four page numbering schemes in the Auto Renumbering area of the Book Publication List dialog box. When used in conjunction with the **Restart page numbering** option box in the Document Setup dialog box, the schemes cover virtually every condition that may be encountered in numbering the pages of a book:

❖ **None**—Choose **None** if you want the page numbers for each chapter and section of the book to begin with 1. Use the **Restart page numbering** option box in the Page Setup dialog box to start a particular chapter with a number other than 1.

❖ **Next page**—Numbers the book consecutively from 1, or whatever number you enter in the Restart page number text box in the Page Setup dialog box.

❖ **Next odd page**—Choose this option if you want each section and chapter entered in the book list to begin on an odd-numbered page. Generally, books begin sections and chapters on right-hand pages, which are normally odd-numbered.

❖ **Next even page**—Choose this option if you want each section and chapter entered in the book list to begin on an even-numbered page.

Restarting Page Numbering

Use the Restart page number text box in the Document Setup dialog box to restart the numbering of any section or chapter listed in the book list. Here's how:

1. Open the document that is the section or chapter in the book list for which you want to restart page numbering.

2. Choose the **Document Setup** command on the File menu to display the Document Setup dialog box, shown in Figure 9.26.

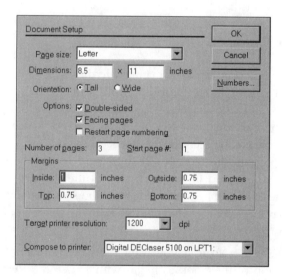

Figure 9.26 *The Document Setup dialog box.*

3. Click the **Restart page numbering** option box and enter the number to start with in the Start page # text box. Normally you will enter **1** as the number to restart with, but you can enter any number you want.

4. Click **OK** or press **Enter** to return to your document.

The page numbers for this section or chapter will now restart from the number you specified. For example, you could have four documents in the book list representing the front matter of the book: the acknowledgment, dedication, preface, and table of contents. These four sections are numbered consecutively, but you want the first page of Chapter 1 to be numbered 1. By opening the Chapter 1 document and choosing the **Restart numbering** feature, Chapter 1 will be numbered the way you want.

Now, let's decide what style page numbers to use.

Defining Numbers for Pages

You can choose a distinct numbering style for the whole book or for individual sections and chapters of the book. For example, you can number the front matter with lowercase roman numerals (i, ii, iii, iv, and so forth), the chapters of the book with Arabic numerals (1, 2, 3, 4, and so forth), and the appendix pages alphabetically.

To change the style:

1. Open the document in which the numbering will begin. For example, if you are establishing numbering for the front matter, open the first document, such as the preface, in the front matter; if you are setting the numbering style for the chapters, open Chapter 1.

2. Open the Document Setup dialog box. Click the **Numbers** button to display the Page Numbering dialog box, shown in Figure 9.27.

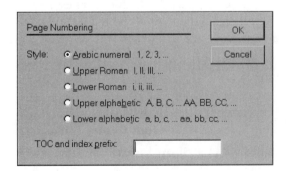

Figure 9.27 *The Page Numbering dialog box.*

3. Choose the numbering style you want for this part of the book.

NOTE

The front matter of a book is usually numbered with roman numerals. The chapters are usually numbered with Arabic numerals.

4. If you have added text to the page number markers ("Page 14" instead of "14"), you can add the same text to the table of contents and index page numbers by entering the text in the TOC and Index prefix text box. Just type the text instead of a page number or the page number marker.

Creating an Index

Indexing books is very complicated. There are people who make their living solely by indexing books for publishers. For an index to be useful, it should contain all the subjects a potential reader will likely search for, as well as All the page references and cross-references for each subject. These tasks are most suitable for a computer (with some advance planning). One of PageMaker's strongest features is its indexing capability.

To create a good index, you must approach the book as if you were a first-time reader. Forget that you just finished writing it or contributed to its production. Now, you are a new reader thumbing through it for the first time. Ask yourself: if I wanted to find a certain subject, what indexed words would I want to see? What cross-referencing would be helpful? Which index entries are frivolous and which have substance? Work through the eyes of the reader and you will build a good index. Work through the eyes of the writer and you may wind up with some gaping holes in your index.

To create an index:

1. Mark each occurrence of the individual words and phrases you want to include in the index using the **Index entry** command.

2. Edit the entries with the **Show index** command, add second- and third-level subentries to further define the index entries. Add cross references where necessary.

3. Build the index using the **Create index** command.

To mark text as an index entry:

1. Switch to the Story Editor to mark index entries (PageMaker shows you the index marks in Story view).

2. Highlight the word or phrase you want to appear in the index.

3. Open the Utilities pull-down menu and choose **Index entry** (or press **Alt+U E**) to display the Add Index Entry dialog box, shown in Figure 9.28.

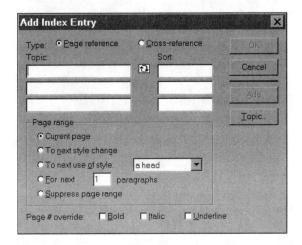

Figure 9.28 *The Add Index Entry dialog box.*

4. Use the dialog box to enter, edit, and configure page-referenced and cross-referenced index entries. In the Type area of the dialog box, click the **Page reference** option button to enter a page reference.

Setting Up Page-Referenced Index Entries

Page-referenced index entries are entries with page numbers referring the reader to text concerning the entry. To set up a page-referenced entry:

1. Enter the index topic and any subtopics for the entry. Notice that there are three text boxes under Topic and three under Sort. These are first-, second-, and third-level areas in which you may enter up to three levels of topics. For example, an automotive repair manual might index the word *steering* as:

Level 1: FWD Steering

Level 2: Adjusting the rack and pinion system

Level 3: FWD minimum wheel clearance

These would be entered in the Add Index Entry dialog box as shown.

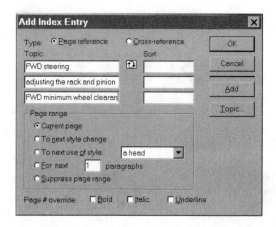

The three sort boxes allow you to specify a different word to sort that is different from the word in the topic box. For example, in the illustration, you could enter the word **front** next to the level 1 topic *FWD Steering*, and the entry would be positioned alphabetically based on *f-r-o*, not *f-w-d*.

2. Change the order of the topic and subtopics by clicking the **looped-arrow** icon. Each time you click the icon, the topics shift down one text box. Any sort terms shift with their associated topics.

3. Choose one of the Page range option buttons:

    ❖ **Current page**—The page number for the current page on which the entry appears will be shown in the index.

    ❖ **To next style change**—Choose this option to show a range of page numbers that includes the current page on which the entry appears and all subsequent pages until PageMaker encounters a style change. This usually means that the whole subsection from the current page number forward will be noted in the index. For example, if you have the word *steering* in a subsection called "Alignment" on page 151, and body copy continues for four additional pages until the next subhead, the index entry with this page-range option would look like: *Steering 151-155.* If the five pages offer a viable explanation of steering, or if this is a crucial area that discusses steering, assign the index entry this page-range option. However, if there is little relevant information about steering on the five pages, don't make the reader wade through the text by using a range of pages. Choose the **Current page** option instead.

❖ **To next use of style**—Choose this option to note where the discussion of the index entry ends (at the change of a style). Choose the style by clicking the **Style** list box arrow to display the list of styles.

❖ **For next _ paragraphs**—Choose this option if you know that the discussion using the indexed entry continues for a known number of paragraphs. Enter the number of paragraphs in the text box.

❖ **Suppress page range**—Choose this to temporarily prevent the page number from being added to the index entry.

4. Choose one of the Page # override options to change the style of the page numbers. If the previously defined page number style is Normal, choosing one of these options will change the style to the option box style. If the page number style is already in one of the option styles, choosing the style here will cancel the style, and the page numbers will revert back to Normal. For example, if the previously defined page number style is Normal, an index entry might look like this:

Steering 151

If you click the **Bold** option box, the page number portion of the entry would change to:

Steering **151**

However, if the previously defined page number style is Bold, the entry would look like this:

Steering 151

If you then click the **Bold** option box, the page number portion of the entry would revert to the Normal style and look like this:

Steering 151

The same rules apply with the **Italic** and **Underline** option boxes.

5. Click the **Add** button to add another index entry without having to close and reopen the dialog box.

6. Click the **Topic** button to display the Select Topic dialog box, shown in Figure 9.29, to move to a different index topic.

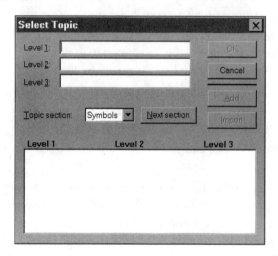

Figure 9.29 *The Select Topic dialog box.*

Managing Page Reference Topics

The Select Topic dialog box gives you a concise view of all existing topics that have been added to the index, as well as the topic you are currently working on. Use the dialog box to add additional topics or a second- or third-level subtopic to an existing topic. Following are some of the ways you can use this dialog box:

❖ **Choose a topic**—Click the **Topic section** list box arrow to open the list box, and scroll down the alphabetic list of letters to choose a topic. As you display a letter of the alphabet in the list box, the topics scroll to that letter. Click the topic, and it and its associated second- and third-level subtopics (if any) appear in the Level 1, Level 2, and Level 3 list boxes.

❖ **Change the names of a displayed topic**—Edit the words in the list box to make them consistent with other similar topics.

❖ **Add subtopics**—For a topic without subtopics, click in the **Level 2** or **Level 3** subtopic list box and type a subtopic. Click the **Add** button to add the subtopic to the lists.

❖ **Capitalize the first letter of every Level 1 topic**—Hold down the **Ctrl** key and click the **Next section** list box arrow to capitalize the first letter of all first-level topics.

❖ **Capitalize the first letter of every Level 2 and Level 3 subtopic**— Hold down **Ctrl+Shift** and click the **Next section** list box arrow to capitalize the first letters of all second- and third-level subtopics.

❖ **Import topics for other documents in the book list**—Click the **Import** button to import the list of topics and subtopics for all other documents in the book list of which the current document is a part. This ensures consistency across all the sections and chapters in the book.

Click **OK** or press **Enter** to return to the Add Index Entry dialog box.

Setting Up Cross-Referenced Index Entries

Cross-referenced index entries refer the reader to other page-referenced index entries. In the cross-referenced entry:

Steering wheel, see Hub assembly

Steering wheel is the index entry, *see Hub assembly* is the cross-reference. To set up a cross-referenced entry:

1. Enter the index topic and any subtopics for the entry described above.

2. Change the order of the topic and subtopics by clicking the **looped-arrow** icon.

3. Choose one of the Denoted by option buttons:

   ❖ **See [also]**—This is the default method of pointing out a cross-refer- ence. If the topic also has a page reference, the wording *See also* is used for the cross-reference. For example, if we use the previous steering example as the page-referenced entry, this option would add the *see also* wording:

   FWD Steering 151–155

see also Tracking control

adjusting the rack and pinion system 44–70

FWD minimum wheel clearance 378

If the topic did not contain a page reference, the word *see* will be used for the cross-reference. In the steering example, the reference would look like this:

FWD Steering, see Tracking control

❖ **See**—Simply refers the reader to another page reference.

❖ **See also**—Like the **See [also]** option, this refers the reader to both the cross-reference and the page reference of the current topic.

❖ **See herein**—Refers the reader to a subtopic page reference within this topic. For example:

Steering, See herein Hub

adding fluid to power steering 9

adjusting power steering belt 12

adjusting toe in 57-60

hub 154

replacing headlight dimmer stalk 231

replacing horn assembly 230

replacing turn signal relay 232

torquing the hub nut 155

removing the steering wheel 153

turns lock-to-lock A32

❖ **See also herein**—Refers the reader to page references for the main topic, plus a subtopic page reference within this topic. For example:

Steering, 9–12, 57-60 151–155, 230–235

See also herein Hub

adding fluid to power steering 9

adjusting power steering belt 12

adjusting toe in 57–60

hub 154

replacing headlight dimmer stalk 231

replacing horn assembly 230

replacing turn signal relay 232

torquing the hub nut 155

removing the steering wheel 153

turns lock-to-lock A32

4. Choose one of the **X-ref override** options to change the style of the cross-reference. If the previously defined cross-reference style is Normal, choosing one of the options will change the style to the option box style. If the cross-reference style is already in one of the option styles, choosing the style here cancels the style, and the cross-references revert back to Normal. For example, if the previously defined cross-reference style is Normal, it might look like this:

    See also Driver's-side air bag

    If you click the **Bold** option box, the cross reference would change to:

    See also **Driver's side air bag**

    However, if the previously defined cross-reference style is Bold and you click the Bold option box, the cross-reference portion of the entry reverts to the Normal style. The same rules apply to the **Italic** and **Underline** option boxes.

5. Click the **Add** button to add another index entry without having to close and reopen the dialog box.

6. Click the **Topic** button to display the Select cross-reference topic dialog box shown in Figure 9.30, to move to a different cross-reference topic.

Figure 9.30 *The Select Cross-Reference Topic dialog box.*

7. Click the **X-ref** button to display the Select Cross-Reference Topic dialog box to mark a topic as a cross reference to the current index entry.

Managing Cross-Referenced Topics

The Select Cross-Reference Topic dialog box, shown in Figure 9.30, gives you a concise view of all existing topics that have been added to the index, as well as the topic on which you are currently working. Use this dialog box to add additional cross-referenced topics or a second- or third-level subtopic to an existing cross reference. You can also use this dialog box in a way similar to the Select Topic dialog box.

Click **OK** or press **Enter** to return to the Add Index Entry dialog box.

Editing the Index

Once the majority of index entries and cross-reference entries have been made, the Show Index dialog box makes it easy to review and modify the list. You can see the entries for the current chapter, or for all the documents in the book list. Follow these steps:

1. To see index entries for the entire book list, open the Utilities pull-down menu and choose **Show index** (or press **Alt+U W**) to display the Show Index dialog box, shown in Figure 9.31.

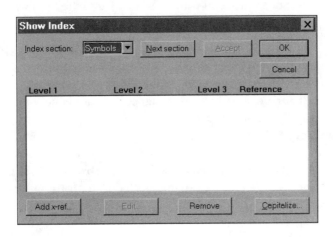

Figure 9.31 *The Show Index dialog box.*

2. Or hold down the **Ctrl** key while performing step 1 to see only the index entries for the current document.

3. Use the Next Section list box to move alphabetically through the list of entries.

4. To change or add a cross-reference, click the **Add x-ref** button. This opens the Add Index Entry dialog box to add or change the reference.

5. To add or edit an index page reference, click the **Edit** button. Again, you'll see the Add Index Entry dialog box, in which you can add or change the reference.

6. Click the **Accept** button to accept the changes made in this dialog box.

7. Click **OK** or press **Enter** to return to your document.

Automatically Marking Index Entries

You can use the **Change** command to search for exact in-text references and automatically mark them as index entries. Here's how:

1. In the Story Editor (use the Story Editor so that you can see the index entry symbols), choose **Change** to display the Change dialog box (see (Using the Change Feature) earlier in this chapter).

2. Enter the index entry you want to search for in the Find what text box.

3. In the Change to text box, enter the caret (**Shift + 6**) and the semicolon.

4. In the Options area, choose the **Whole word** option box. To automatically add proper names to the index, enter the name as it appears in the text (for example, **John Doe**) in the Find what text box. Then enter **^Z** in the Change to text box. All instances of the name will automatically be marked as index entries and will appear in the index as last name, first (**Doe, John**). If the name has a middle name or initial, add the characters **^s** between each of the first two names or between the first name and the middle initial (for example, **John^sQ. Public**). The name will appear in the index last name first (**Public, John Q.**).

5. Click the **Find all** button to locate all entries and mark them with the index symbol.

Once the items are marked as index entries, they are displayed in the Show Index dialog box. Review the marked entries and edit or delete them as necessary.

Generating the Index

Now comes the fun part: generating the index you worked so hard to develop. Here's how:

1. Open the Utilities pull-down menu and choose **Create index** (or press **Alt+L I**) to display the Create Index dialog box, shown in Figure 9.32.

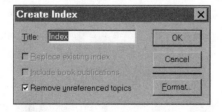

Figure 9.32 *The Create Index dialog box.*

2. In the Title text box, type the title for this index (the default title Index is displayed).

3. To replace an existing index with this new index, click the **Replace existing index** option box.

4. To include all documents in the book list, click the **Include book publications** option box.

5. To remove any referenced topics, click the appropriate option box.

6. To generate the index, click **OK**. PageMaker compiles the index, returns you to your document, and displays a loaded-text icon. Move to the page you want for your index and click the left mouse button to place the text block.

Creating a Table of Contents

The table of contents is created automatically from the heading and subheading styles you marked using the **Include in TOC** option (see Chapter 6, "Setting Up Custom Styles"). To generate the table of contents:

1. Open the Layout pull-down menu and choose **Create TOC** (or press **Alt+O T**) to display the Create Table of Contents dialog box, shown in Figure 9.33.

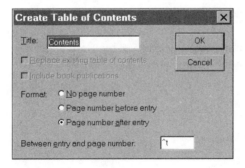

Figure 9.33 *The Create Table of Contents dialog box.*

2. Enter a title for the table of contents in the Title text box or accept the default title **Contents**.

3. If you want the table of contents you're about to generate to replace an existing table of contents, click the **Replace existing table of contents** option box.

4. If you want to include heads from all the documents in the book list, click the **Include book publications** option box.

5. Choose a format for the table of contents:

    ❖ **No page number**—Click this option button to prevent page numbers.

    ❖ **Page number before entry**—Click this option button to position the page number before the heading in the table of contents.

    ❖ **Page number after entry**—Click this option button to position the page numbers after the heading.

6. Specify how you want to format the space between the table of contents entry and the page number. The default ^t tells PageMaker to insert a tab.

7. Click **OK** or press **Enter** to generate the table of contents. In a few moments, the mouse pointer changes to a loaded-text icon. Position the icon where you want the table of contents to begin, and click the left mouse button.

To Sum Up

In this chapter, you have seen PageMaker's straightforward approach to creating professional publications with all the trimmings. Regardless of your publishing requirements, PageMaker can handle layout and production with ease. If you use styles and templates and print to a high-resolution PostScript imagesetter, you will have a book ready for the printer.

In the next chapter you learn how easy it is to use PageMaker's powerful Help system.

CHAPTER 10

Using PageMaker Help

- ❖ Accessing help
- ❖ Getting help with the help index
- ❖ Getting help with shortcuts
- ❖ About PageMaker

If you've read this far and have used PageMaker to work through some of the examples in this book, you realize PageMaker has a powerful help system. Windows help systems are standardized across applications, so if you know how to use help in another application, you'll find it very familiar in PageMaker.

Help is not only easy to access in PageMaker, it is *text-sensitive*—the help you request relates specifically to what you're doing at the moment. For example, if you are about to choose the 25% page view size from the View pull-down menu, the text-sensitive help gives you a brief explanation of what the 25% view is and refers you to some related topics (in this case, explanations of the other view sizes).

Accessing Help

Choose the **Help** pull-down menu to reveal the Help commands. The commands provide help by function or topic. There is also specific help in using PageMaker's Help system.

Text-sensitive help is available by pressing **Shift+F1**. A question mark replaces the mouse pointer or toolbox tool you're currently using. Select any menu command to see help messages relative to that command.

Text-sensitive help inside any dialog box is available by holding down the **Shift** key and clicking the right mouse button. The help window offers two types of icons that further define and explain dialog box functions.

Help from the Menu

To gain access to the PageMaker Help system, follow these steps:

1. Choose the **Help** pull-down menu (or press **Alt+H**) to see the Help submenu, shown in Figure 10.1.

Figure 10.1 *The Help submenu.*

2. Select one of the commands from the menu:

    ❖ **Contents**—Just like the table of contents of a book, the **Contents** command takes you to a functional listing of PageMaker's Help system.

    ❖ **Search**—Lets you search through help topics to quickly retrieve the help text you want.

    ❖ **Shortcuts**—Shows you a clever way to reference all of PageMaker's powerful keyboard shortcuts.

    ❖ **Using PageMaker Help**—Gives you help to use Help.

    ❖ **About PageMaker**—Displays the registered name of the owner and the serial number. There is also a hidden function that is discussed later in this chapter.

Using the Help Window

Regardless of which command you select on the Help submenu, PageMaker displays the Help window shown in Figure 10.2.

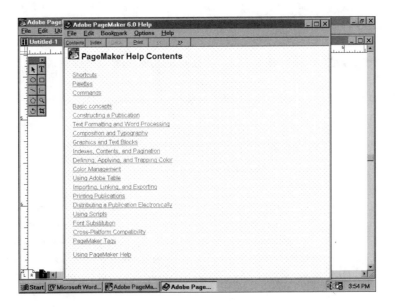

Figure 10.2 *The Help window.*

If you think the Help window resembles a miniature Windows application with its own File, Edit, and Help pull-down menus, you're right. It is an application and can be run in tiled or cascaded windows along with PageMaker, as shown in Figure 10.3.

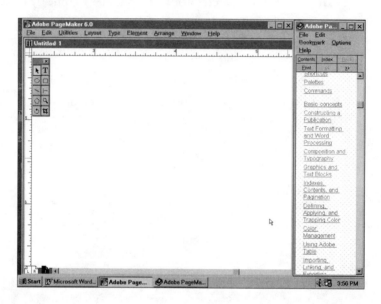

Figure 10.3 *Displaying the Help window in a tiled fashion.*

The Help commands offer a number of features to make Help easier to use and customize to your situation. Let's look at them briefly.

USING THE HELP FILE MENU

The File menu contains the following commands:

❖ **Open**—Opens another application's help system instead of Page-Maker's. When you choose this command you're presented with the File Open dialog box, shown in Figure 10.4. All help files end with the extension **.HLP**, which is preset in the File name text box. Use the Files and Directories list boxes to find the help file you want.

Figure 10.4 *The Open dialog box.*

❖ **Print topic**—Immediately prints the Help text for the currently displayed topic. Choose this command only after selecting the correct printer with the following command.

❖ **Printer Setup**—Displays the Printer Setup dialog box, listing the active printers. Choose the printer you want or change options for the printer by clicking the **Options** button.

❖ **Exit**—Closes the Help window and returns to PageMaker. You can also double-click the window's Control-menu box to close the window.

USING THE HELP EDIT MENU

The Edit pull-down menu contains the following commands:

❖ **Copy**—Copies the currently displayed topic to the Clipboard. You may also press **Ctrl+Ins**.

❖ **Annotate**—Adds your comments, instructions, or other types of annotations to the current Help topic. Choose **Annotate** to display the Help Annotation dialog box, shown in Figure 10.5.

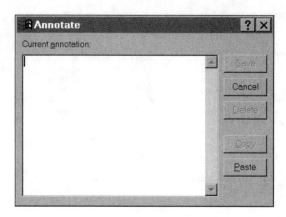

Figure 10.5 *The Help Annotation dialog box.*

Add whatever text you want in this dialog box to further explain or enhance the currently displayed Help text. When you click **OK**, a paper clip icon is shown at the beginning of the Help text to indicate the annotation, as shown in Figure 10.6.

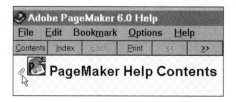

Figure 10.6 *A paper clip icon at the beginning of the Help text indicates annotation.*

In situations where you are introducing new users to PageMaker or Windows, you can add company-specific annotations. For example, in discussing Windows, you could annotate the Help text to include steps to verify the operating mode of Windows, as shown in Figure 10.7.

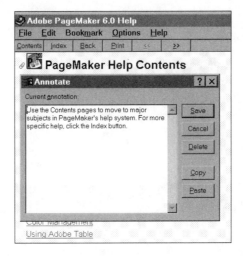

Figure 10.7 *An example of custom annotation.*

You can edit the annotation by merely clicking on the appropriate paper clip and changing the text. You can delete the annotation by opening the annotation and choosing **Delete**.

USING THE HELP BOOKMARK MENU

Help system bookmarks offer a means of returning to specific Help text. You can use a bookmark to temporarily hold your place, or you can set up permanent bookmarks. To create a bookmark, move to a window of Help text you want a bookmark for and choose **Bookmark > Define**. You will see the Bookmark Define dialog box, shown in Figure 10.8.

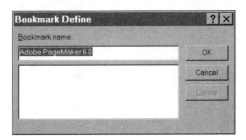

Figure 10.8 *The Bookmark Define dialog box.*

Enter the name of the bookmark in the Bookmark Name text box. Note that the default name already entered in the box is the Help system name for the topic or command you're currently viewing. You can enter a series of unique bookmark names to guide a new user through a self-teaching session. Like the annotation feature just described, setting up uniquely named bookmarks can be useful in training new users in specific areas of PageMaker. For example, by setting up bookmarks as *Step 1*, *Step 2*, *Step 3*, and so on, you can prepare a self-paced tutorial in specific Help text you want a new user to read. When you add the bookmark name, the Bookmark pull-down menu adds the name to the menu, as shown in Figure 10.9.

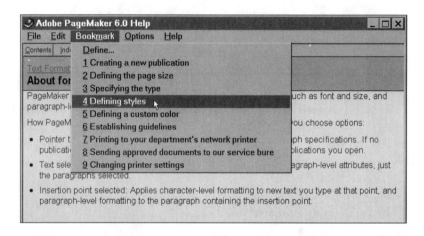

Figure 10.9 *The Bookmark pull-down menu.*

USING THE HELP MENU

As you can see, the Help system also has its own help. To get help about Help, choose **Using Help F1**. The command displays a Help file that walks you through the basics of using the mouse and keyboard in Windows.

The **About Help** command displays a title window showing the current version of the Help system and a copyright notice.

Getting Help with the Help Index

The Help Index walks you through the hierarchy of PageMaker's pull-down menus and commands. To use the index, click the **Index** button while in the Help system (see Figure 10.10).

Figure 10.10 *The Help system showing the Index option.*

Select the subject you want from the list or click a different index letter to see additional subjects. When you click on the subject line, you'll see a Help screen of pertinent information. If you have trouble locating the appropriate subject, click the **Find** tab to use Windows' powerful search capabilities.

To use the Find feature:

1. Click the **Find** tab to open the Find dialog box, as shown in Figure 10.11.

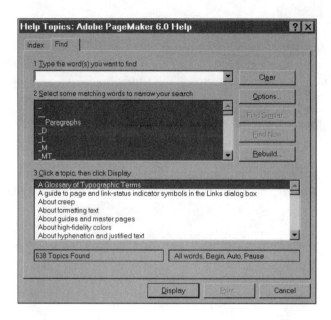

Figure 10.11 *The Help system showing the Find option.*

2. In the Search for text box, type the word or the beginning letters of a word for which you wish to search. For example, if you want help with kerning, type **k** or **ker** to display and highlight *kern* in the word and phrase list. Alternately, you can scroll down the list box of available search topics and double-click the one you want to add to the box.

3. Select the matching topics from the list PageMaker presents. Click the topic you want to read.

Getting Help with Shortcuts

It seems like PageMaker includes about 10 million keyboard shortcuts. Some (and I've tried to include them in this book) are useful time-savers, but there are too many to try to remember. Instead, the Help system includes a series of windows to display all of PageMaker's shortcuts. Open the Help system and choose **Shortcuts** on the Help menu. You will see the PageMaker Shortcuts window, shown in Figure 10.12.

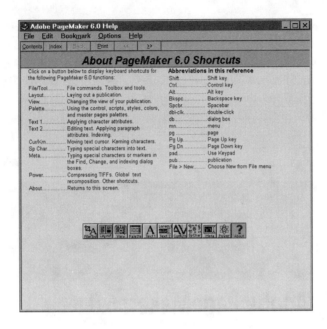

Figure 10.12 *The PageMaker Shortcuts window.*

To use the shortcut Help, click the icon button at the bottom for the type of shortcuts you want. For example, if you want to see font-related shortcuts, click the **Text1** icon and you'll see the following:

About PageMaker

Every Windows application has an About window, and PageMaker is no exception. The About PageMaker window, shown in Figure 10.13, displays the name of the registered user and the serial number of the software. The software's version number is also shown.

Figure 10.13 *The About PageMaker window.*

Click **OK** or press **Enter** to return to your document.

Listing Installed Additions, Filters, and Dictionaries

The About PageMaker window also reports all of the currently installed plug-ins, import and export filters, and dictionaries. To see the list, hold down the **Ctrl** key while choosing **About PageMaker** from the Help pull-down menu. You'll see a window similar to the one in Figure 10.14.

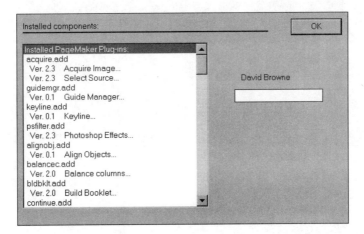

Figure 10.14 *The Installed Components list available through About PageMaker.*

The plug-ins are displayed first. You may have to scroll down the list to see the import and export filters. Click **OK** or press **Enter** to return to your document.

APPENDIX A

Hardware and Software Issues

- ❖ Improving your system
- ❖ Computer viruses
- ❖ Backing up important files
- ❖ Transferring PageMaker files between PCs and Macintoshes

Improving Your System

If you have put off upgrading that old 486 system to a faster 486, you may want to consider doing so. Prices are ripe for the picking and are sure to continue their downward spiral in the coming months. If you are using an overloaded 80486 system, you might want to consider upgrading to a computer with a Pentium processor, which will make a drastic improvement in speed. Short of replacing your system, let's look at ways to make what you have run faster.

If your computer is running Windows 95, you are operating about as quickly as you can. And, since PageMaker 6.0 is a 32-bit Windows 95–compliant application, you will find it considerably faster than previous versions.

Adding Memory

The single greatest improvement you can make to your system is to add more memory. How much? As much as you can afford. I think 8 MB of memory is a minimum configuration for Windows; 16 MB is more reasonable. With that much memory, you can set up a 5 MB or 6 MB disk cache, dedicate several megs to expanded memory and several to a RAM drive, assign a 2 MB font cache for Adobe Type Manager, and still have plenty of memory for Windows to play with. The best source for computer memory is H.Co. Computer Products, Inc. (800-726-2477). Most manufacturers and suppliers buy memory from that company, which will sell to anyone over the phone. Since different computers require different types of memory chips, it's a good idea to buy from knowledgeable people. H.Co. manufactures its memory chips and offers a 100% guarantee.

With enough memory, you can disable Windows' permanent or temporary swap files. *Swap files* are overflow files that Windows sets up to juggle the memory requirements of multiple programs. They dedicate part of your hard disk as a swap area to read and write data in memory. If you have the disk space available and your computer is short on memory, you can set up a large swap file. Windows adds it to the available memory and thinks that it has much more memory than it actually does. The only problem with this arrangement is that it slows down the computer. Now, instead of keeping data in memory, the system has to look in the swap file and read parts of the file back into memory before it can be used. If the swap file is large (5 MB or larger), the disk-access time means a long wait while Windows puts back into memory what the application expects to find.

Adjusting the Swap File Size

If you are not running Windows 95, here's how to adjust Windows' swap file. In the Program Manager, choose the **Control Panel** icon to open the Control Panel. Then click on the **386 Enhanced** icon to open the 386 Enhanced dialog box.

Click the **Virtual Memory** button to set up either a permanent or temporary swap file. The difference between the two is:

❖ A *permanent swap file* dedicates a contiguous section of your hard disk for its exclusive use. In fact, a 20 MB permanent swap file might as well be a 20 MB document or graphic. If you set up a permanent swap file you permanently lose that amount of space on your system. The swap file is identified by two hidden files: **SPART.PAR** and **386SPART.PAR**. Leave these files alone.

❖ A *temporary swap file* dedicates the same amount of space on your disk but only while you are running Windows. When you exit Windows the swap file is deleted and the space on the disk it occupied is returned. The temporary file is named **WIN386.SWP**.

NOTE One of the things you should keep in mind with a permanent or temporary swap file is its size—remember it takes just as long for Windows to read a 20 MB swap file as it does to read any other file of that size. The larger the file, the longer it will take to read and write data to and from the file. So keep your files a reasonable size. I would suggest between 16 MB and 20 MB, unless you are working with extremely large graphic files.

Speeding Up Your Drive with Disk Caching

Again, for those not using Windows 95, Windows 3.1 comes with an excellent disk-caching program called SmartDRIVE. For those of you who aren't familiar with *disk caching*, it's a way of materially speeding up your hard drive by taking what the hard drive reads, plus data in areas immediately adjacent to what the hard drive reads and storing that data temporarily in memory. The cache works on the assumption that you will probably ask the hard drive to read the data again or possible data in areas close to that data. Since the information is held in the cache, it can be accessed much quicker than having to reread the data from the disk.

Increasing the cache size of your disk-caching program can significantly increase the speed of Windows and PageMaker. Depending on the amount of extended memory, set up the **SMARTDRV.EXE** program with at least a 768 to 1024K buffer size. If SmartDRIVE is not installed, add this line to your **AUTOEXEC.BAT** file:

```
C:\WINDOWS\SMARTDRV.EXE 1024
```

Remember to change the path to the actual path of the Windows subdirectory (it may be in **D:** drive instead of **C:**). The 1024 indicates the size of the caching buffer. If you are using a more advanced caching program (such as Multisoft's Super PC-Kwik, 503-644-5644), give it as much memory as possible. With Super PC-Kwik you can reduce the buffers statement in your **CONFIG.SYS** to **BUFFERS=2**, which frees up some conventional memory (each buffer equals 512 bytes).

Another way to drastically increase the access speed of your hard disk is to replace the disk controller with a hard disk caching controller. The caching controller does what SmartDRIVE does, only much more efficiently. The draw-back of caching controllers has always been that they are expensive and require reformatting your hard drives, once they are installed. You don't have to reformat your drives with caching controllers from Alpha Research (512-836-0709). Alpha Research has IDE controllers in the $200 range that can reduce the access time of your drive down to .5 milliseconds. Generally all hard disk controllers support only two physical hard drives in a computer; Alpha Research cache controllers support up to four!

Computer Viruses

Computer viruses are hidden programs that reside in your computer (stored on a hard drive or floppy diskette) and do something that shouldn't be done. Some viruses are simply mischievous; others do physical damage to files or even erase or reformat your hard disk. Each time PageMaker starts, it looks for any changes a virus may have made to the program. If it finds anything different, it warns you and gives you a chance to cancel starting the program. Some of the ways to prevent viruses include:

❖ Purchase a program that identifies and eradicates viruses, such as Symantec's Norton AntiVirus.

❖ Back up your data files onto floppies or a tape cartridge system on a regular basis. Important files should be backed up daily.

❖ A computer virus isn't transmitted through the air. It gets into your computer as part of a program. Be very careful downloading shareware from bulletin boards and electronic mail systems.

❖ Be cautious about shareware. I recommend getting your software only from reputable companies whose success demands quality control and rigid testing.

❖ Be discriminating about whom you allow to use and work on your computer. If you deal with reputable companies, you shouldn't have any problems.

❖ Insure your hardware and software against loss. Many business insurance policies now offer riders for such protection. At least one company, Safeware (800-848-3469), specializes in insuring small computer systems, covering the loss of both hardware and data.

❖ In an office environment, password-protect your computer so that only you and your supervisor can gain access. Most modern BIOS setups have a password feature; use it. Password protection not only keeps a potential hacker from fooling around, but in the event that the computer is stolen, it offers little resale value if no one can use the system.

❖ If you are using MS-DOS 6, you can use the virus scanning utility to scan your hard disk for potential viruses. Also, a number of backup utilities, including Central Point Backup from Central Point Software (503-690-8090), include virus scanning utilities.

Backing Up Important Files

There are two sets of files in Windows and Windows applications that should be backed up daily: group files ending in **.GRP** and initiation files ending in **.INI**. I strongly suggest making a subdirectory in the root directory of your drive called **WINBACK**, and adding the following lines to the end of your **autoexec.bat** file:

```
copy \windows\*.ini c:\winback
copy \windows\*.grp c:\winback
```

Copy the files each time you boot your computer; then if you inadvertently edit an **.INI** file incorrectly, it's a simple matter of closing Windows and copying the copy of the **.INI** file in the **WINBACK** subdirectory back to the **\WINDOWS** subdirectory. On rare occasions, Windows will eat one or more of its **.GRP** files, and as it is starting, Windows will announce that it can't open the damaged group. If that happens, you will have a current backup of the **.GRP** file in the **WINBACK** subdirectory.

For Windows 95 users, be sure to back up the **SYSTEM.DAT** and **USER.DAT** registry files, found in the **\WINDOWS** directory.

Transferring PageMaker Files between PCs and Macintoshes

PageMaker 6.0 files are interchangeable between the Macintosh and Windows versions of the application (both Macs and PCs were used in the development of this book). All you have to do is transfer them via modem or a null modem cable. There are a number of programs on the market that handle such transfers. My favorite is MacLink Plus, by Dataviz, Inc. MacLink runs in the Macintosh that is connected to the PC with a serial cable. The files are transferred in either directory. Another way of transferring files is by using the Apple SuperDrive that comes in all currently available Macs. The SuperDrive can read DOS 1.44 MB floppy disks, so you can transfer files to and from the disks in the Mac with ease.

You can create a SuperDrive equivalent on your PC by using Mac-in-DOS software from Pacific Micro (415-948-6200). The program, which costs approximately $60, lets you read Macintosh files on any Macintosh-formatted double-density floppy with your PC's 1.44 MB, 3.5-inch floppy drive. Not only can you copy any file on the Mac floppy onto your system, you can just as easily copy PageMaker for Windows files onto the Mac floppy. You can even start the program, insert a blank floppy in your drive, and format the floppy as a Macintosh floppy!

NOTE
If you want to transfer earlier versions of either PageMaker for Windows or PageMaker for the Macintosh across platforms, you must first convert the file to the current version of PageMaker. In other words, if you have a PageMaker for Mac 5.0 file that you wish to open in PageMaker 6.0 for Windows, you must first open the file in PageMaker 6.0 for the Mac, save the file as a Mac 6.0 file, and then transfer it to the Windows computer. The same is true for moving files from Windows to the Macintosh.

APPENDIX B

Menu and Command Reference

- ❖ The File menu
- ❖ The Edit menu
- ❖ The Utilities menu
- ❖ The Layout menu
- ❖ The Story menu
- ❖ The Type menu
- ❖ The Element menu
- ❖ The Arrange menu

This appendix is designed to give you the basics of how each command in PageMaker works. Often, you will have read much more involved explanations in the preceding 10 chapters, but this appendix can give you a quick reminder of what a particular command does. The commands are presented in the order that they appear on PageMaker's menus.

Before a document is opened, if a menu command is not dimmed it means you can choose the command, open the dialog box, and adjust the settings, which then become the new default settings for PageMaker.

N O T E

The File Menu

Use the File menu, shown in Figure B.1, for all file-management chores, including opening and closing documents, importing and exporting documents, and defining linked files. You also print files with this menu, and you can exit the program from this menu.

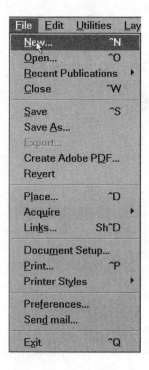

Figure B.1 *The File menu.*

New (Ctrl+N)

Choose the **New** command to open a new document in PageMaker. Selecting the command opens the Document Setup dialog box, where you can set up the parameters for the page. When you close the Document Setup dialog box, a new page is created and displayed in the Fit in Window view. Choosing **New** while working in an existing document signals PageMaker to start a second document. See **Close** and **Document Setup**.

Open (Ctrl+O)

Choose the **Open** command to open an existing PageMaker document or template. PageMaker displays the Open Publication dialog box (Figure B.2) so that you can select a document to open. The opened document is displayed in the same view size and at the same page as when it was closed.

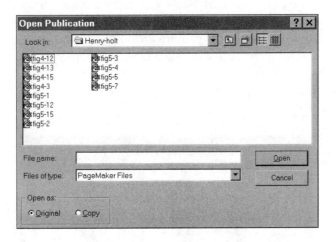

Figure B.2 *The Open Publication dialog box.*

In the Open Publication dialog box, choose an existing PageMaker document or template from the list of files (only files with **.PM6** or templates with **.PT6** extensions will be displayed) or type the name of the document in the Name text box. Choose the **Original** option button to open the original document. Choose the **Copy** option button to open a copy of the document, leaving the original intact. See **Save** and **Save As**. To view PageMaker 5.0 files, choose **Older PageMaker files** in the Files of type list box.

Close

Choose **Close** to close the current document. If changes have been made to the document since the last time it was saved, PageMaker asks if you want to save the document before closing. If you choose **No**, you will lose the work you have done to the document since the last time you used the **Save** command.

You can also close any document by double-clicking its Control-menu box in the upper-left corner of the document window or its Close box in the upper-right corner. Again, if you haven't saved your work, PageMaker reminds you to do so. See **Save** and **Save As**.

Save (Ctrl+S)

Choose the **Save** command whenever you want to save your work. The first time you choose **Save** with a new document, PageMaker displays the Save Publication dialog box, shown in Figure B.3. Enter a name for the document up to eight characters long (don't include asterisks, question marks, forward or backward slashes, or periods). If you are creating a document, PageMaker adds the extension **.pm6**. If you are creating a template, PageMaker adds the extension **.pt6**. You can change to a different directory by using the Directories list box. Double-click the directory name you want or double-click a different drive letter to change drives.

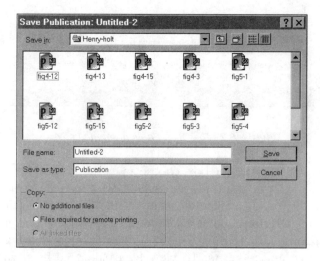

Figure B.3 *The Save Publication dialog box.*

If you are creating a publication, choose the **Publication** option in the Save as type list box; if you are creating a template, choose the **Template** option. In the Copy area of the dialog box, click the **No additional files** button if you do not want to save an additional copy of the linked external files to the same directory that the new publication is saved to (see **Links**). If you want to include copies of all external files with your document, click the **All linked files** option and the linked files will be copied to the same directory as the new document. PageMaker will warn you if there is not enough room in the directory for all the files.

If you will be printing this document at a service bureau or if you have selected a floppy drive to save the document to, click the **Files required for remote printing** option to ensure that all necessary linked files or special files (like the Track-Kerning Resource file) are included with the document.

Save As

When you want to save a copy of an existing document or template as another document or template with a different name, choose the **Save As** command. PageMaker displays the Save Publication dialog box for you to enter a different name. The **Save As** command also reduces the size of the document, which can grow in size as revisions, spelling corrections, resizings, and the like are made. **Save As** eliminates the excess and compresses the file, making it smaller, faster, and more efficient.

To simply compress the size of the current document, choose **Save As**, give the current document a new name, and click **OK** to save the first document as the second document. Then choose **Save As** again and give the second document the first document's name. Now the first document is compressed. If you want this compression to take place each time the **Save** command is used, choose the **Smaller** option button in the Preferences dialog box (see **Preferences**).

Revert

Use the **Revert** command to revert your current document to the last-saved version of the document. In other words, if you save changes you make to your document, begin working on a new page, or alter an existing page and then choose **Revert**, PageMaker changes the document back to the way it was when you last saved it.

PageMaker has its own internal backup scheme to offer some protection between times that you choose the **Save** command. The program saves a miniature version of the current document whenever the following actions occur: printing, copying, inserting or deleting one or more pages, moving from one page to another, switching between the Story Editor and the Layout Editor, clicking the current page icon, or changing parameters in the Document Setup dialog box. If you choose the **Revert** command while holding down the **Shift** key, you restore to the last mini-saved version of the document.

Mini-saved versions of the document are made even before you save a new document the first time. Until you name and save the document, PageMaker gives it a temporary name that begins with **~PM** and saves it in the **WINDOWS\ TEMP** subdirectory, where all other Windows temporary files and print spool files are saved. If you lose power to your computer while working in a newly created but not yet saved document, open the **~pm**-named mini-saved version and use the **Save As** command to give it a proper name.

Export

Choose the **Export** command to save your PageMaker document in a word processor–like format or a format that can be understood by a word processor. Please note that not all of PageMaker's features will be converted, because word processors do not have the sophisticated layout and typographic control that PageMaker does. For example, Word 2.0 for Windows does not understand leading, so any leading specified in the PageMaker document will be lost when the document is exported to a Word file. Word does understand PageMaker's discretionary hyphens, but WordPerfect doesn't. Refer to the list of importable and exportable features in PageMaker's Windows Supplement manual.

When you choose **Export**, PageMaker displays the Export Document dialog box, shown in Figure B.4.

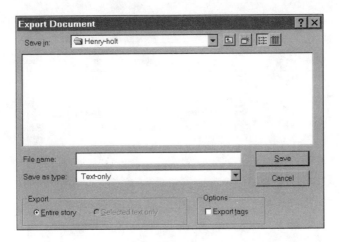

Figure B.4 *The Export Document dialog box.*

Choose the drive and directory for the exported document by clicking open the **Save in** list box or enter the path, along with the file name, in the File name text box. Choose the type of export file in the Save as type list box. (The formats displayed in the list box reflect the export filters you have loaded with the PageMaker Setup program.) If you have selected some text from a document to export, the **Selected text only** option will be checked. Otherwise, the **Entire story** option is checked. To export style tags that carry the PageMaker style names, click the **Export tags** option box.

Place (Ctrl+D)

While working in the Layout Editor, choose the **Place** command to import a text or graphic file and place it on the page (or pages) of the document. When you choose **Place**, PageMaker displays the Place Document dialog box, shown in Figure B.5. In the Name text box, type the name of the word processing, database, spreadsheet, or graphics file you wish to import. Or use the Directories list box to locate the file name. Then double-click the name to add it to the File name text box.

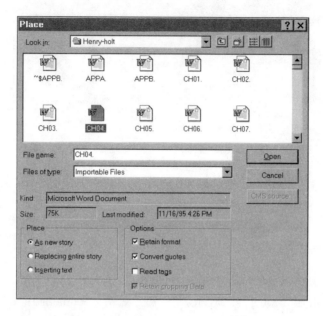

Figure B.5 *The Place Document dialog box.*

If you have not selected a text block with the Pointer tool or clicked the Text tool insertion point in a text block, the **As new story** (or **As new graphic**) option button will be checked. To replace the current text in the text block with the new text, select the text block with the Pointer tool and choose **Open**. The **Replacing entire story** (or **Replacing entire graphic**) option button will be checked. To insert new text or place a graphic as an in-line graphic, position the Text tool insertion point in the text block where you want the new text or graphic to be inserted. Choose **Open** and the **Inserting text** (or **Inserting graphic**) option will be checked.

Click the **Retain format** box to retain the file's formatting and style sheet (if applicable). For example, if the file was formatted in WordPerfect in 12-point Courier, checking this option box would format the file in PageMaker in 12-point Courier. If you do not check this option box, the default PageMaker formats and specifications will be added to the file. The **Convert quotes** option box, when checked, converts word processor–style quotation marks to the "curly" quotation marks found in real typesetting and converts double dashes to em dashes.

N O T E

Some fonts may not have curly quotation characters. In that case, PageMaker will not attempt to convert the characters. Also, word processor–style quotation marks following numbers (indicating feet or inches) are not converted to curly quotes.

If you check the **Retain tags** option box, PageMaker looks for style names enclosed at the beginning of paragraphs in angled brackets (<>) that match named styles in the PageMaker document. If the names match, the paragraphs will be formatted in the appropriate PageMaker style. If PageMaker cannot find a matching style, it adds the file's style name with an asterisk to the styles in the Style palette. The text will be formatted in the default style for the document. Edit the style name (see **Type > Define Styles**) to add the attributes you want for the style.

When you have selected the options you want, choose **Open** or press **Enter** to return to your document. The pointer changes to a different "loaded" icon, depending on what kind of file you are placing. Position the icon on the page and click the left mouse button to place the text or graphic.

In the Story Editor, the **Place** command places the current story in the document. When you choose the command from the File menu, the mouse pointer changes to a loaded-text icon and the document in the Layout Editor is displayed. Position the icon and click the left mouse button to place the text on the page. See **Layout > Autoflow**.

Links (Ctrl+Shift+D)

Choose the **Links** command to see all the current links in your document. Whenever you place text or graphics in PageMaker, a link is created to the external application's file. You can see the status of the document's links with the Links dialog box, shown in Figure B.6. This dialog box displays the name of the linked file, the type of file, and the page number the file starts on. A status indicator and a status explanation line indicate whether there is a problem with the link (the external file can't be located, for example) and whether the external file or the internal linked element needs to be updated.

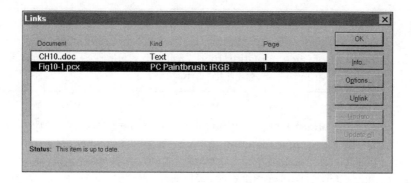

Figure B.6 *The Links dialog box.*

The Links dialog box leads to two other dialog boxes: the Link Info dialog box and the Link Options dialog box. Choose the **Update** button to update only the selected file in the dialog box. Choose the **Update all** button to update all files that need to be updated.

LINK INFO

Choose the linked file in the Links dialog box you want and click the **Link Info** button to display the Link Info dialog box, shown in Figure B.7.

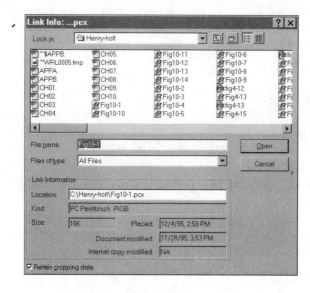

Figure B.7 *The Link Info dialog box.*

The Link Info dialog box shows pertinent information about the file, including its size and location, the date and time it was placed, and the date and time the original or internal copy was last changed. You can enter a different linked file name in the Name text box to see its link information. You can also enter a new unlinked file in the dialog box and link the file by clicking the **Link** button. Choose **Cancel** to go back to the Links dialog box.

LINK OPTIONS

Choose the **Link Options** button in the Links dialog box to display the Link Options dialog box, shown in Figure B.8.

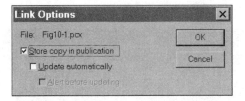

Figure B.8 *The Link Options dialog box.*

This is a smaller version of the Link Options: Default dialog box (see **Element > Link Options**). In this dialog box you can set the options for the linked file highlighted in the Links dialog box.

You can store a complete copy of the linked element inside the PageMaker document by checking the **Store copy in publication** option box (this is the default option for text files and encapsulated PostScript files, in which case the option is checked and dimmed). Storing a copy inside the publication increases the size of the publication. For graphic files, especially full gray-scale or color TIFF files, this option could drastically increase the size of the document (PageMaker warns you if the file exceeds 250K in size).

If the externally linked file has changed, checking the **Update automatically** option means the internally linked file will be automatically updated whenever the PageMaker document is opened. Once checked, if the document is opened and PageMaker cannot locate the externally linked file, you'll see the Cannot Find dialog box, informing you that the file in question cannot be found. Use the Directories list box to find the file or enter the path and file name in the File name text box. Click the **Link** button to re-establish the link to this file. To unsuccessfully end the search for the file, choose the **Ignore** button. Choose the **Ignore all** button if more than one file cannot be located.

Checking the **Update automatically** option allows you to choose to be alerted before the updating occurs. Check the **Alert before updating** option box if you want to be notified before the linked element is updated. Click **OK** or press **Enter** to return to the Links dialog box.

Preferences

The **Preferences** command allows you to set certain preferences for PageMaker's operation. The preferences may be changed at any time without affecting the layout of the document. Choose **Preferences** to display the Preferences dialog box, shown in Figure B.9.

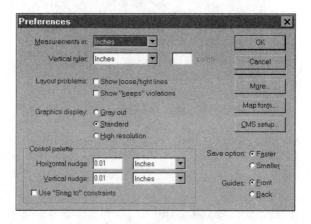

Figure B.9 *The Preferences dialog box.*

Changing the measuring system affects all text boxes in the system that require or display measurement values (like the margin text boxes in the Document Setup dialog box). The ruler also displays the currently selected measurement system. If you set the Vertical ruler list box to **Custom**, you can specify the amount of leading in the Points text box, and by choosing **Snap to rulers** in the Layout menu, the baselines of your text line up with the tick marks on the vertical ruler.

In the Show layout problems area, checking the **Show loose/tight lines** option displays any lines that are either under or over the spacing parameters established in the Spacing Attributes dialog box (accessed by choosing the **Paragraph** command in the Type menu, then choosing **Spacing** from the Paragraph Specifications dialog box). The lines will be highlighted with a gray background. Clicking **Show "keeps" violations** highlights any lines of text that do not adhere to the widow and orphan controls or the Keep with lines control (set up in the Paragraph Specifications dialog box). PageMaker sometimes violates these controls in order to compose the page. When PageMaker highlights the inconsistencies, it's easy to find and correct them manually.

If you choose the **Guides in Front** option, the guidelines will be seen in front of text and graphic elements. If you choose **Guides in Back**, the text or graphics will partially cover the guidelines. Choose the level of resolution at which you want to display graphics. **Gray out** shows a gray shape the size of the graphic. **Normal** renders an accurate display of the graphic, but without the fine detail of the **High resolution** setting. The high setting takes the most time for the screen to redraw.

In the Save option area, the **Faster** option means that mini-saved versions of the file are included when you choose the **Save** command. **Smaller** means that each time the file is saved with the **Save** command it is compressed the same way it is with the **Save As** command (see **Save As**). Click **OK** or press **Enter** to return to your document.

If you click the **More** button, PageMaker displays the More Preferences dialog box, shown in Figure B.10.

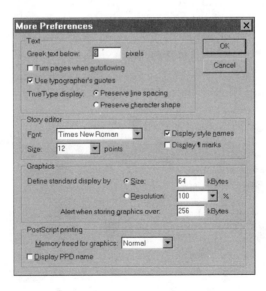

Figure B.10 *The More Preferences dialog box.*

To display all pages as text is autoflowed into the pages (using the **Place** command), click the **Turn pages when autoflowing** check box. Normally, with the box unchecked, the autoflow option only displays the final page text is flowed onto. The **Display PPD name** check box means that the actual file name for the PPD is displayed in the Print dialog box, rather than the nickname for the printer.

Set the size of the internal graphic bitmap using the Size of internal bitmap text box. The larger the value you enter in the text box, the crisper the resolution and the more memory PageMaker devotes to displaying the bitmap (and the slower the screen redraws the graphic while scrolling on the page). To lower the size of graphic files below PageMaker's internal file size, rather than linking to an external original, change the value in the Auto include images under text box.

The **Use typographer's quotes** check box substitutes typographer's curly quotes instead of straight quotes. You have to uncheck this check box if you want to enter " or ' for inch or foot symbols. The two TrueType options preserve the shape and leading of TrueType fonts used in your document. Set the size, in pixels, below which text will be *greeked* (the text is displayed as a shaded bar). The higher the resolution of your monitor, the more pixels it has and the smaller the type size will be before it is greeked. Greeking the text speeds the rate at which the screen redraws its image.

Finally, set the font and size you want to use in the Story Editor with the Font and Size list boxes. Click the **Display style names** check box to display styles assigned to text in the Story Editor. To display invisible paragraph, tab, and space marks, choose the **Display ¶** check box. Click **OK** or press **Enter** to return to the Preferences dialog box.

Choose the **Map fonts** button to display the PANOSE Font Matching dialog box, shown in Figure B.11.

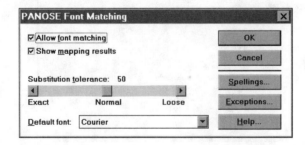

Figure B.11 *The PANOSE Font Matching dialog box.*

This dialog box allows PageMaker to look at the fonts in your document and determine how closely they match Macintosh fonts. To disable the feature, click **Allow font matching** to remove the **X** from the check box.

Document Setup

Choose the **Document Setup** command to establish the page size, page orientation, margins, and related parameters for the document. This command opens the Document Setup dialog box, shown in Figure B.12.

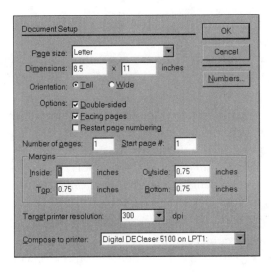

Figure B.12 *The Document Setup dialog box.*

First, set the page type by clicking the **Page size** list box arrow and choosing the page type from the list. Different printers, depending on what size paper they can handle, will demand different page type settings in the list box (the current printer is named at the bottom of the dialog box). The page types listed are tied to the printer selected with the **Target Printer** command. If you select a different printer, the page types may change.

The Page dimensions text boxes for width and height will reflect the size of the chosen page type. Enter different dimensions if the listed page types don't suit your job requirements. The Page list box will reflect your nonstandard dimensions by saying **Custom**. Choose **Wide** orientation if you want to print landscape. The dialog box defaults to the **Tall** option, which prints portrait. If you change the dimensions after you begin laying out your page, PageMaker does not adjust text or graphics to the new dimensions. The text or graphics may overlap onto the pasteboard.

N O T E

You can enter dimensions smaller than the selected printer can handle. If you enter larger dimensions, the printed page has to be reduced to fit on the maximum size paper the selected printer can handle, or you have to use the **Tile** option.

To start page numbering with a number other than 1, enter the starting number in the Start page # text box. If you have built a book list using the **Book** command and you have selected the **Next page** option to number the pages of the book consecutively, entering a starting number of **1** in this text box renumbers the book from this document forward.

Increasing the starting page number by an odd-numbered amount forces left-hand, odd-numbered pages to become right-hand, even-numbered pages. Increasing the starting page number by an even-numbered amount forces the opposite. If you have *double trucks* (layouts that continue across the break between facing pages), changing the odd/even orientation changes the pairing of facing pages. The double trucks may overlap onto the pasteboard.

When you create a new document using the **New** command, PageMaker starts you off in the Document Setup dialog box. You are free to set up as many pages as you think you need for the publication. Once you have created the document, you can no longer use the # of pages text box to adjust the number of pages in the document. Instead, use the **Insert Pages** or **Remove Pages** command on the Page pull-down menu.

In the Options area of the dialog box, choose whether you want **Double-sided pages** (printed on both sides), or **Facing pages** (think of an opened book, the two pages facing each other with the binding in the middle). If you choose **Facing pages**, then increasing the inside margin size adds a wider binding width to the right margin of left-hand pages and to the left margin of right-hand pages.

Set margins to the values you want. The left margin changes to the inside margin when you choose the **Facing pages** option. Press **Tab** to move the insertion point to each margin text box. When you are finished, click **OK** or press **Enter** to return to your document.

Finally, choose the printer this document should be composed for in the Compose to printer list box. Where applicable, you can choose a DPI resolution in the Target printer resolution list box.

NUMBERS

Before returning to your document, you can set up how page numbers will be handled in your document by clicking the **Numbers** button. You'll see the Page Numbering dialog box, shown in Figure B.13.

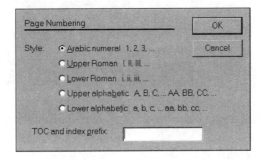

Figure B.13 *The Page Numbering dialog box.*

Use this dialog box to set the numbering style for your document. Please note that if you choose **roman numerals**, PageMaker changes to Arabic numerals after 5000 pages. If you choose **letters**, PageMaker changes to Arabic numerals after 53 pages.

The page number is created automatically by inserting page number markers where you want the page numbers to appear. The markers are created by pressing **Ctrl+Shift+3**. On right-hand pages you'll see the marker *RM* (for right marker), on left-hand pages there will be an *LM* (for left marker). You can add the marker individually to each page, but a faster way is to add the marker to the master page (or, if you have selected **Facing pages**, to both the left and right master pages). When the document is printed, PageMaker adds the actual page number wherever it encounters a page number marker.

To add text to page numbers in the table of contents and index, type the text in the TOC and Index prefix text box. When you are finished, click **OK** or press **Enter** to return to the Document Setup dialog box.

Print (Ctrl+P)

Choose the **Print** command when you are ready to print draft copies, print to a high-resolution imagesetter, or prepare your document to be sent to a service bureau. PageMaker displays the Print Document dialog box, shown in Figure B.14.

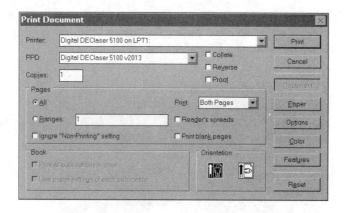

Figure B.14 *The Print Document dialog box.*

Use the Print Document dialog box to set the parameters you want for your print job. For example, at the top of the dialog box, open the two list boxes and select the printer and the PPD you want to use for this print job. Then enter the number of copies you want printed, and whether you want them collated or printed in reverse order. To print quick copies of pages without graphics, click the **Proof** check box. Click the **Reverse order** option box to reverse the order in which your printer prints. To print selected pages of your document, enter the range of inclusive page numbers in the Ranges text box.

Click the **Paper**, **Options**, **Color**, or **Features** command buttons to move to additional dialog boxes of parameters and features you can invoke to customize your print job. You can read about these dialog boxes in detail in Chapter 7, "Printing."

Exit

Choose the **Exit** command to close the application and return to the Windows desktop. PageMaker prompts you to save the current documents if you have not done so.

The Edit Menu

The Edit menu, shown in Figure B.15, handles a variety of editing chores, including copying, cutting, and pasting; finding and changing words and phrases; checking spelling; and toggling between the Layout Editor and the Story Editor.

Figure B.15 *The Edit menu.*

Undo (Ctrl+Z)

Basically, the **Undo** command undoes whatever you most recently did. Although the **Undo** command doesn't work with some functions (for example, you can't undo scrolling or changing the page view size), there are many things that can be undone. You can undo the resizing of a text block or graphic element. If you change the size of a text block, then immediately choose the **Edit** menu, you will see that the **Undo** command has changed to **Undo stretch**, because PageMaker knows that the last action you took can be undone; thus it labels the command with the reverse of the action. The secret to the **Undo** command is that if the action can be undone, the command will tell you.

Cut (Ctrl+X)

Cutting a text or graphic element removes the element from its present position and transfers it to the Windows Clipboard. The cut element remains in the Clipboard until you cut or copy something else to the Clipboard, which copies over the element, until you save the element as a Clipboard file, or until you exit Windows.

When you highlight text with the Text tool and cut the text, the text following the cut reflows to fill in the gap. When you select text with the Pointer tool and cut the text, the gap remains where the text had been.

Almost all Windows applications have cut, copy, and paste commands; they are fundamental to the mutual functionality of Windows applications. You can cut text or graphics from PageMaker and paste it into another application, like Word for Windows, and you can cut text from Word and paste it into PageMaker.

Copy (Ctrl+C)

Copying is similar to cutting, except the element that is copied remains where it was and a copy of it is transferred to the Clipboard. You can then paste the copied element anywhere else in PageMaker or into another Windows application. Again, remember that the Clipboard holds only the most recent text or graphics cut or copied.

Paste (Ctrl+V)

The **Paste** command moves whatever is currently in the Clipboard to the document or pasteboard in PageMaker.

If you have the Pointer tool selected when you paste, the position of the pasted element will be slightly offset from its original position if the original position is known, or it will be centered on the page. Text and graphics pasted with the Pointer tool become independent text blocks or independent graphics.

If you have the Text tool selected when you paste and you click an insertion point in a text block, the pasted text is threaded into the text block. A graphic is inserted as an in-line graphic (part of the text block). Text pasted onto the pasteboard or a new area of the page, but not in an existing text block, assumes the maximum width that it can. In other words, pasting a word at the insertion point of the left margin creates a text block that extends across the column or page (the text block seeks the right margin). To create a more reasonably sized text block, first *drag-place* the text (hold down the left mouse button and drag a box the width you want). Then choose the **Paste** command; it fills the box that you dragged open with the mouse.

Clear (Delete Key)

Using the **Clear** command is the same as pressing the **Delete** or **Backspace** key. The selected text is deleted but not copied to the Clipboard. You can undo cleared or deleted text or graphics by immediately choosing the **Undo** command.

Multiple Paste

Use the **Multiple Paste** command to repeatedly paste the same contents of the Clipboard a number of specified times. Choose **Multiple Paste** to display the Multiple Paste dialog box, shown in Figure B.16.

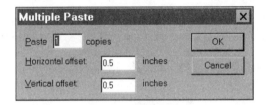

Figure B.16 *The Multiple Paste dialog box.*

Enter the number of times you want to paste the contents in the Copies text box. The two Offset text boxes are used to define the location of the multiple pastes relative to the first pasted item. To paste items horizontally across the page on the same line, change the vertical offset to **0**. To paste items vertically down the page in a straight line, change the horizontal offset to **0**.

Select All (Ctrl+A)

In the Layout Editor, the **Select All** command selects all elements, text, and graphics on the page. In the Story Editor, **Select All** selects the entire story. To select all threaded text blocks on all pages of one story, choose the **Text** tool and click the insertion point anywhere in the story that has text blocks you want to see. Choose **Select All**, and all of the threaded text blocks for the story are highlighted. To deselect the elements, click anywhere in any selected element.

If you have selected all of the text and graphic elements on the page and wish to selectively deselect them, hold down the **Shift** key while you click the elements you don't want selected.

Paste Link

Unlike the **Paste** command, **Paste Link** pastes the contents of the Clipboard as an OLE object. This command is dimmed unless you have copied an object from an OLE server application. Use the command exactly like **Paste**, with the exception that you can double-click on the pasted object to automatically open the application that created it.

Paste Special

Paste Special presents a dialog box, shown in Figure B.17, that allows you to select the type of object you want to paste. Some OLE servers present different types of OLE objects for you to select from. Choose the file type you want from the list in the dialog box.

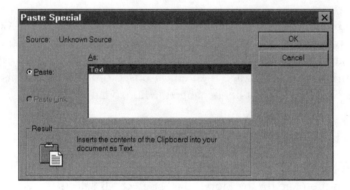

Figure B.17 *The Paste Special dialog box.*

Insert Object

When you want to embed rather than paste an OLE object, choose the **Insert Object** command. You will see the Insert Object dialog box, shown in Figure B.18.

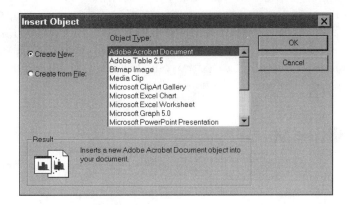

Figure B.18 *The Insert Object dialog box.*

The Insert Object dialog box lists all of the OLE server applications currently installed in your system. Scroll down the list to find the application you want. Double-click the application to start it and create the object you want to insert. When you are finished, save the object in the server application and close it. The object is inserted in your PageMaker document.

Edit Story and Edit Layout (Ctrl+E)

PageMaker has two editors and two views of your work. The *layout view* is what you see when you start PageMaker and open a file or create a new file. In this view you are working in the Layout Editor. The page is laid out before you; stories, headlines, and graphics are all visible. If you choose the **Edit Story** command from the Edit menu, you switch to the *story view*. In this view you are working in the Story Editor. You can see only one story at a time, but many word processing tools that are not available in the Layout Editor are available here. When you are in the Story Editor, the command on the Edit menu reads **Edit Layout**; when you are in the Layout Editor, this command reads **Edit Story**. Choose the view and editor that suits the work you need to do.

Edit Original

Choose the **Edit Original** command when you wish to edit text or graphics you have added to your pages either with the **Place** command or through an OLE link. For example, if you have placed a Word for Windows story in your document, click the story to select it, open the Edit menu and choose **Edit Original**. Word will start, the Word document will be opened, and you can make any changes to the story that you want. When you move back to PageMaker and update the link for the story placed in your document, you'll see the changes you just made to the original document in Word.

The Utilities Menu

The Utilities menu, shown in Figure B.19, holds a number of vital tools and utilities for controlling text.

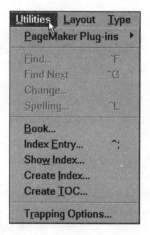

Figure B.19 *The Utilities menu.*

Find (Ctrl+8)

The **Find** command is a powerful feature that searches for words, phrases, text attributes, and hidden characters and codes. The **Find** command and its cousin, the **Change** command, can be used only in the Story Editor. Choose **Find** to display the Find dialog box, shown in Figure B.20.

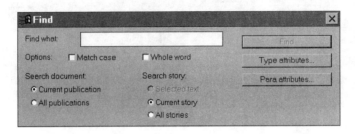

Figure B.20 *The Find dialog box.*

Enter the word or phrase (searched-for words are sometimes called the *search string*) in the Find what text box. Choose **Match case** to match the uppercase or lowercase presentation of the word. Choose **Whole word** to prevent PageMaker from identifying partial word matches (such as searching for *ring* and locating *string*). You can enter a wildcard character to replace specific characters in the search string; wildcard characters are useful if you are not sure of the spelling of a word for which you are searching. The wildcard character is the caret and the question mark together (**^?**). You can also enter a number of special characters to search for, including hard return codes, discretionary hyphens, and many more. See Chapter 9 for a complete listing of these characters.

The **Find** command normally searches the entire story from the insertion point forward. When it reaches the end of the story, PageMaker asks if you want the **Find** command to wrap back to the beginning and search from the beginning up to the insertion point. To search selected text, highlight the text with the Text tool and choose **Find**. To search all stories in a document, choose the **All stories** option button.

Choose the **Find** button to start the search. After the first occurrence of the search string, the **Find** button changes to **Find Next**. To find the next occurrence, choose **Find Next**. The **Find Next** command on the Edit menu also becomes available after finding the first occurrence of the search string.

TYPE ATTRIBUTES

To add type attributes to your search string, click the **Type Attributes** button. This will open the Find Type Attributes dialog box, shown in Figure B.21.

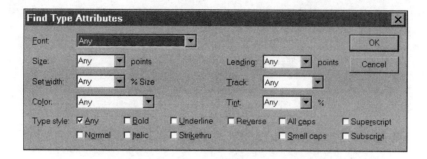

Figure B.21 *The Find Type Attributes dialog box.*

To search for text in a specific font, open the Font list box and click one of the fonts. The **Find** command then searches for all occurrences of the search string in the font specified. When you are finished defining the type attributes, click **OK** to return to the Find dialog box and begin your search.

Find Next (Ctrl+Shift+9)

Also available only in the Story Editor, the **Find Next** command is dimmed until after the **Find** command has found the first instance of a searched-for word or phrase. You can then choose the **Find Next** command to search for more occurrences of the same word or phrase.

Change (Ctrl+H)

The **Change** command is also available in the Story Editor. It is really an extension of the **Find** command: After you find what you are searching for, the **Change** command lets you change it to something else or delete it. The **Change** command's dialog box is very similar to the Find dialog box; it is shown in Figure B.22.

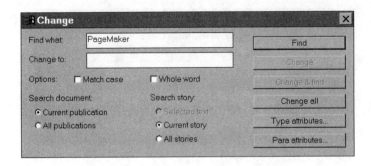

Figure B.22 *The Change dialog box.*

Enter the search string in the Find what text box. Enter into the Change to text box what you want to change the search string to. The remaining options are the same as in the Find dialog box.

Choose **Find** to find the first occurrence of the search string. Choose **Change** to change that occurrence to what you entered in the Change to text box. Choose **Change & find** to make the change and immediately find the next occurrence of the search string. Choose **Change all** to find all occurrences and change them. The **Attributes** button takes you to a dialog box very similar to that used in the **Find** command.

Spelling (Ctrl+L)

PageMaker's speller, available only in the Story Editor, works much like any spelling program—if you have used one before, you will find this one familiar enough. It is remarkable not so much in its functions but in its speed. It is much faster than spellers in any other Windows applications I've used. Choose the **Spelling** command to display the Spelling dialog box, shown in Figure B.23.

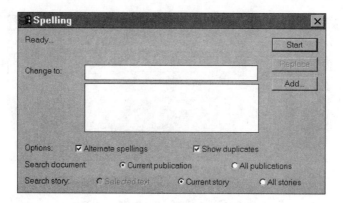

Figure B.23 *The Spelling dialog box.*

If you want to spell check only part of a story, highlight the text with the insertion point and choose **Spelling**. Otherwise, the speller begins checking at the location of the insertion point and continues forward to the end of the story. When it reaches the end, PageMaker asks if you want the speller to wrap back to the beginning and spell check from the beginning up to the insertion point. To spell check all of the stories in the PageMaker document, click the **All stories** option.

ADD WORDS

If you would like to add words to or delete words from the spelling dictionary, choose the **Add** button, which opens the Add Word to User Dictionary dialog box, shown in Figure B.24.

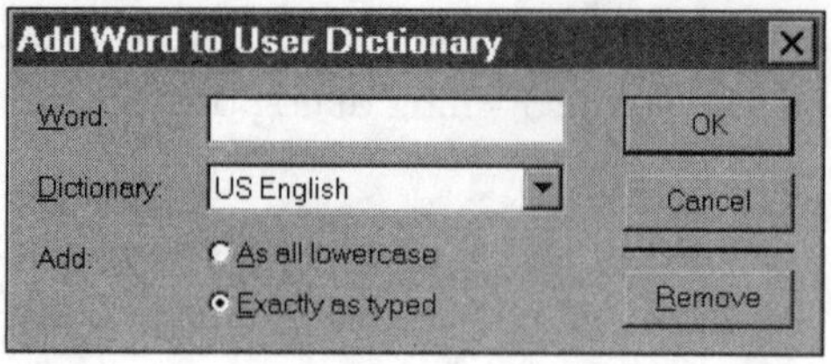

Figure B.24 *The Add Word to User Dictionary dialog box.*

The Add Word to User Dictionary dialog box is shared with the **Hyphenation** function. Use it to add or remove words or to hyphenate words for the User Dictionary. To indicate the most favorable place to hyphenate the word you are entering, break the word with the tilde symbol, located above the number 6 on your keyboard. One tilde signifies the best place to hyphenate, two tildes signify the next best place to hyphenate, and three tildes signify the least desirable but still acceptable place to hyphenate.

If you have purchased other dictionaries from Adobe Systems, you can select the dictionary you wish to use in the Dictionary list box (dictionaries are installed using the Setup program). To add the word in all lowercase letters or to add it exactly as entered in the Word text box, choose the appropriate option. To remove a word from the dictionary, type the word in the Word text box and click the **Remove** button. Click **OK** or press **Enter** to return to the Spelling dialog box.

Book

Choose the **Book** command to create a list of PageMaker documents, that, when combined, comprise a book. For example, if you have PageMaker documents called **CHAP1.pm6**, **CHAP2.pm6**, **CHAP3.pm6**, **CHAP4.pm6**, **INTRO.pm6**, **CONTENTS.pm6**, and **INDEX.pm6**, the **Book** command puts them together in the proper order. Choosing this command displays the Book Publication List dialog box, shown in Figure B.25.

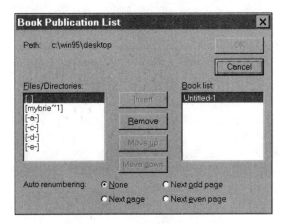

Figure B.25 *The Book Publication List dialog box.*

For each document you want to include in the book, find the document in the Files/Directories list box, click the document name, and choose the **Insert** button to add it to the Book List list box. After you have inserted all of the documents into the book list, use the **Move up** or **Move down** button to adjust the order of the documents in the list, if necessary. If you want to remove a document from the list, click the **Remove** button.

N O T E
If for some reason you move a document included in a book list, the book list will still include the name of the document, even though PageMaker won't be able to find it. You'll be notified of the missing document when you perform any book-oriented tasks, such as printing the book or compiling the index or table of contents. To fix the problem, go back to the Book Publication List dialog box, remove the document name that cannot be found from the book list, find the document in the Files/Directories list box, and reinsert it using the **Insert** button.

The Book Publication List dialog box also controls how PageMaker numbers pages in the book. For example, if you choose the **None** option button in the Auto renumbering area of the box, PageMaker does not number the pages of the documents in the book list in consecutive order. Each document has its own independent numbering.

Check the **Next page** option to provide consecutive numbering throughout the book. If the last page of Chapter 1 is 38, then the first page of Chapter 2 will be 39, and so forth. If you want the page numbering to restart at a particular point (for example, to number the front matter sections consecutively, then restart the page numbering for the chapters), open the Document Setup dialog box and choose **Restart page #** for the first chapter receiving the new number (see **Page Setup**).

If you want all new chapters or sections to start on an odd page number, check the **Next odd page** option button. If the chapter or section would normally fall on an even-numbered page, PageMaker will add a blank page to the end of the previous chapter or section to force the next chapter to start on an odd page. Likewise, if you want the chapters or sections to start on even pages, check the **Next even page** option button. When you are finished with the dialog box, click **OK** or press **Enter** to return to your document.

Index Entry (Ctrl+;)

Choose the **Index Entry** command to create entries for a publication's index, to edit existing entries, and to add cross-references to the entries. This command displays the Add Index Entry dialog box, shown in Figure B.26.

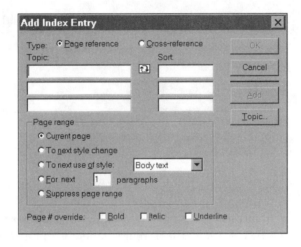

Figure B.26 *The Add Index Entry dialog box.*

Use this dialog box for a variety of activities, including marking text as index entries or as cross-references, adding second- and third-level subentries to the entry, and choosing the page range for the page number of the entry. Choose the **Add** button to add the entry to the list of index entries without closing the dialog box. Choose the **Topic** button to see a second dialog box that allows you to enter and edit index topics. If the entry is a cross-reference, you can also display a special Cross-Reference dialog box. Detailed instructions on indexing are found in Chapter 9.

Show Index

Choose the **Show Index** command to display a very useful dialog box, shown in Figure B.27, that lists, alphabetically, all current entries for the document.

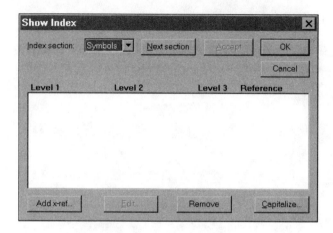

Figure B.27 *The Show Index dialog box.*

The Show Index dialog box is a handy way to review your index entries, check for consistency, and spot any potential problems. You can add cross-references to entries directly from this dialog box by clicking the **Add x-ref** button. You can also edit entries by choosing **Edit** or remove them with the **Remove** button. See Chapter 9 for complete details about the **Show Index** command.

Create Index

This command actually generates an index. It gathers the entries and cross-references, compiles the page numbers, and arranges everything in alphabetical order. Choosing this command opens the Create Index dialog box, shown in Figure B.28.

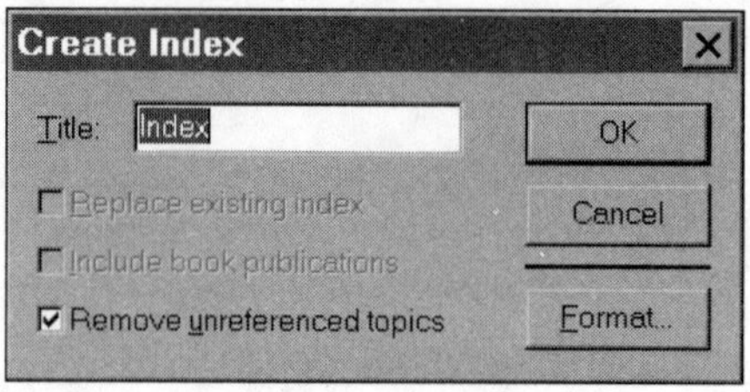

Figure B.28 *The Create Index dialog box.*

You may enter the title for the index in the Title text box. If you have already generated an index and this index supersedes it, choose the **Replace existing index** option. If you are working with documents in a book list, choose the **Include book publications** option to create an index that includes all of the publications in the book list. If you are not working with a book list, this option will be dimmed. If you check **Remove unreferenced topics**, the index removes any topics that aren't tied to index references or cross-references. Choose **Format** to display the Index Format dialog box, which is used to set the actual format of the index pages. See Chapter 9 for complete instructions about formatting and generating the index.

Create Table of Contents

Chapter titles, headings, and subheadings are marked as table of contents entries in the Paragraph Specifications dialog box. (Since PageMaker defines a paragraph as text followed by a hard return, chapter titles and headings are considered paragraphs.) You can mark each heading manually by opening the dialog box and checking the **Include in table of contents** option box, or you can add the option to the style specification for chapter titles and headings.

Once the headings are marked, choose the **Create table of contents** command to generate the table of contents. You will see the dialog box shown in Figure B.29.

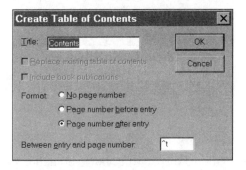

Figure B.29 *The Create Table of Contents dialog box.*

The Create Table of Contents dialog box is very similar to the Create Index dialog box. Choose whether you want to replace an existing table of contents or whether to include all book publications entries in the table of contents, by clicking the appropriate options. You can format the table of contents without page numbers or with numbers to the right or left of the entries. Finally, you can specify a character other than the default tab character to be inserted between the entry and the page number. See Chapter 9 for complete information about creating a table of contents.

The Layout Menu

Use the Layout menu, shown in Figure B.30, to establish the basic layout for your document.

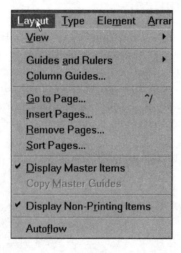

Figure B.30 *The Layout menu.*

View

Click the **View** command to display the View submenu, shown in Figure B.31. The submenu displays the different view percentages you can choose to see your document page.

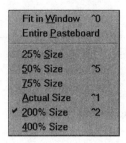

Figure B.31 *The View submenu.*

FIT IN WINDOW (CTRL+0)

The Fit in Window page view size reduces the page, regardless of how large it is, to a size that fits in the document window. If you reduce the size of the window, the view of the page reduces an equal amount. The Fit in Window view gives a good overall view of the page layout.

ENTIRE PASTEBOARD

The Show Pasteboard view shows the entire pasteboard. It is useful when you've temporarily placed an element on the pasteboard and you can't find it in a larger view.

25% SIZE

The 25% page view gives you a slightly larger page size than the Show Pasteboard view. The 25% view also displays much, but not all, of the pasteboard.

50% SIZE (CTRL+5)

The 50% page view size is half of the original size. With a 14-inch monitor, you'll see about two-thirds of the height of an 8.5-by-11-inch page.

75% SIZE

The 75% page view size offers a happy medium between keeping the page small enough to move around in quickly and large enough to read body copy.

ACTUAL SIZE (CTRL+1)

The Actual Size page view size is a one-to-one representation of the page.

200% SIZE (CTRL+2)

The 200% page view size doubles the actual size of the page. This is a good size to use when manually kerning letters or adjusting type to critical measurements. Graphics displayed in high resolution will be slower to redraw as you scroll up or down the page. You can change the display resolution of graphics in the Preferences dialog box.

400% SIZE

The 400% page view size is four times the actual size of the page. At this size you are looking at a very small portion of the page. Moving about the page is tedious, and high-resolution graphics are very slow to redraw. This is an excellent page size for minute kerning and very fine adjustments.

Guides and Rulers

Choose the **Guides and Rulers** command to display the Guides and Rulers submenu, shown in Figure B.32.

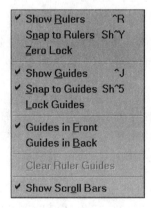

Figure B.32 *The Guides and Rulers submenu.*

Show Rulers (Ctrl+R)

The **Rulers** command turns on and off the display of the rulers. If the rulers are visible, the command is checked. Choosing the checked **Rulers** command turns the rulers off.

Snap to Rulers (Ctrl+Shift+Y)

When the **Snap to Rulers** command is checked, text, graphic elements, and guidelines are pulled to the nearest tick mark on the ruler. Change the definition of the ruler by changing the page view size (the larger the view, the finer the definition of the rulers). Choosing the checked **Snap to Rulers** command turns the command off.

Zero Lock

Choose the **Zero Lock** command to lock the zero points of the vertical and horizontal rulers. Once locked, the zero points cannot be moved until you choose the command again, unlocking the rulers.

Show Guides (Ctrl+J)

When the **Guides** command is chosen and checked, guidelines, margins, column borders, and column gutters are displayed. To hide all of the alignment marks, choose **Guides** again to uncheck the command.

Snap to Guides (Ctrl+Shift+5)

Choose the **Snap to Guides** command to have text and graphic elements accurately align with (*snap to*) the nearest guideline. Turn the snap feature off by choosing the checked command again.

Lock Guides

Once guidelines have been established where you want them, choose the **Lock Guides** command to lock them in place so they cannot be moved inadvertently. You can unlock them at any time by choosing the checked command again.

Guides in Front/Guides in Back

This command determines whether guides will be positioned in front of or behind objects on the page.

CLEAR RULER GUIDES

This command automatically clears all guides you have "pulled" out of rulers off the page.

SHOW SCROLL BARS

To gain a little more room on the document layout page, you can click the **Show Scroll Bars** command to uncheck the option and hide the scroll bars. Click the option again to show the scroll bars.

Column Guides

The **Column Guides** command displays the Column Guides dialog box, shown in Figure B.33.

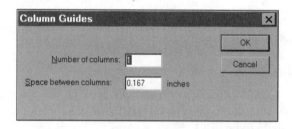

Figure B.33 *The Column Guides dialog box.*

Use the Column Guides dialog box to set up multiple columns for the page or document. Enter the number of columns you want in the Number of columns text box. Then enter the gutter width in the Space between columns text box. Choosing the **Column Guides** command when you are on the master page sets the columns definition for all pages in the document. Choosing the command from any page in the document sets the new column definition for only that page. The **Column Guides** command automatically creates equal-width columns. You can create unequal-width columns by clicking the column guides and dragging them left or right to the position you want.

Go To Page (Ctrl+/)

The **Go to** command is an easy way to move to a specific page in your document. Choosing it displays the Go to Page dialog box, shown in Figure B.34.

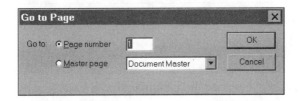

Figure B.34 *The Go to Page dialog box.*

Use this dialog box to enter the page number to which you want to move. Or choose the appropriate option button to move to the master pages. Click **OK** or press **Enter** to move to the page you want.

Insert Pages

You can add pages to your document at any time. Choosing this command displays the Insert Pages dialog box, shown in Figure B.35.

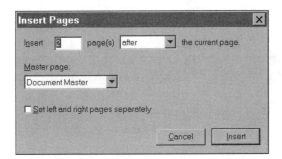

Figure B.35 *The Insert Pages dialog box.*

Enter the number of pages you want to add to your publication in the Insert pages text box. Then decide whether you want the pages added before the page you are currently on, after the current page, or (if you are working with facing pages) between the current pages. Choose **Insert** or press **Enter** to add the pages. The specifications of paragraphs and type for the current pages will be carried over to the newly added pages. Threaded text that is split by the inserted pages remains threaded.

If you are working with a double-sided publication, adding pages between the current pages or adding an odd number of pages can change the left/right orientation of the document's pages. If the left and right margins are not the same measurement, you may have to realign text and graphics to the new margins.

Remove Pages

You can remove pages just as easily as you can insert them. Choosing **Remove Pages** displays the Remove Pages dialog box, shown in Figure B.36.

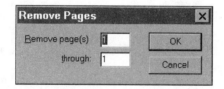

Figure B.36 *The Remove Pages dialog box.*

In the two text boxes, enter the beginning and ending page numbers for the pages you want to remove. Click **OK** or press **Enter** to remove the specified pages. If you are working with double-sided pages, you may have problems with unequal-width margins, depending on how many pages are removed. Text and graphics may have to be realigned on some pages.

Sort Pages

This command lets you rearrange the order of your document pages; page 3 can become page 7 or page 1 and 2 can be swapped, for example. **Sort Pages** shows icons representing the pages, and you simply click and drag the icons to reorder them. Choose **Sort Pages** to see the Sort Pages dialog box, shown in Figure B.37.

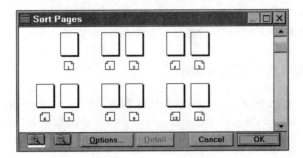

Figure B.37 *The Sort Pages dialog box.*

You can vary the size of the page icons by clicking the **plus** or **minus** magnification buttons. If the icon pages are grayed, you can show true thumbnail sketches of your document pages by clicking the **Options** button and choosing **Show detailed thumbnails**.

When you have rearranged the icons the way you want them, click **OK** to return to your document, and the real pages will be sorted to reflect the arrangement you set up in the addition.

Display Master Items

The **Display Master Items** command controls whether master page items are imposed or waived for a specific page in your document. For example, you can set up a master page header to be printed on every page of your document. If you toggle off the **Display Master Items** command (so that its box has no check mark), you will not see the header on the current page, nor will it print on the current page.

Copy Master Guides

If you have established guidelines on the master pages of your document and you move one or more of the guidelines on a specific page, the **Copy Master Guides** command becomes available. If you later want to return the moved guide to its original position, choose the command and the guides will be reset to their master page positions.

Display Nonprinting Items

Toggle this command on to see items you have marked as nonprinting (**Element > Nonprinting**). Toggle the command off to hide nonprinting items.

Autoflow

When the **Autoflow** command is checked, text placed on a document page automatically flows to as many consecutive pages in the document as the size of the text file dictates. You do not have to have the pages available; Autoflow creates the pages as it needs them. Choose **Autoflow** again to turn the command off.

The Story Menu

The Story menu, shown in Figure B.38, is available in the Story Editor only.

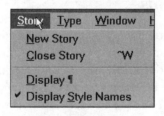

Figure B.38 *The Story menu.*

New Story

The **New Story** command opens a new story window labeled *Untitled*. You can stack up a number of new stories—each will be numbered. Move between the story windows by choosing the window you want in the Window pull-down menu.

Close Story (Ctrl+W)

To close a story, choose the **Close Story** command. If the story has not yet been placed on the document page, PageMaker warns you with a small dialog box. Choose **Place** to place the document and the story window closes, the Layout Editor is displayed, and the mouse pointer changes to the loaded-text icon. Click it to place the story.

Display

While working in the Story Editor, you can display several hidden symbols, including paragraph marks, spaces between words, and tab marks. Choose the **Display** command to display the symbols. Choose the command again to hide them.

Display Style Names

To open a left margin in the story view window and display the style names of all paragraphs marked with a style, choose **Display Style Names**. You can click the style name to highlight the entire paragraph. Paragraphs without names will be marked with a small bullet in the margin. Clicking the bullet highlights the paragraph. To close the left margin, choose the checked command again.

The Type Menu

The Type menu contains commands and dialog boxes that precisely control how type is displayed on the page. To change the default type values for the document, make your choices without positioning the Text tool insertion point in the document. To have the settings you choose affect only selected text, highlight the text first with the Text tool. To have the settings affect text you are about to type, click the insertion point, then choose a command from the Type menu, shown in Figure B.39.

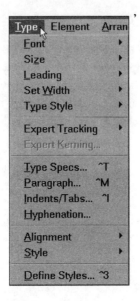

Figure B.39 *The Type menu.*

Font

Choose the **Font** command to display a submenu of all the fonts you currently have installed. (If your list of fonts is long enough, this command runs off the bottom of the window; Windows menus do not scroll the way Macintosh menus do.) If you don't see the font you want, select it in the Type Specifications dialog box.

Size

Choose the **Size** command to display a submenu of preset sizes from 6 to 72 points. If you don't see the size you want, choose **Other** and enter the size in the dialog box. You can enter type sizes as small as 4 points or as large as 650 points, in .1-point increments.

Leading

Choose the **Leading** command to display a submenu of selected leading sizes based on the size currently selected in the Size submenu. For example, if you select **10 points** as the type size, the leading selections will range from 9 to 30 points. Choose **Auto** to allow PageMaker to automatically calculate the correct amount of leading, based on the size of the type. Choosing **Other** allows you to enter a leading value that is not displayed. You can enter leading values from 0 to 1300 points, in .1-point increments.

Set Width

Choose the **Set Width** command to display a submenu of selected width settings from 70% to 130% of normal. Choose **Other** to enter a different width, from 5% to 250%, in .1% increments.

Style

Choose the **Type Style** command to display a submenu showing the different available styles that can be applied to the selected typeface.

Expert Tracking

Choose the **Expert Tracking** command to display a submenu that displays five different tracking settings. Choose **No Track** to prevent tracking adjustments.

Type Specs (Ctrl+T)

Choose the **Type Specs** command to display the Type Specifications dialog box, shown in Figure B.40. It contains all the options in the six submenus just listed.

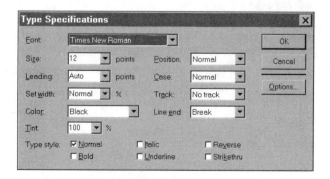

Figure B.40 *The Type Specifications dialog box.*

Instead of using the Type submenus, you can make your selections in the Type Specifications dialog box. In addition, you can specify the position (normal, subscript, or superscript) of the type by clicking the **Position** list box arrow and the case (normal, all caps, or small caps) style by clicking the **Case** list box arrow.

OPTIONS

Choose the **Options** button in the Type Specifications dialog box to display the Type Options dialog box, shown in Figure B.41.

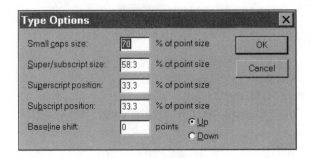

Figure B.41 *The Type Options dialog box.*

Use this dialog box to enter different values for the proportional size of small caps, superscript, and subscript characters, and the proportional positioning of superscript and subscript characters. Click **OK** or press **Enter** to return to the Type Specifications dialog box.

Paragraph (Ctrl+M)

Choose the **Paragraph** command to display the Paragraph Specifications dialog box, shown in Figure B.42. All of the information about how paragraphs will be handled is included in this dialog box and the two dialog boxes that branch from it.

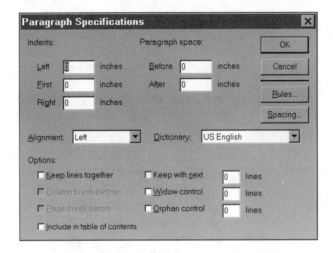

Figure B.42 *The Paragraph Specifications dialog box.*

In the Indents area, specify how left, right, and hanging indents will be arranged. The Paragraph space area determines the amount of space before and after paragraphs. Type alignment can be set in the Alignment list box (which is the same as setting the alignment with the Alignment submenu). In the Options area, you can determine exactly how the beginning and ending lines of the paragraph will be handled with respect to page and column breaks. Check the **Include in table of contents** option box to mark headings and chapter titles for inclusion in the table of contents.

RULES

Choosing the **Rules** button opens the Paragraph Rules dialog box, shown in Figure B.43. This dialog box is used to set parameters for adding lines (*rules*) to your paragraphs.

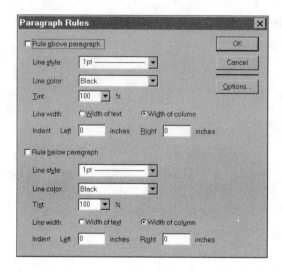

Figure B.43 *The Paragraph Rules dialog box.*

For rules either above or below the paragraph, you can decide the weight of the line, its color, and its width. Press the **Options** button to determine how far above or below the baseline the line will be positioned. Click **OK** or press **Enter** to return to the Paragraph Specifications dialog box.

SPACING

Choose the **Spacing** button in the Paragraph Specifications dialog box to open the Spacing Attributes dialog box, shown in Figure B.44.

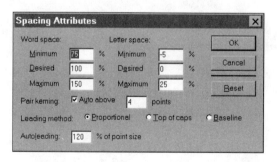

Figure B.44 *The Spacing Attributes dialog box.*

This dialog box sets minimum, desired, and maximum spacing values for letter spacing and word spacing. You can also decide whether leading is calculated proportionally or by the top of caps method. Press the **Reset** button to reset the default values in the text boxes. Click **OK** or press **Enter** to return to the Paragraph Specifications dialog box.

Indents/Tabs (Ctrl+I)

Choose the **Indents/Tabs** command to show the dialog box in Figure B.45. Use this dialog box to set tab stops for your document.

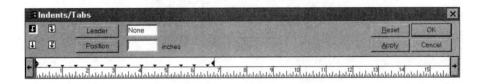

Figure B.45 *The Indents/Tabs dialog box.*

If you are using the Pointer tool when you open the Indents/Tabs dialog box, the settings made to the dialog box change the default indent and tab settings for the document and apply to the next paragraph you type. If you have clicked the **Text** tool insertion point in a text block and then opened the dialog box, the changes you make affect tab settings in the paragraph that contains the insertion point. If you highlight more than one paragraph of text with the Text tool, the tab settings made in the Indents/Tabs dialog box affects all the highlighted paragraphs.

To set a tab stop, click the tab icon you want to move and drag it to a new position. To remove the tab stop, drag the tab icon off the ruler. To add a new tab, click the tab icon in the left corner to highlight it, then click the pointer where you want the tab to be placed. Or choose the **Position** button to add, delete, move, or repeat a tab stop. Select a leader character by choosing the **Leader** button. To reset the tabs to their default positions, choose **Reset**. You can see the results of your settings by pressing the **Apply** button, which affects the text in view (if the Indents/Tabs dialog box is partially blocking the text, click the title bar of the dialog box and drag it to another part of the screen). Click **OK** or press **Enter** to return to your document.

Hyphenation (Ctrl+H)

Choosing the **Hyphenation** command opens the Hyphenation dialog box, shown in Figure B.46. In it you can turn hyphenation on or off and specify how words should be hyphenated.

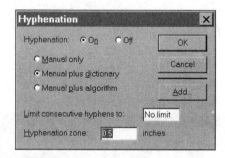

Figure B.46 *The Hyphenation dialog box.*

Choose the **On** or **Off** option button to toggle hyphenation on or off. Select **Manual Only** if you want to decide how to hyphenate words in the publication based on discretionary hyphens you have inserted. Choose **Manual plus dictionary** to find words with discretionary hyphens plus words in the hyphenation dictionary. If you choose **Manual plus algorithm**, PageMaker uses the discretionary hyphens, the dictionary, and a mathematical formula to determine how words should be hyphenated. You can also decide how many consecutive lines can end with a hyphen, and you can set the hyphenation zone. Choose the **Add** button to display the Add Word to Dictionary dialog box (see the **Spelling** command in the Edit menu for a description of this dialog box).

You can use the **Hyphenation** command to help repair corrupted files. Simply hold down the **Ctrl** and **Shift** keys while choosing the command, and PageMaker tries to fix the file. If the file is okay, you will hear one beep; if the problem is identified and corrected, you'll hear two beeps; if the problem can't be fixed, you'll hear three beeps.

Alignment

Choose the **Alignment** command to display the Alignment submenu, in which you can select an alignment configuration for your text: align left, align center, align right, justify, or force-justify.

Style

Choosing the **Style** command displays the Style submenu, which lists the default or custom styles established for the current document. Highlight the text you want to mark with a style, then choose the **Style** command and select the style from the menu. You can also choose styles from the Style palette.

Define Styles (Ctrl+3)

To create new styles, change existing styles, or remove styles, choose the **Define Styles** command to display the dialog box shown in Figure B.47.

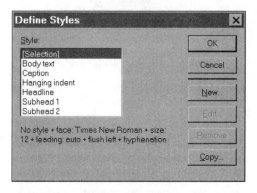

Figure B.47 *The Define Styles dialog box.*

The Define Styles dialog box lists the styles defined for the current publication. Choose the **New** button to define a new style. You can base new styles on elements of existing styles and change existing styles, which will change characteristics of all text marked with the style. You can also remove styles from the list or copy custom styles from other publications. See Chapter 6 for a complete description of this dialog box.

The Element Menu

The commands on the Element menu, shown in Figure B.48, control the display and orientation of text and graphic elements.

Figure B.48 *The Element menu.*

Line

Choose the **Line** command to display the Line submenu. If the line or shape you have drawn with one of the drawing tools is selected, the choice you make in the menu affects only the selected element. If you choose a line style without first selecting an element, the choice becomes the default style for shapes and lines that will be drawn.

Fill

Choose the **Fill** command to display the Fill submenu. If a shape you have drawn with one of the drawing tools is selected, the choice you make in the Fill submenu affects only the selected element. If you choose a different fill pattern without first selecting an element, the choice becomes the default style for shapes that will be drawn. *Paper* is a solid fill pattern the color of the paper. *Solid* is normally black. The percentage shades represent screens of 100% solid (black).

Fill and Line

This command combines the characteristics of the Line and Fill submenus into one simple dialog box, shown in Figure B.49.

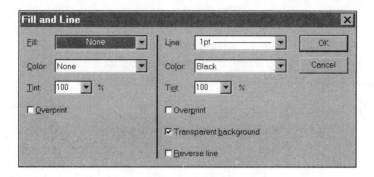

Figure B.49 *The Fill and Line dialog box.*

Polygon Settings

Choose this command when you have drawn a polygon and you want to change the shape or the number of sides. The Polygon Settings dialog box is shown in Figure B.50.

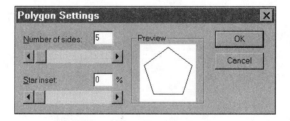

Figure B.50 *The Polygon Settings dialog box.*

Use the Number of sides scroll bar to set the total number of sides for your polygon. To create inset midpoints (and effectively double the number of sides) use the Star inset scroll bar. Adding insets to the polygon sides creates star points.

Rounded Corners

Choose this command to display the Rounded Corners dialog box, shown in Figure B.51. To change the radii of round-cornered rectangles and squares, select the shape and choose the **Rounded Corners** command. This opens a small dialog box in which you can choose among the different corners. Choose the one you want and click **OK** or press **Enter** to return to your document. Selecting a different radius in the dialog box without selecting a round-cornered shape changes the default corner radius for the document.

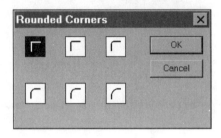

Figure B.51 *The Rounded Corners dialog box.*

Image

Choose the **Image** command to open the Image submenu, shown in Figure B.52. Use the menu to make small corrections to grayscale TIFF images, choose a Color Management System source for the image, save color separations of the image, or apply special effects.

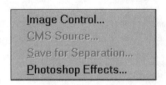

Figure B.52 *The Image submenu.*

IMAGE CONTROL

When you select a graphic, the **Image Control** command becomes available. Choose the command on the Image submenu to display the Image Control dialog box, shown in Figure B.53.

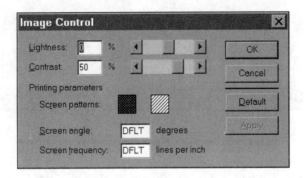

Figure B.53 *The Image Control dialog box.*

Use this dialog box to alter the image of black-and-white and full grayscale TIFF files and paint-type files. The slide bars adjust the *lightness*, which lightens or darkens the image, and *contrast*, which changes the contrast of foreground to background images.

Choose either the dot or line screen pattern. The dot pattern is used for most images, while the line screen creates special effects.

Change the screen angle and lines-per-inch frequency of the image. PageMaker normally sets the screen angle at 45 degrees. However, you can choose any angle from 0 to 360 degrees. The more lines per inch, the finer the resolution and detail. The screen frequency is a factor of the printing device; a 300-dpi laser printer can print only 53 lines per inch, a Linotronic L330 imagesetter can output screens at 150 lines per inch.

Choose **Apply** to try your choices on the image. Press **Default** to change the settings back to the default values. Click **OK** or press **Enter** to return to your document.

PHOTOSHOP EFFECTS

When you select a graphic, the **Image Control** command becomes available. Choose the **Photoshop Effects** command on the Image submenu to open the Photoshop Effects dialog box, shown in Figure B.54.

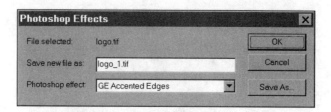

Figure B.54 *The Photoshop Effects dialog box.*

The dialog box applies some of the same special effects to images that Photoshop does. PageMaker automatically creates a special copy of the image, named numerically for each effect you apply. Accept the default name or change it in the Save new file as text box. Then choose the effect you want from the Photoshop effect list box.

Text Wrap

The **Text Wrap** command controls the way text flows around an independent graphic element. Select the graphic with the Pointer tool and choose **Text Wrap** to display the Text Wrap dialog box, shown in Figure B.55.

Figure B.55 *The Text Wrap dialog box.*

Pick the wrap option you want by clicking the icon. The first icon represents text flowing over the graphic. The second icon flows text around the graphic's boundary. If you have modified the boundary to mask the shape of the graphic, then the third icon will be selected.

To change the area and shape of the boundary, click the graphic to select its boundary. Notice the diamond-shaped handles. Drag a handle to change the shape of the boundary. You can create more sizing handles by clicking along the boundary where you want them to appear.

Choose the text flow icon you want. The first icon is called the *column-break icon.* Choose it and text stops flowing when it encounters a graphic and begins again in the next column. The second icon is called the *jump-over icon.* Choose it and text stops when it encounters a graphic but starts again immediately after the graphic (it jumps over the graphic). The third icon is called the *wrap-all-sides icon.* Choose it and text flows around all sides of a graphic. Finally, enter the amount of standoff around the graphic. The *standoff* is the margin between the graphic and the wrapped text. Click **OK** to return to your document.

Link Info

The **Link Info** command displays the same dialog box as the File menu's **Links** command.

Link Options

Use the **Link Options** command to set up certain parameters concerning linked text and graphic files. If neither a linked text nor a graphics file is selected, choosing this command displays the Link Options dialog box, shown in Figure B.56.

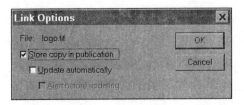

Figure B.56 *The Link Options dialog box.*

First choose how text and graphic links will be stored: as a separate file or internally as part of the PageMaker file. Then select for both text and graphics whether you want PageMaker to update the internally linked files automatically whenever you open the document. The **Alert before updating** option means that PageMaker will ask if the files should be updated before performing the update.

If you select a linked text file and choose **Link Options**, the dialog box will contain only the text options. Select a linked graphic and you'll see the graphics options in the dialog box.

Define Colors

The **Define Colors** command displays the first of several dialog boxes, shown in Figure B.57.

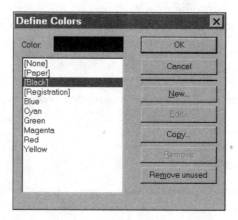

Figure B.57 *The Define Colors dialog box.*

This dialog box is used in editing existing colors and creating new ones. You can choose from any of three color models and up to five color matching libraries to define a new color, or you can copy a custom color from another document. See Chapter 8 for a full description of the Color feature.

The Arrange Menu

Commands on the Arrange menu (Figure B.58) control the relative positions of objects on the page.

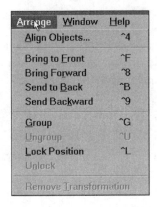

Figure B.58   *The Arrange menu.*

Align Objects

Choose this command when you want to arrange two or more objects on the page in an organized manner. The Align Objects dialog box is shown in Figure B.59.

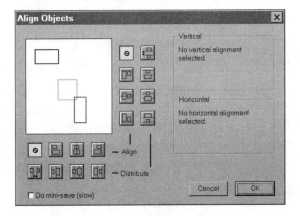

Figure B.59   *The Align Objects dialog box.*

To use the dialog box, click the **Align** and **Distribute** buttons to arrange the objects in the preview window the way you want them. Click **OK** to reshuffle the objects and return to your document.

Bring to Front (Ctrl+F)

When two or more elements are stacked on top of one another, select each element by holding down the **Shift** key and clicking the elements. Each in turn will be selected. To move a selected element to the top of the stack, choose **Bring to front**.

Bring Forward (Ctrl+8)

Use this command when you want to move an object in a stack of objects one place forward.

Send to Back (Ctrl+B)

In a stack of two or more elements, send the top element to the bottom of the stack by selecting the element and choosing **Send to back**.

Send Backward (Ctrl+9)

Use this command to move an object in a stack of objects one layer farther back in the stack.

Group (Ctrl+G)

The **Group** command connects individual objects together as a group and treats it as a single object. For example, if you have created a logo consisting of a name, several rules, and a graphic, you can group them all together, save the group to a library, and use it in designing stationery.

Ungroup (Ctrl+U)

Use the **Ungroup** command to separate grouped objects.

Lock Position (Ctrl+L)

Once you have grouped objects together, use this command to lock their position on the page.

Unlock

Use the **Unlock** command to remove the position lock on a group.

Remove Transformation

Use this command to remove skewing, rotation, or reflection applied to an object. Once you invoke this command you can't undo it with the **Undo** command. However, if you save the document before choosing **Remove Transformation**, if you don't like what you've done, you can choose the **Revert** command on the File menu to revert to the transformations you removed.

GLOSSARY

A

alignment
The arrangement of type in lines between column or page margins. The alignment in PageMaker can be left, right, center, justified, or force-justified.

ascender
The part above the *x-height*, or body, of a lowercase letter (the stems of the *b*, *h*, *d*, and *k*, for example).

ASCII files
Files of text without any word processing codes. ASCII files, also called *text files*, have a carriage return (**CR**) code and a line feed (**LF**) code at the end of each line and end in a Control-Z (**^Z**) code. Almost all programs can strip away their proprietary coding and generate an ASCII file. Some programs call this *writing the file to disk*. You can place ASCII files in PageMaker using the ASCII filter.

ATM
Stands for Adobe Type Manager, a type manager that controls and oversees the operation of screen fonts and

matching downloadable printer fonts. ATM enhances the look of screen fonts in larger sizes, eliminating the jagged edges that you would normally see.

B

base art

In a hand-done mechanical, the base art is the art (type and graphic elements) pasted on the art board, as opposed to the art on overlays aligned to the base art. In PageMaker, the base art is the black-printing art to which you add color overlays.

baseline

An invisible line on which type characters rest, with the characters' descenders extending below the baseline.

BCF

Stands for binary color file, a file that contains a collection of colors for the Colors palette that you have assembled yourself and saved to disk.

book

In PageMaker, a linked compilation of related stories or chapters. A book is compiled with the **Book** command in order to renumber chapters consecutively and to generate a complete table of contents and index.

byline

Originally newspaper jargon for the name of the person who wrote a story. The byline is usually set in a smaller type size and a different style under the story's headline.

byte

Usually 8 bits (ones and zeros in base two that comprise the machine language of the computer). A byte represents a single character. The size of files is measured in bytes, kilobytes (1024 bytes or more), or megabytes (1024 kilobytes or more).

C

check mark

Commands in pull-down menus and submenus are activated when you see a check mark beside them;

choosing the command again removes the check mark and toggles the command off. In dialog boxes, you can turn certain options on and off by clicking the mouse in an options box, which adds or removes a check mark (actually an **X**). If the **X** is present, the option is on.

cicero   A unit of measurement you can assign to the Page-Maker rulers. One cicero equals 4.55 millimeters; 5.58 ciceros equal 1 inch.

click   To quickly press and release the mouse button.

Clipboard   An application that comes with Windows and runs automatically in the background. When you use the **Cut** or **Copy** command in PageMaker or any other application, you are actually moving what was cut or copied to the Clipboard. The Clipboard holds only the item most recently cut or copied.

CMS   Stands for color management system, a way of calibrating devices, such as monitors and printers, so that precise colors can be specified, viewed, and output. PageMaker supports Kodak's Precision Color Management System and other methods.

Colors palette   A small window you can add to the PageMaker document window. The Colors palette holds the standard-defined colors in PageMaker (red, green, blue, cyan, magenta, and yellow), as well as any special colors that you add with the Define Colors dialog box. When you select or highlight text or graphic elements and click a color in the Colors palette, you assign that color to the item selected.

Close box   The small box in the upper-right corner of most windows. Click the box to close the window.

copy   A command that copies to the Clipboard text or graphics selected with the Pointer tool or text highlighted with the Text tool insertion point.

crop   To cut or trim part of a photo or graphic. In Page-Maker, select the **Cropping** tool from the toolbox to crop graphic images.

crop marks   Small lines added to artwork to indicate the trim size of the page. PageMaker adds crop marks when you set up crop marks in the Print dialog box.

cut   A command that deletes from the PageMaker document and transfers to the Clipboard text or graphics selected with the Pointer tool or text highlighted with the Text tool.

D

default   Default settings in PageMaker are the settings in effect at the time the program is purchased and loaded as a new system. After starting PageMaker, whatever settings are in effect when you create a new document will be the default settings for that document.

descender   The part of a letter that hangs below the baseline (for example, the "tails" of the g, p, j, and y).

discretionary hyphen   Hyphens added to words in PageMaker so that if the hyphenation program decides it must hyphenate a word, it will do so at the discretionary hyphen.

dots per inch   See **dpi**.

downloadable fonts   Laser printers have some fonts stored in nonvolatile memory, which are called *resident fonts*. The printer can also make use of fonts stored in your computer, if they are first *downloaded*, or copied to the printer. Then the printer can receive a print job using the font. Downloadable fonts have screen and printer versions of the font: the screen version displays the font on the screen; the printer font is downloaded to the printer. Also called *soft fonts*.

dpi   Stands for dots per inch, the resolution of laser printers and imagesetters is measured in dpi. The more dots, the higher the resolution and the finer the "grain" of the printed image. PostScript laser printers typically have from 300 to 600 dpi resolution; some higher-priced laser printers have as much as 1200 dpi; and some PostScript phototypographic imagesetters can have resolutions higher than 3000 dpi.

drag To reposition an object on the screen by selecting the appropriate tool, positioning the mouse pointer on the object, depressing the mouse button, and dragging the mouse to the desired location.

drop cap An oversized first letter of the first word starting a paragraph, extending several lines down into the paragraph, as opposed to the *initial raised cap*, also a first letter set in larger type, but it extends up from the first line of the paragraph.

drop shadow A silhouette of the image above it that is offset enough to give a shadow effect.

E

em dash The typographic equivalent of the double dash. The em dash is the size of one em space, which is the width of the letter *m* in the typeface and size you're working in.

em size The size of the width of the letter *m*, the widest letter in any given typeface. The origin of the term was an old typographer's term *emquad* or *mutton*, a metal square the height and width of the type size.

Enter The **Enter** key is located where the carriage return key is on an electric typewriter. The key is labeled **Enter** or **Return** and may show the arrow symbol. When a button in a dialog box (normally the **OK** button in PageMaker) has a black border around it, you can activate the button by pressing the **Enter** key. The term is synonymous with *type*—to enter text in a text box, type the text.

export Exporting a file replaces the proprietary formatting codes of the application that created it with the codes of the destination application. PageMaker uses *export filters* to replace the codes. Export filters are installed and are moved with the Adobe Setup program.

F

filters
PageMaker uses import and export filters to convert foreign documents to PageMaker documents and vice versa. Filters are loaded with the Adobe installation program and can be loaded or unloaded at will. See **export**. Another type of filter, Photoshop-compatible plug-ins, can process and manipulate bitmapped images in PageMaker. These are accessed through the **Element > Image > Photoshop Effects** menu choice.

font
Comprises all the letters (uppercase and lowercase), numerals, and special characters in one size and typeface (for example, the 12-point Times Roman font).

footer
Recurring text at the bottom of the page. A footer can contain a page number, a book's title, a current chapter title, or a heading that preceded the text on a given page.

G

guidelines
Nonprinting, adjustable lines to which you can align text and graphics. You can turn the display of guidelines on and off. If you add guidelines to master pages, they will be precisely the same for every page in your document.

H

header
Repeating text at the top of the pages of a document. See **footer**.

high-fidelity colors
Hues produced using more than four process inks. The standard cyan, magenta, yellow, and black might

be augmented with colors such as orange and green to produce a wider range of those colors than can be produced by mixing the four traditional subtractive primary colors alone.

highlight
In PageMaker, you highlight text with the Text tool (as opposed to selecting it with the Pointer tool). Position the insertion point of the Text tool over a word and double-click the mouse button to highlight the word. Triple-click the mouse button to highlight the paragraph.

I

icon
A small graphical symbol that represents a document, application, or utility (or even a tool within applications).

imagesetter
PostScript typesetters are called *imagesetters* because they "set" both text and graphics as images of the page, as opposed to non-PostScript typesetters that can normally only set type.

indent
Moves a line or paragraph of text in from either the left or right margin.

independent graphic
Not part of a text block like an in-line graphic; occupies a fixed position on the page and is not anchored to any text.

initial cap
See **drop cap**.

in-line graphic
Part of the text block in which it is placed. The graphic is anchored to the text; if the text moves because of editing changes, the in-line graphic moves with it.

insertion point
The working end of the Text tool. The insertion point, also called an *I-beam*, is a blinking vertical bar that indicates where text will be typed, deleted, or highlighted.

J

jump page Originally a newspaper term, stories are continued (or *jumped*) to a jump page. Often the jump page will hold continuations of several stories.

K

kern Reduce the space between two letters, sometimes so much that the letters begin to overlap. PageMaker can automatically kern certain pairs of letters where normal spacing looks awkward. You can also manually kern any pairs of letters.

kilobyte Abbreviated *KB* or *K*, 1024 bytes. The size of computer files is sometimes referred to in kilobytes—32K is about the same as 32,000 bytes.

knockout If you print one color on top of another, it will be altered by the color beneath it. To prevent such color changes and a number of other similar problems, a hole is cut out of the color element on the bottom. The hole is called a *knockout*—it knocks out the color. In PageMaker, knockouts are easier to do than they are to explain.

L

layout view One of two views of your work available in PageMaker. In the layout view of your document, you work in the Layout Editor to create and arrange text and graphics on the pages of your document. In the story view, you work in individual stories in the document. See **story view**.

leading Pronounced "ledding," the amount of space between the lines of type, measured from baseline to baseline. Leading is proportionally larger than the type size (normally about 120% of the type size). If the leading

link   were the same as the type size, you would not have any padding: the descenders of the line above would touch the ascenders of the line below.

When you place or import a document into Page-Maker, an invisible link is established between the file in PageMaker, called the *internal element*, and the application the file came from (called the *external application*). If you change the external application's file, the internal linked element changes as well.

M

master pages   Every PageMaker document has one or more master pages (depending on how the document is configured). Anything added to a master page is duplicated in the same position on every page in the document.

masthead   The title of a newspaper or newsletter.

measure   The length of a line of text.

mechanical   The camera-ready compilation of your document—type aligned, colors registered, screens in place—ready to hand to a commercial printer for printing.

megabyte   1024 kilobytes, abbreviated *MB* or *meg*). Large files are often referred to in megs instead of kilobytes (335 megs instead of 335,000 kilobytes).

monospacing   In a monospaced font, such as Courier, the letter spacing is the same for all characters. In a *proportional font*, such as Times Roman, narrow letters like the *i* and the *l* are given less space than wider letters like *m* and *w*.

N

nested dialog boxes   In PageMaker, a dialog box that is activated by a dialog box, usually by clicking a button. Dialog boxes can nest several layers deep.

nonbreaking hyphen   A hyphen normally indicates to PageMaker a favorable place to hyphenate a word, even if the hyphen falls in a hyphenated last name, like Worthington-Smythe. A nonbreaking hyphen prevents such words from breaking at the end of a line.

O

orphan   The last line of a paragraph that is split by a page break and winds up all by itself at the top of the next page.

outdent   The opposite of an *indent*, an outdent normally extends the first line of a paragraph to the left of the left margin, while the rest of the paragraph is flush with the left margin.

overlay   In PageMaker, a separate page containing text and graphic elements that will be printed in a color other than black. A separate overlay is printed for each color.

P

Page Description Language (PDL)   A proprietary language that the laser printer is programmed to understand. Different brands of printers recognize different PDLs. The most successful and popular PDL is PostScript.

paste   Copying into a PageMaker document whatever is currently in the Clipboard. You can paste the same material from the Clipboard as often as you wish—pasting doesn't clear what is in the Clipboard; it copies it into your document.

pasteboard   Pasteboards or artboards were used in the manual composition of a page. Rules were drawn on the pasteboard, type was pasted to it, and spot color overlays were taped to its edge. PageMaker applies the analogy of the pasteboard to the working area in the layout editor. It makes a logical and easy transition from the old manual way to PageMaker's way of page composition.

PCL

Stands for Printer Control Language, Hewlett Packard's proprietary page description language. PCL can understand and print scalable fonts and shares some similarities with the PostScript page description language.

photo credit

The name of the photographer, located underneath or positioned vertically along one side of a printed photo.

pica

A measurement system; 12 points equal one pica, and 6 picas equal one inch. See **points**.

place

When you place text or graphics in PageMaker, they are imported from the application that created them (normally a word processor, spreadsheet, or graphics program), formatted for use in PageMaker, and loaded into an icon. You place the icon where you want the text or graphic to be located and click the icon to flow the text or graphics onto the page. Once the text or graphic is placed, it is linked back to the application that created it; if the application changes its file, PageMaker can automatically change the placed file. See **link**.

point

Type and leading are measured in points; 72-point type is approximately one inch tall. See **pica**.

pointer

The mouse used with the Macintosh is represented on the screen by a pointer icon and any number of other icons. The pointer is used to select text or graphics and open dialog boxes, pull-down menus, and list boxes.

PostScript

Developed by Adobe Systems, PostScript is a page description language that a laser printer or imagesetter containing a PostScript raster image processor can understand. PostScript is successful partly because the PDL is device-independent—any PostScript file prints on any PostScript device.

print spooler   Computers operate much faster than printers. To keep the printer from holding up the application when you print a file, the file is formatted for the printer and sent to a print spooler. The spooler is a separate program that talks to the printer and feeds it pages of the document at a speed the printer can accept. Meanwhile, the application can go about doing other things.

proportional spacing   Assigns more letterspacing to wider characters in a font, and less spacing to narrower characters. For example, if the letters *i* and *m* were both given the space required of the larger character, the *i* would have too much space around it in relation to other characters (especially another *i*, as in the word *skiing*). See **monospacing**.

R

registration bullets   When colors are added to the page, they must be aligned properly with the type and artwork on the page. PageMaker prints registration bullets (or marks) outside the image area of the page. The printer uses these to check the alignment of color overlays.

resident fonts   Fonts permanently installed in your printer. See **downloadable fonts**.

resolution   See **dpi**.

rule   In page composition, lines are often referred to as rules.

S

sans serif   Literally meaning "without serifs." See **serif**.

screen fonts   The part of a font system necessary to display fonts in actual size on the screen. Screen fonts can be controlled and enhanced with a type manager. See **ATM**.

scroll bar   A tool along the right side and bottom of a document window that scrolls or moves the displayed document. You move the document by clicking the scroll box in the scroll bar and dragging the box in the direction you want the document to move.

scroll box   See **scroll bar**.

select   In PageMaker, click text or graphic elements with the Pointer tool in the toolbox to select them. Text blocks display sizing handles and top and bottom windowshade handles; graphics display sizing handles. To execute a command, often an element must be selected.

Select All   A PageMaker command that selects every text and graphic element on a page, as well as any elements moved to the pasteboard.

serif   The finishing strokes of the characters in some typefaces. Serifs help to lead the eye from letter to letter, so that body text, especially in smaller sizes, is easier to read. Sans serif typefaces lack these finishing serifs and tend to be used in headlines, headings, and subheads. See **sans serif**.

sidebar   In newspapers, a related story located beside the main story.

sizing handles   Graphic elements in PageMaker, when selected, display sizing handles that allow you to resize by simply grabbing a handle with the mouse pointer and dragging it.

small caps   Capital letters sized so that the height of the letter is the same as the x-height of lowercase letters in the same type size. See **x-height**.

snap   A PageMaker feature that helps you to align text or graphics accurately to the ruler or guidelines. When **Snap to Rules** or **Snap to Guides** is invoked, the element being aligned actually jumps to the closest ruler tick mark or guideline.

Story Editor	One of two editors in PageMaker, the Story Editor offers many word processing features to use in writing and editing individual stories in a document (as opposed to the Layout Editor, in which you can lay out multiple stories on a page).
style	A compilation of type and formatting attributes assigned for a specific purpose; for example, headline style, byline style, photo caption style, body text style. Styles allow you to make global changes that affect many groups of text tied to the changed style.
Style palette	PageMaker uses a small window that can be moved anywhere on the page to display the current names of all styles. The window is called the Style palette.

T

tab	Press the **Tab** key to move the text insertion point to the next tab stop or to indent a line of text.
template	A document that is formatted to act as a guide to create similar documents.
text files	Another name for *ASCII files*, which have no formatting codes. See **ASCII files**.
thin space	Half an *en space*, which is the size of the width of the letter *n*.
thumbnail	A miniature rendering of the page. PageMaker can print thumbnails of the pages of a document in varying sizes, based on how many thumbnails you want printed on a page.
tiling	A PageMaker feature that allows you to lay out pages larger than your laser printer can print. PageMaker will subdivide the page into printable *tiles* (or regions), annotate each region so it can be put back together, and print crop marks proportionally.

toggle	Toggle commands work like light switches. Choose the command to turn it on; choose it again to turn it off.
toolbox	The small window containing six different tools that work with text and graphics. The toolbox can be positioned anywhere on the document page.
tracking	In some ways, tracking is like kerning; you are increasing or reducing the space between letters. However, with tracking you're working with words instead of letters. Tracking increases or reduces letterspacing and the spaces between words in whole lines or sections of text.
type size	In PageMaker, type can be sized from 4 points to 650 points in 1/10th-point increments.
type style	Any typeface can be configured in a number of different styles in PageMaker, including bold, italic, underline, strikethru, and reverse.

W

widow	Created when a paragraph's first line winds up at the bottom of a page by itself, because a page break pushed the rest of the paragraph to the next page.
width	A type specification feature that adjusts the width of letters.
windowshade handles	Selected text blocks display windowshade handles at the top and bottom. The handles are used to move and adjust the text block. Symbols are displayed in handles to indicate certain conditions of the text block.

X

x-height	The height of the lowercase *x* in a given typeface; the portion of a letter that rests on the baseline, exclusive of ascenders and descenders.

Z

zero point   The point on either PageMaker ruler that establishes
                       the zero-measurement tick mark.

teach yourself...
PageMaker 6
for Windows 95

INDEX